UNMUTED

Unmuted

Conversations on Prejudice, Oppression,
and Social Justice

Myisha Cherry

Foreword by Cornel West

OXFORD
UNIVERSITY PRESS

OXFORD
UNIVERSITY PRESS

Oxford University Press is a department of the University of Oxford. It furthers
the University's objective of excellence in research, scholarship, and education
by publishing worldwide. Oxford is a registered trade mark of Oxford University
Press in the UK and certain other countries.

Published in the United States of America by Oxford University Press
198 Madison Avenue, New York, NY 10016, United States of America.

Library of Congress Cataloging-in-Publication Data
Names: Cherry, Myisha, author. | West, Cornel, author of foreword.
Title: Unmuted : conversations on prejudice, oppression, and social justice /
Myisha Cherry ; foreword by Cornel West.
Other titles: UnMute (Podcast)
Description: New York, NY : Oxford University Press, [2019] |
Includes bibliographical references and index.
Identifiers: LCCN 2018032484 (print) | LCCN 2018050199 (ebook) |
ISBN 9780190906788 (updf) | ISBN 9780190906795 (epub) |
ISBN 9780190906771 (cloth : alk. paper)
 Subjects: LCSH: Prejudices—Philosophy. | Oppression (Psychology) |
Racism—Philosophy. | Social justice—Philosophy. |
Philosophers—Interviews.
Classification: LCC HM1091 (ebook) | LCC HM1091 .C44 2019 (print) |
DDC 303.3/85—dc23
LC record available at https://lccn.loc.gov/2018032484
ISBN 978-0-19-090677-1

9 8 7 6 5 4 3 2 1

Printed by Sheridan Books, Inc., United States of America

For my mother,
Vernell Cherry,
who taught me the importance of service
and showed me the genius of everyday people.
(Rest in Power)

Contents

Foreword: Unmuting Philosophic Voices in Our Time

Cornel West

Academic philosophy in America—despite the heroic efforts of some—remains a professional discourse removed from the harsh realities of poor and working peoples here and abroad. If Martians were to visit philosophy departments in order to be informed of our major crisis, these aliens would have little exposure to or knowledge of impending ecological catastrophe, escalating white and male supremacy, expanding transphobia and homophobia or US imperial decline and decay. Instead, the educated guild of philosophy in our universities puts a premium on sustaining the hegemony of analytic philosophy along with a few historians of modern philosophy (Descartes, Spinoza, Leibniz, and Kant) and classical philosophy (Plato and Aristotle). This hegemony has yielded some brilliant figures and texts—yet it falls far short of meeting the challenges of wrestling with the realities of empire, capitalism, patriarchy, white supremacy, homophobia, and transphobia. Furthermore, the blindness of our fellow analytic philosophers has made it difficult to pursue wisdom and truth in other philosophic modes and traditions—especially those that highlight existential issues, historical sociology, and artistic ways of engaging the world.

This powerful and propitious book is part of a new wave of young philosophers unwilling to be muted by the silences of the philosophy guild. Instead, these serious and substantive thinkers lift their philosophic voices in regard to issues too often on the back burner of their profession. The rich conversational style that embraces the call-and-response forms of black music takes us on an unpredictable and unprecedented voyage through language, art, politics, sexuality, love, activism, economics, hope, and other themes. The Socratic guide and interlocutor Myisha Cherry—true to her precious mother Vernell Cherry's lesson of service to and example of the genius of everyday people—is superb. She moves and weaves through subtle arguments and narratives without easy resolutions or weak conclusions. Cherry's brilliant queries and probings accent not only the possible inconsistency and incoherence of claims but also the tone and temper of those who make the claims. In this way, this special book is not just a fascinating record of active minds but also a fecund expression of aching souls in love of truth, goodness, and beauty. How rare it is to encounter a philosophic book—a vital and vibrant cacophony of wise and soulful voices—that would put a smile on W. E. B. Du Bois's face in the grave. And in these bleak days, we need more such books and voices!

Introduction
A Revolution of Ideas

The idea for the UnMute podcast started in the summer of 2014. I met a friend at a cafe in Fort Greene, Brooklyn. There we shared lifestyle podcasts that we had recently fallen in love with and could not live without. Soon after this geeky exchange, I told him, "I think I want to start a philosophy podcast. And I want it to appeal to my former students."

The students I was referring to were not my university students but rather were a group of formerly incarcerated young people that were part of a philosophy institute that I had organized at John Jay College of Criminal Justice in 2013. These students were not philosophy majors but were interested in what philosophy had to say and the ways they could engage with it. After a year, I wanted to create a way for them to *stay* engaged with philosophy. I knew that in order for this to happen, I needed to find some way of making philosophy accessible in addition to being relevant. That is to say, the format and content had to be something that would grab and keep the attention of these brilliant black and brown twenty somethings—the majority of whom had never gone to college.

Now living in Chicago, I thought a podcast would be an ideal medium to keep in touch with these students in New York City. In that cafe, my friend Mike gave me the initial support I needed to begin planning for the first episode that would be released six months later in 2015.

When I returned to Chicago, I created a list of twelve contemporary philosophers whose work addresses topics in social and political philosophy *and* also excites me (there is nothing wrong with being selfish as long as it benefits others). This list consisted of people like Rachel Ann McKinney, Jason Stanley, Amir Jaima, Joel Michael Reynolds, Rachel McKinnon, and others. I sent each of them an email inviting them to record interviews. The first line read as follows: "I am embarking on a new project in 2015 that I think will aid in the revolution." An ambitious opener, I know, but it continued with more realistic aims:

> Recently, I've been getting the itch to do a podcast focused on giving an ear to voices and/or topics that are not given much attention in mainstream philosophy and to also have informal and accessible conversations about philosophy for non-philosophers. The name of the podcast is UnMute. It will be a place where philosophy and real world issues collide. It will begin as a monthly podcast and will alternate with diverse voices each month.

It was important that the guests be diverse. I wanted my future audience (my students) to know that people who looked like them also did philosophy. I wanted them to know that there are black and brown philosophers; women philosophers; philosophers with disabilities; gay, lesbian, and trans philosophers; and young philosophers. They needed to know that philosophy was not only an old white man's enterprise.

I was surprised that every email response I received read, "Yes, I will participate." I do not know how I gained their trust, but I am grateful for it and thank all of my participants.

The structure of the podcast was just as important as the participants. When someone pressed play, I wanted it to sound like they had just turned on an urban radio station. So I hired an announcer and commissioned music. I also knew that it was important for the listeners to know how the philosophers got into philosophy as well as who the philosophers were behind *and* beyond the work. This was important in making the philosophers not only relatable but human. Through the podcast I discovered that Elizabeth Barnes is a gamer, Rachel McKinnon is an athlete, Denise James is a painter, and Luvell Anderson is a musician. If he could have any basketball player's game and attitude, Tommie Shelby would choose Kobe Bryant over LeBron James because of his work ethic (this was personally hard to hear as a LeBron fan). And Jason Stanley thinks that rapper and actor Ice Cube is a political philosopher. So the podcast questions started out and remain focused on the philosophers' journeys, their philosophical work, and their identities beyond philosophy.

After the release of the first episode, I quickly realized that the podcast was not only for my students. I was surprised to learn that there are UnMute listeners within the activist community and the podcast community who are not necessarily interested in philosophy per se but are interested in the podcast's content. There are also professional philosophers and students of philosophy across the world who listen each month. I am grateful to those who incorporate UnMute in their courses. I am also grateful to the interviewees who continue to say, "Yes, I will participate" in sharing ideas with me as I assume the role of questioner, interlocutor, and student during our forty-minute conversations. I still do believe UnMute aids in the revolution—even if the revolution is only a revolution of ideas.

However, while many people have found the UnMute podcast interesting and helpful, an audio podcast is not accessible to the hearing impaired. Also, not everyone listens to podcasts or retains information in this way. If I want the podcast to really be accessible, I needed to provide additional ways to make the conversations available. In response to this accessibility dilemma, a book of transcripts sounded like a good idea.

In your hands is that idea. The UnMute book consists of thirty-one interview transcripts from diverse philosophers talking about the social and political issues of our day. They have different perspectives and take different approaches to responding to these issues. Some take an analytic, continental, feminist, historical, or critical-theoretic approach––naturally, these are not mutually exclusive. The topics covered in this book focus on six areas: politics and society; language, knowledge, and power; social groups and activism; race and economics; gender, sex, and love; and emotions and art in public life. The interviews in this book comprise the first three seasons of the UnMute podcast, which were recorded during my four years of graduate school. I felt that the interviews were a perfect supplement to my educational journey and they still are today. I'm happy to share that rewarding experience with you in this format.

I cannot guarantee that you will agree with everything written in the following pages. But I am certain that the content will encourage you to think more deeply, perhaps even differently about our world. Many of the philosophers in this book are widening the scope of what philosophy is, the questions it can pose and answer, and the contributions philosophical thought can make to the "real world." They have made me believe that it is indeed an exciting time to read philosophy, do philosophy, and be a philosopher. I hope they do the same for you.

The Conversations

In the first section of the book, we talk about politics and society. I speak with Meena Krishnamurthy, Denise James, Lori Gruen, José Mendoza, and Wendy Salkin. The questions we explore include the following: What is valuable about political distrust? In what ways does race contribute to global poverty? What are our duties to the global poor? We then turn to talk about political illusions. We examine four political illusions according to writer Lorraine Hansberry. We then transition to the prison system. More specifically, we talk about carceral spaces, teaching philosophy in prisons, and the "animal, prisoner, and blacks" analogy. Afterward, we talk about immigration. We do so by tackling four questions: (1) Is Mexican immigration a problem or a myth? (2) What's problematic about the terms "aliens" and "illegals"? (3) What is our obligation to the undocumented? (4) Should states control borders? We end with considering informal political representation and who has the standing to unofficially represent groups of people.

The second section of the book is concerned with language, knowledge, and power. I talk with Rachel Ann McKinney, Cassie Herbert, Luvell Anderson, Jason Stanley, and Winston Thompson. We explore these questions: How might we explain the power of words? What is extracted speech and how do the police use it in their interactions with the public? We also look at "risky speech," discuss the difference between accusations and reports, and talk about how to respond to accounts of racism, sexism, and so on. We then turn to slurs and "bad" words. We wonder if the n-word can be appropriated. What gives curse words their power? And how do we make sense of the nature and rules of racial humor? We then turn to discussions about the relationship between satire and liberalism as well as public intellectualism. This section ends with a discussion on educational justice by asking, "Is what is owed to persons and polities a matter of *educational* rather than *political* justice?"

Our focus in the third section of the book is on social groups and activism. The social groups we highlight are women, the disabled, indigenous peoples, blacks, and the trans community (although what is discussed may be transferrable to other groups). I begin by chatting with Serene Khader, Joel Michael Reynolds, and Elizabeth Barnes. We begin by looking at women in the Global South and imagine what a transnational feminist ethic would look like. We then turn our attention to disability. We examine stigmas and oppressions surrounding disability, sex and disability, and reading philosophy through a disability lens. Other topics discussed are inspiration porn, theories of disability, abnormal bodies and well-being, disability pride, and valuing disability.

The second part of this section focuses on activism. I talk with Douglas Ficek, Rachel McKinnon, Kyle Whyte, and Andrea Pitts. We begin by asking several questions: What does Frantz Fanon say about social protest? What is the difference between #BlackLivesMatter and #AllLivesMatter? What are the virtues of present-day activism? Other questions include the following: What is an ally and what is the problem with ally culture? How do we truly support others' lived experiences? We then explore activism in the context of indigenous communities. We talk about the problems and possibilities Indigenous peoples face regarding climate change, environmental justice, and food sovereignty. We also analyze the historical ways that indigenous women in Central America have resisted neoliberalism. We end by looking at ways we can end colonialism and resist settler-colonial logics.

In the fourth section of the book we talk about race and economics. This is not to say that the two are always connected, but as we will see, they can overlap. I talk with David Livingstone Smith, Linda Martín Alcoff, Chike Jeffers, Lawrence Blum, Tommie Shelby, David McClean, and Vanessa Wills. First we attempt to get at the root of dehumanization by asking how and why we demean, enslave, and exterminate others. We also look at how race plays a part in dehumanization. We then examine whiteness, white exceptionalism, white double-consciousness, and the future of whiteness. We also take a look at the history of black political thought, its themes, the intellectual contribution of W. E. B. Du Bois, and tools and tips for teaching race in the classroom. In moving the themes of race and economics closer together, we examine black ghettos. We also reflect on integration, the moral permissibility of crime, and the obligations of the ghetto poor. Other economic questions raised and answered are: What is the root of hip-hop culture's materialism? What should a virtuous person's relationship with money be? Why does what happens on Wall Street matter to the poor? With all this talk about money, we conclude this section with a conversation on Marxism. We discuss Marxism and its misconceptions and what today's social movements can learn from Marxist thought.

The fifth section of the book is concerned with gender, sex, and love. I talk with Nancy Bauer, John Corvino, Tom Digby, and Justin Clardy. We start by discussing pornography, the sexiness of taboos, feminism and porn, and hookup culture. Then we turn to homosexuality, traditional marriage, religious liberty, and the similarities and differences between the civil rights movement and the LGBTQ movement. We move from sex to gender by exploring masculinity and militarism, how masculinity contributes to rape culture, and the ways in which masculinity is culturally programmed. Finally, we talk about love by examining the nature of it, arguments for and against monogamy and polyamory, and the possibility of love in politics.

The sixth and final section of the book explores emotion and art in public life. I talk with Paul C. Taylor, Amir Jaima, and Adrienne Martin. We first discuss race and aesthetics by focusing on black invisibility, art and politics, authenticity and cultural appropriation, and beauty and race. We then to turn to literature. We ask, what can philosophy learn from literature? What makes black literature so philosophically rich? Why is Toni Morrison a philosopher? Lastly, we take up the issue of hope. We ask: What is hope? How does it motivate? How is it connected to faith and optimism? Why should we hope in humanity?

Final Note

The interviews have been edited for brevity and style. The conversations are stand-alone discussions; however, they do connect well with other chapters in their section. This is not to imply that chapters cannot be paired with other chapters from other sections. For example, chapter 7 on risky speech can be paired with chapter 15 on allies and ally culture. Chapter 2 on political illusions can be paired with chapter 22 on black ghettos. I leave it up to readers to decide for themselves what order they would like to read and what other connections they can make between a particular chapter and other parts of the book. The purpose of the sections is to serve as an organized guide and not as a rule.

If you plan to use this book in the classroom, it is important to note that about thirteen of the interviews conducted are based on books while some of the other interviews are based on published articles and essays. This book can therefore serve as an introduction or supplementary material to the original work. Recently, for example, graduate students at an unnamed institution used Paul C. Taylor's UnMute interview as a supplement to his book on black aesthetics. Students found the interview to be useful in helping them to understand the book as a whole. This book can serve a similar role.

Although we have attempted to talk in everyday language and break down complex terms in our conversations, I recognize that not everyone reading the book shares the same understanding of certain concepts and references. For that reason, I have provided a glossary of terms, or more appropriately, a *Say What?* chapter to assist readers.

Lastly, you will notice in the following chapters that interviewees are referred to by their first name and not by their last name or by "Doctor." This is not a mistake. It is very much intentional. Nor is it a sign of disrespect. In our original interviews, I informed all guests that they would be referred to by their first names. This was a subtle way of getting us out of the academy *and* not allowing their titles to serve as a barrier between them and listeners. Remember the aim of the podcast is accessibility. I wanted to level the "conversation" field. Whether this was and is effective is an empirical matter.

Before we get to the thematic interviews, the next chapter dives briefly into who the philosophers are and how they got interested in philosophy. For some philosophers it occurred because of a class they took, a book they read, or an obsession and fear that they could unintentionally do horrible, immoral things. For other philosophers, working mindless jobs helped them discover that they enjoyed thinking. While another philosopher suggests that she ended up a philosopher due to job availability. The question serves several purposes, but one important one is that it allows us to see the various ways that people from different economic, racial, geographic, generational, and other social backgrounds come to philosophy as a practice.

So lets begin our journey with a salutation that I use at the beginning of every podcast episode. *"Hello and Welcome to UnMuted! This is the place where I have the opportunity to talk to young, diverse philosophers about the social and political issues of our day. Today I chat with . . ."*

Notes on Contributors

Linda Martín Alcoff

Research: **Epistemology, Feminism, and Race Theory**

Affiliation: **Professor of Philosophy | The City University of New York**

Philosophical Journey: **I took a course . . . and I got addicted . . . [There] were the influential works out there, and they were so wrong about so many things that I just got hooked on wanting to be part of the conversation.**

Research: Philosophy of
Language and
Philosophy of Race
Affiliation: Assistant Professor
of Philosophy |
Syracuse University

Philosophical
Journey: I started reading
Cornel West's *The
American Evasion
of Philosophy*, and
from there I was
hooked . . . I started
talking to a few
folks at different
universities in
the area about
philosophy.

Luvell Anderson

Research: Metaphysics,
Social
Philosophy, and
Ethics
Affiliation: Professor of
Philosophy |
University of
Virginia

Philosophical
Journey: I first started
reading about
philosophy just
because I wanted
to understand
more about
the novels that
I was really into,
and I wanted a
deeper sense of
these ideas.

Elizabeth Barnes

Research: Feminism, Existentialism, and Phenomenology

Affiliation: Professor of Philosophy and Dean of Academic Affairs for Arts and Sciences | Tufts University

Philosophical Journey: I started attending ethics rounds at a children's hospital. The person who ran that was a professor at Harvard Divinity School . . . [He encouraged me to go to Harvard and attend a medical ethics program]. . . . I basically just hung around until the philosophy department kind of got weary of me and just let me into the PhD program.

Nancy Bauer

Research: Philosophy of Race and Moral Psychology

Affiliation: Emeritus Professor of Philosophy & Distinguished Professor of Liberal Arts & Education | University of Massachusetts, Boston

Philosophical Journey: I took an ethics course. Somehow the whole idea of thinking philosophically about ethical questions and trying to figure out what made something right or wrong . . . just blew my mind and I just was completely obsessed with it.

Lawrence (Larry) Blum

Research: Moral Psychology, Social
and Political Philosophy,
and Philosophy of Race
Affiliation: Assistant Professor of
Philosophy | University
of California, Riverside

Philosophical
Journey: When I got to college, it
was the first time I was
able to have time to just
think about the world.
I knew then that I wanted
to explore this "thinking
life," so without taking a
class, I changed my major
from telecommunications
to philosophy my second
semester.

Myisha Cherry

Research: Ethics and Social &
Political Philosophy
Affiliation: Thinking Matters
Postdoctoral Fellow |
Stanford University

Philosophical
Journey: [When] I went to elementary school in Compton
and high school in
Gardena, it was just
easy for me. . . . I was
kind of lazy . . . [But
when I encountered]
philosophy and had to
grapple with some of the
questions, [it became]
the first subject that really challenged me.

Justin Clardy

Research: Ethical Theory, Applied
Ethics, and LGBT Studies
Affiliation: Professor of Philosophy |
Wayne State University

Philosophical
Journey: I was planning on
going into the priest-
hood . . . then when I decided not to go, I thought,
"What am I going to do
with all these philosophy
credits?" And I went, "Oh,
I'll teach philosophy." [But
I was also] taking some
courses at Saint John's
University from some re-
ally wonderful professors
who got me excited about
philosophy.

John Corvino

Research: Gender Studies
Affiliation: Professor Emeritus
of Philosophy |
Springfield College

Philosophical
Journey: At the end of my first
year of college, I fell in
love with someone who
was majoring in phi-
losophy. I had no idea
what philosophy was,
having grown up in
Arkansas, so I signed
up for an intro class.
And that started the
process of liberation,
which continues to this
day.

Tom Digby

Research: Africana Philosophy and
Philosophy of Existence
Affiliation: Visiting Assistant Professor
in Philosophy | University
of New Haven

Philosophical
Journey: When I was a kid . . . I read
Umberto Eco's mystery
novel *The Name of the Rose.*
It's this really remarkable
story with this complex theological and philosophical
backdrop . . . [There were
two characters] illustrating
the difference between Plato
and Aristotle's theory of
forms . . . [and] I just found
it fascinating.

Douglas Ficek

Research: Ethics and Feminist
Philosophy
Affiliation: Professor of
Philosophy |
Wesleyan University

Philosophical
Journey: I took a philosophy
class and I didn't have
any idea what was
going on. But because
I didn't, I was motivated
to try to figure out what
was going on. I kept at
it and then I realized,
"Wow, there is tremen-
dous liberatory potential
in thinking about these
philosophical questions
in systematic ways."

Lori Gruen

Research: Philosophy of Language,
Feminist Philosophy, and
Philosophy of Sex

Affiliation: Visiting Assistant Professor
of Philosophy | Hobart and
William Smith Colleges

Philosophical
Journey: I've always really had this
strong commitment towards
social justice ever since I was
a little kid. I also was really
worried about getting things
wrong in an important way.
So I used to have these sorts
of existential nightmares. . . .
I found that philosophy gave
me a space to explore these
questions such as "What is
right and wrong?"

Cassie Herbert

Research: Aesthetics and Africana
Philosophy

Affiliation: Assistant Professor of
Philosophy | Texas A&M
University

Philosophical
Journey: At some point [in a philosophy course] we read Fanon
and that really surprised
me. [I said] "This could be
philosophy?" I [also] de-
cided I wanted to write a
novel . . . I thought, "I'm
missing something." The
ideas weren't grounded
enough. So I just did a
master's [in philosophy]. And
then eventually . . . I went
on to graduate school for a
doctorate.

Amir Jaima

Research: Pragmatism, Feminism,
and Social Justice
Affiliation: Professor of Philosophy
| University of
Dayton

Philosophical
Journey: I went to college and
I knew I was going to be
a lawyer. . . . I took a
philosophy class and my
professor converted me
to philosophy. He told me
I didn't want to really be
a lawyer, that I wanted
to sit with the books and
ideas, and that I should be
a philosopher.

Denise James

Research: Africana Philosophy and
Philosophy of Race
Affiliation: Professor of Philosophy |
University of Dalhousie

Philosophical
Journey: I was interested in philosophy
from very early . . . not knowing
it under that name. On Sundays
while listening to the pastor, I was
thinking about the philosophical
aspects of what I was hearing.
I wasn't clear on whether philosophy was a way that someone who
is black and cares about his community . . . whether philosophy
is a vehicle for that. [But reading
George Yancy's "African-American
Philosophers: 17 Conversations"]
helped push me into philosophy.

Chike Jeffers

Serene Khader

Research: Ethics, Political Philosophy, and Feminist Philosophy

Affiliation: Jay Newman Chair in Philosophy of Culture | Brooklyn College

Philosophical
Journey: It has a lot to do with my experiences having parents who are immigrants. I always felt not at home in any world. So because I was always in that space of wondering, "What are the norms that apply here?" and "Why are conventions worth following?", those questions brought me into philosophy.

Research: Political Philosophy

Affiliation: Assistant Professor of Philosophy | University of Michigan

Philosophical
Journey: Like many other people of Indian descent, I thought that I was going to go into medicine. . . . But I took a philosophy course and right away I loved everything about it. Analyzing arguments is something I did around the dinner table with my family ever since I was a child. So I think it felt like love at first sight, but in many ways I think my own life kind of geared me towards philosophy.

Meena Krishnamurthy

Adrienne Martin

Research: Moral Psychology and
Medical Ethics

Affiliation: Akshata Mary '02 and Richi
Sunak Associate Professor of
Philosophy, Politics, and Economics
and George R. Roberts Fellow |
Claremont McKenna College

Philosophical
Journey: In high school, I started reading
things like *The Tao of Physics* and
The Dancing Wu Li Masters and
wanted to figure out the meaning
of existence. . . . I went abroad to
Italy and had a culture shock. . . .
I decided that the meaning of life
was to be understood through
ethics; that it was about how
people can live together, not about
the fundamental, metaphysical
constituency of the universe.

Research: Pragmatism and
Business Ethics

Affiliation: Lecturer in Philosophy and
Business Ethics | Rutgers
University, Newark

Philosophical
Journey: I was rummaging through a
library shelf in the philosophy section when I was an
undergraduate. And I came
upon a book by Sarvepalli
Radhakrishnan. . . . It's a
classic work on Indian philosophy. I was really impressed
by all of the issues that were
addressed, the subjects covered.
Although I could not have articulated it at the time, I liked the
fact that the philosophical stuff
was blended into the religious
and spiritual dimension.

David McClean

Research: Philosophy of Language and
Feminist Philosophy
Affiliation: Assistant Professor of Philosophy
| Suffolk University

Philosophical
Journey: I think I was sort of always interested in philosophical questions,
but I didn't know there was this
thing called philosophy. I remember
reading Neil DeGrasse Tyson when
I was little and just being so enthu-
siastic about all the stuff having
to do with science, free will, and
whether God existed . . . [Later
in college] I figured out that I was
interested in philosophy, and that
there was a name to the mass
of questions that I had been
curious about.

Rachel Ann McKinney

Research: Epistemology and Feminist
Philosophy
Affiliation: Assistant Professor of
Philosophy | College of
Charleston

Philosophical
Journey: While I was on a work term
for chemistry, I found the lab
life a little mind-numbing and
found myself rereading some
of the philosophy books that
I didn't read when I took
Intro to philosophy. I just
decided that the sorts of
questions that philosophers
were asking were the types
of questions I was having at
that time about science.

Rachel McKinnon

Research: Political Philosophy, Philosophy of Immigration, and Latin American Philosophy

Affiliation: Assistant Professor of Philosophy | University of Massachusetts, Lowell

Philosophical Journey: As a nineteen-year-old kid, I kept losing arguments. When I would take a philosophy class, I noticed my professors were really good at arguing. . . . It was sort of like if you get picked on in school, you take up a martial art. I was getting intellectually picked on, I felt like. So I wanted to take an intellectual martial art and I thought it was philosophy.

José Mendoza

Research: Social Epistemology and Latin American and US Latinx Philosophy

Affiliation: Assistant Professor of Philosophy | University of North Carolina, Charlotte

Philosophical Journey: I went to university for jazz . . . [There was this] analogous relationship between jazz music as a history of ideas. Someone like Charlie Parker and the bebop era was this precursor and influence on people like Cannonball Adderley in the hard-bop era. . . . I started thinking about these subtle shifts between genres. . . . [I noticed] that kind of showed up in interesting ways through philosophy.

Andrea Pitts

Research: Bioethics and Medical
Humanities
Affiliation: Assistant Professor of
Philosophy | University of
Massachusetts, Lowell

Philosophical
Journey: I must have been around ten
years old and reading a passage probably from Psalms
90 about eternity, or as I
interpret it, infinity. And I
could imagine that something
never ended, but I couldn't
imagine something never
beginning. . . . And I didn't
know it then, but I was
philosophizing.

Joel Michael Reynolds

Research: Political Philosophy and
Black Political Thought
Affiliation: Assistant Professor
of Philosophy |
San Francisco State
University

Philosophical
Journey: The first philosophy book
I ever got was when
I was in sixth grade. It
was Plato's *Republic*. . . .
In high school, we
had a little philosophy
reading group. And we
would read mostly pre-
Socratics and Plato and
Aristotle.

Wendy Salkin

Tommie Shelby

Research: Social & Political Philosophy and Africana Philosophy
Affiliation: Caldwell Titcomb Professor of African and African American Studies and of Philosophy | Harvard University

Philosophical
Journey: I took classes in sociology, psychology, and religion. I had a couple of religion professors who said, "You really ought to consider taking a class in philosophy. I think it would suit you better than studying religion." And so I did. I took a couple of philosophy classes; one in political philosophy, one in logic. And I just loved it immediately. It just suited me.

Research: Philosophy of Psychology
Affiliation: Professor of Philosophy | University of New England

Philosophical
Journey: I was a psychotherapist and a psychotherapy educator. I thought, "I kind of like this academic stuff. I should go get a PhD." It was recommended to me to visit Jim Hopkins, a philosopher who was interested in Freud. Hopkins was so delighted to find a student who was interested in Freud that he made the case for the University of London to take me on as a grad student in philosophy despite my having zero background in philosophy. So I kind of fell into philosophy. It was entirely accidental.

David Livingstone Smith

Jason Stanley

Research: Philosophy of Language, Epistemology, and Political Philosophy

Affiliation: Jacob Urowsky Professor of Philosophy | Yale University

Philosophical Journey: My father was teaching in the sociology department, and he also had a biweekly reading group on philosophy where they read philosophy of education, Dewey, and the classics—Plato, Aristotle, Kant. I knew philosophy was something that was greatly admired, but of course, analytic philosophy not so much. But at the time, at the table he was often discussing the German philosopher Jürgen Habermas, who had greatly influenced him at the time.

Research: Philosophy of Race, Aesthetics, and Pragmatism

Affiliation: W. Alton Jones Professor of Philosophy | Vanderbilt University

Philosophical Journey: Philosophy was the only thing that really interested me in college. I was meant to be a medical doctor because that's what my father was and that's what his father was, and that's what I started out on my way to being. I suddenly realized halfway through freshman year of the biology-for-major sequence that I was bored out of my mind. And the first class I took after I realized that was Intro to Philosophy. And I realized, "I get to think about stuff instead of just memorizing things." And the rest is history.

Paul C. Taylor

Research: Philosophy of Education
Affiliation: Assistant Professor of
              Philosophy of Education |
              The Ohio State University

Philosophical
Journey: I discovered philosophy
         while I was in middle school.
         I came across some books at
         home, my father had some
         philosophical books in his
         library . . . so it felt to me
         as though I'd sort of dis-
         covered a secret world; this
         world where people were
         asking questions of the sort
         that I had always asked and
         found productive, rewarding
         and fulfilling.

Winston Thompson

Research: Pragmatism and Social &
          Political Philosophy
Affiliation: Professor of the Practice
             of Public Philosophy |
             Harvard University

Philosophical
Journey: I got interested in philos-
         ophy simply by wrestling
         with the catastrophe of
         evil in the world!

Cornel West

Kyle Whyte

Research: Environmental Political Theory, Climate and Environmental Justice, and Indigenous Philosophy and Research Methodology

Affiliation: Associate Professor of Philosophy & Community Sustainability | Michigan State University

Philosophical Journey: I was volunteering and doing work for a number of different activist-type projects. I had applied for a range of jobs with nonprofits and I'd applied to grad school to programs that I thought were places I could talk about social and political questions. And so I ended up going to grad school . . . I then realized I was sort of tracked into this and it might be a good place for me to explore a lot of the issues that I was concerned with on indigenous matters.

Research: Nineteenth-Century German Philosophy (especially Karl Marx), Political Philosophy, and Philosophy of Race

Affiliation: Assistant Professor of Philosophy | The George Washington University

Philosophical Journey: The first time I encountered the work of an academic philosopher was Wittgenstein at a nerd camp when I was sixteen. . . . I was really intrigued by it, and it seemed deep and profound somehow. In college there was a class being offered by Jeffrey Stout in the Department of Religion called "Dewey, Heidegger, and Wittgenstein." That struck my fancy. After that, I was well on my trajectory towards becoming a philosopher.

Vanessa Wills

Section 1

POLITICS AND SOCIETY

1

Meena Krishnamurthy on Political Distrust

MYISHA: In your view, Meena, what do you think is a true democracy and what values underwrite it?

MEENA: I think at its most basic, democracy is really sort of two things. It's sort of that idea of formal equality where people have equal rights to vote, but I also think it's something more substantive in the sense that it's not just about having equal votes; it's also about having an equally effective or influential vote. So I think those two things really comprise the basics of democracy.

The second question, which was, "What are the values," I think I'm a pluralist about the value of democracy or the justifications behind democracy. So I think there are a number of values that underwrite or justify it. My own work has developed from arguments in favor of democracy based on John Rawls's work. And I've argued that there are sort of three really core values: self-respect, autonomy, and then ownership. And I think all of these values actually give rise to democracy.

MYISHA: So is the United States democratic?

MEENA: I think my answer probably won't surprise you. I mean, in part I think democracy is on a sliding scale, so some things are more democratic than others, and in some ways the US is democratic. But when we ask, "Is it sort of genuinely democratic," I think the question is whether it reaches a certain threshold. And I think the answer is probably, "No, it's not genuinely or robustly democratic." And I think that's because in many ways, I guess, America has become an oligarchy. I think it's ruled by the interests of a small group of people. So in that sense, while people might—in terms of the law–have equal rights to vote, they don't have substantive political equality. I don't think that people have an equally influential vote in this country.

I was looking at some recent work by Martin Gilens and Benjamin Page. They've done some work showing that the preferences of the rich have a greater impact on policy decisions than middle-income and poor Americans. So this is suggesting that rich Americans have more political influence. When we think about the ways in which campaign finance and lobbying work, again, it gives people with more money more say. I think if we were to look in terms of racial minorities, I think we would see something similar: that people of color have less influence in this country, particularly African Americans. So I think in this way America is not a democracy.

MYISHA: Some may argue that distrust is a barrier to a truly democratic institution. But you are currently developing a theory of what you call "valuable distrust." So tell us: How is distrust valuable, and how has Martin Luther King, Jr. helped you to develop a theory of valuable distrust?

MEENA: My inquiry into valuable distrust really starts with Dr. King's work. Really, I mean, people think of King as that mushy, gushy fellow; he was all about love and friendship and forgiveness. But when I read King, his work in detail, there is actually a really strong current of what we could say were negative attitudes, an attitude of distrust.

In my own work, I started with writing mostly about the "Letter from a Birmingham Jail." But looking now at his work more broadly, there's this current of "I distrust the white moderates." And for me, I'm talking here about political distrust. Political distrust consists of beliefs. It's a belief that basically another person or group of people will not act as justice requires. And King is confident in his belief that the white moderates will not do what justice requires despite the fact that they have really good commitments. The white moderates represent what Shannon Sullivan has called "good white people." They believe in racial equality, they believe that segregation is bad. But King just doesn't believe that they're going to do anything about it.

And in turn, I think distrust understood in this sense played a pivotal, motivational role in the civil rights movement. I think distrust motivated Dr. King and his supporters to engage in a social movement that changed the democratic landscape of America. So for me, this is where the moral value comes from. In a sense, distrust plays this moral motivational role, in that it moves people to act as justice requires.

MYISHA: Should distrust always remain? Or should we always, at least, attempt to transform it into something else? That is to say, should we try to transform our distrust into social action with change as the end goal, or is the end goal to transform distrust into trust?

MEENA: I think one thing to say here, since I'm talking about political distrust, is that I think it's really important to maintain at least some level of distrust. In my work, I argue that in a sense political distrust is part of that system of checks and balances. It's a way of making sure that democracy and justice stay on the straight and narrow, so to speak, so that we are pushing forward and trying to make progress. And because of our own biases, and the way vested interests come into play in politics, we need another check. I think this element of distrust can serve as that important check and point us in the right direction.

MYISHA: You gave the example of Martin Luther King Jr. and the white moderates. Let's try to change things up a little bit. Let's think about the present-day feminist movement. There is this notion of white feminism and then there are other women of color. Although white feminism believes that there needs to be equal rights for women, issues of intersectionality have not really been taken up. So, some women of color believe that when it comes down to it, white feminists may not have their back to a certain extent. They have distrust. When women are together fighting for a particular cause, *should* a level of distrust be there, or will it eventually be poisonous to the movement?

MEENA: I think that part of the answer, at least for King, comes from some of his other views about what underwrites distrust. Another part of my work is trying to figure out why King really thinks that we should distrust people, the white moderates.

For him, part of it is an epistemic claim, which is that, "Look, they can't know what it's like to be black in America and to suffer, particularly suffer the way that we have suffered." And because there isn't this knowing of what it's like, as a result there's always a kind of epistemic gap. I think because of that gap, we have to be a bit distrustful. Even when we have allies or active bystanders on our side, I think we have to be distrustful. Again, things are scalar. We don't have to have a full-fledged sense of distrust, but there might be a little bit of guardedness there.

If we see King in this light, it brings him in some ways closer to Malcolm X, who had kind of a similar view: that even the people who are acting on your side, maybe you can't fully trust them. In this sense, I think that King's commitments actually lead him to reaching a somewhat similar conclusion.

MYISHA: You also have done work on the global poor, particularly, our duties to aid the global poor. In what ways do you believe the global poor's distrust of the West is warranted?

MEENA: It's interesting because I haven't really thought about distrust in the global sphere, but certainly, there is some. A lot of my own work is focused on international aid as distributed by international institutions such as the World Bank and the International Monetary Fund (IMF). I think there is a kind of distrust of these institutions and the people that work for them, because people in the developing world have felt that they were pushing their own interests and their own agenda and not really promoting justice. So I do think there is a kind of distrust at the global level around development.

And I do think it's warranted. The reason that I think it is warranted is because of history. This is one of the other things that King appeals to in his work about why he distrusts the white moderates; looking again and again historically and seeing how the white moderates didn't act when they probably should have. In this global case, I think people in these agencies are representing developed countries but acting in the wrong way. We know that for example, aid, when it's distributed by these institutions is typically done on the basis of conditions, economic policy conditions. There've been some very important studies by Breelyn and Pajorsky that have shown that countries that adhered more closely to these conditions, as prescribed by the IMF and the World Bank, typically actually did worse with respect to growth. In fact, they actually had decreased growth as a result of following these conditions.

Part of the reason we know this is that a lot of the conditions that were attached to these loans, at least historically, weren't really there to address the problems that were causing the poverty and the economic disruption in the first place. Because of this history, there is a kind of distrust and it seems warranted because we know that these conditions failed so systematically.

Of course, things have gotten somewhat better in the sense that there are much fewer conditions attached, but again, there's still a lot of worries that these conditions aren't properly tailored to the needs of those countries that are borrowing. And so distrust seems warranted as a result.

MYISHA: When global disasters or injustices happen across the world, there is a part of me as an American that says, "Our government is going to do something about it, and I can't wait to see our government do something about it, to stand up for those who are facing atrocities, or stand up for those who are facing tragedies because we have the resources to do so and the power to do so."

I don't know where that comes from. A part of it comes from it feeling good to see an institution that I distrust—the government—take an ethical and a normative stand against something I perceive as unjust. But then I wonder how much of their decision to take a stand is motivated, not by moral reasons, but political reasons. There are some instances in which I feel like our government should speak out about things that they never speak out about. But I'm concerned that they will only act out of economic reasons. Do you think the US's efforts to aid the poor or other nations are motivated by philanthropic or political reasons? Is it ever ethical for the US government to respond for political reasons alone?

MEENA: My ideas on this are that I think people have mixed motives. I think it's philanthropic in the sense that people really do want to do good. I think the government officials who work in these kinds of international institutions and distribute aid, there is a part of them that ultimately wants to do good.

But is it purely altruistic? I don't think that's the case. Countries need to promote—they do promote—their own interests in these kinds of institutions. And to some extent, they're elected to do so. The people that represent America in international institutions, that distribute international development aid, are often finance ministers. They're people who have been elected to represent American interests. So in some sense, they're doing their job. In that sense, I think it complicates the issue of whether this is really altruistic or not. In some sense it is and in some sense, it isn't; but even though it isn't, they're doing it to represent American interests. It's only when the people of America say, "Well, actually, we really think that it's important that we prioritize the interests of the global poor" will things, I think, fundamentally change.

I am generally a bit skeptical about international institutions and international aid. I have at least suggested in some of my work that maybe we should think about dismantling the IMF and the World Bank. Instead, we should promote other lending institutions or look at other kinds of solutions. We know that things like direct cash transfers actually alleviate individual poverty fairly well. And so maybe that's just something we can think about doing on a larger scale. In doing so, maybe we avoid some of the politics involved in the aforementioned solutions.

MYISHA: So let's talk about duties to the global poor. Institutionally, what do you think are our duties to the global poor, and where do they come from? And also, individually, what do you think are our duties to the global poor, and where do those duties come from?

MEENA: I think that there are two different types of duties that we may have. Some duties we might just have as individuals or humans. I think that gets us to a certain level of duties, which is to establish basic human rights for everybody across the globe; those are human-itarian duties. And those are duties that we might have just as mere individuals. There are also institutional duties to aid the global poor. And so one of the main questions in global justice is how strong are those duties, if there are any. Are they as strong as the duties that you have to your fellow American citizens or are they weaker than that?

In my own view, the kinds of principles that apply within a country are the same kinds of principles that ought to apply more globally. For example, one principle of justice advocated for by John Rawls and many of his followers is the "difference principle," which says that any ine-quality in income and wealth has to be distributed such that the worst off are made as well off as they can be. And similarly, I think that that kind of a principle—basically, make the worst off as well off as they can be—ought to be implemented globally. Of course, there's the question of why. Why would someone think that? And one of the reasons we've given, at least at the local level, is that we think we have these really strong, demanding duties, what's referred to as egalitarian duties, to our fellow citizens because we're in this kind of coercive relationship. The only way we can justify that coercive relationship that we have to each other—coercive, that is, through the state—is by implementing egalitarian duties of justice.

I think something similar holds at the global level. International financial institutions are actually coercive, and the only way to pos-sibly justify the coercion to everybody is by saying that the system ac-tually makes you as well off as you can be. And so that's what I've been writing about recently.

MYISHA: Let me flip the question a little bit: Do the global poor have duties? And in what ways can we, or have we, blocked their agency in fulfilling these particular duties?

MEENA: I do think that individuals within poor countries have duties to each other—to arrange their society so that it meets the principles of distributive justice. They have duties to help each other. Of course, they may not be able to do so because of the poverty that they're in. I think one of the other duties that they definitely have is a duty of resistance, a duty to resist global arrangements that promote injustice in their countries. So there are duties to fight these systemic problems, I think.

MYISHA: Let's talk about race for a moment as we talk about the global poor. How is race relevant to discussions of global poverty?

MEENA: This is an issue that's really not discussed at all. I know this because I am now teaching a course this term called "Global Justice, Race, and Gender," and the emphasis is really on race. And I looked around trying to see what other people have been teaching or writing about this issue. I talked with Charles Mills, and with other people to see what they thought, and we all collectively agreed that there really isn't a lot of work being done on global justice and race. So I've been thinking about how race matters to global economic injustice.

One thing is that we don't have a lot of data. We know that there are a large number of people who live on less than $1.25 (equivalent to US dollars) a day. And we know about 1.3 billion people are living with less than $1.25 a day. What we don't know is how many of those people are of color. The best we can do is look at the data that we have on countries. We know there's a certain amount of people from Asia and Africa that fall under this $1.25 metric. And if we put those people together, we get something like a little more than or a little under 70 percent of the people that suffer from extreme deprivation—that is, having $1.25 a day—are likely people of color. And again, there's no real data. I can just glean this from the data that we have about countries and then make inferences about the race of people in those countries. But roughly 70 percent of the people living with less than $1.25 a day are people of color, and yet this isn't something that's really being talked about in philosophy. So I think it is an important issue that's been ignored.

What's the relevance of race to questions about global justice? Well, I think we have to look historically at the process of colonialism, which has really been one of the core processes that has led to global economic deprivation. And I think if we look at a lot of the justifications around colonialism, they're often steeped in a kind of racist ideology. When the British were colonizing India, for example, there was often talk about Indians being a barbaric people; they needed the British rule, despite the fact that India was a long, well-established civilization with a certain degree of wealth. Despite that fact, apparently Indians were barbaric and needed to be conquered and ruled by the British. And we see similar kinds of ideology around the colonialization of various parts in

Africa. I think in that sense, racism is really important to think about in these issues.

And then I think—and this is something I'm thinking through now as I'm teaching this class: How have these kinds of ideologies filtered into the way that international financial institutions have been set up and designed? In the IMF and the World Bank, essentially, votes are handed out on the basis of economic status, so richer countries have more votes than poorer countries. The US usually, predominantly, has the greatest amount of votes. For example, in the IMF, the US is the only country with single veto power. But the important thing here to note is that when you look at who has lesser votes, yes, it's the countries that are less rich, the ones that are poor, but also the countries that predominantly consist of people of color. So some people have suggested that the arrangements within these institutions are also racist. Some of the dialogues around why it's this way has a similar ideology: "Oh, these people don't know what they're doing. They don't know about economic development, they need us to kind of lead the reins so that we can make progress, et cetera." And dialogues like this leave out the point that a lot of the poverty we see now is a result of colonialism, coercion, and all kinds of other morally objectionable processes. It's not just because these people don't know what they're doing.

MYISHA: Do you think that, as a result of this, we are actually getting further away from solving global poverty and not closer?

MEENA: I don't think we've made enough progress on the question of how do we design institutions and alleviate global poverty. And I think part of it is because some of these important features like race and colonialism are being left out of the conversation. On the other hand, I look at work by people like Banerjee and Duflo, and others, who are development economists doing good work on the ground, working to randomize controls. They help us to see that we can target specific problems and we can make progress.

Can we alleviate or eliminate global poverty as just one big phenomenon? Maybe not. But can we get people some anti-malaria drugs, can we get them to stop having rotavirus, et cetera, et cetera? Yes, definitely. I think those are all part of the problem of global poverty. If we see them as smaller problems, then they are problems that we can target. And I do feel hopeful about making progress on those issues, even if I'm more skeptical about progress in some deeper, institutional structural way.

2

Denise James on Political Illusions

MYISHA: You are a philosopher that has been quite interested in a particular playwright for the last six years. How did you get interested in Lorraine Hansberry, whom I love, and what do you find philosophically interesting and insightful about her and her work?

DENISE: I can admit that I didn't start out thinking, "You know what, I'm going to pick up Lorraine Hansberry and do some philosophy with her." I had been at my current job for two years, and well, I had a colleague—he's since passed on—who was in the law school. And he was putting together a panel for Black History Month on *A Raisin in the Sun*. They were going to screen the play and watch part of a film, and it was a big deal at the time. I think this was when hip-hop music mogul, Puffy, was reprising his role as Walter Lee Younger, so it was a thing.

So my colleague contacted me and he said, "Be on this panel and talk about Lorraine Hansberry's play and her deep ethical ideas and all of this radicalism." And I was like "No, I don't want to be on a panel about Lorraine Hansberry." One, I had read the play and some other things as a college kid, and I didn't have any real sense of her as a thinker. I told him that I didn't necessarily want to do it. And he was like "Oh, you don't have a choice. I've asked." I work at an institution where at the time there were fewer than twenty tenure-line black faculty. Now that has actually shrunk since then, but there were just so few of us. And he was like "My students need to see you, so come be on this panel about Lorraine Hansberry." So he didn't really give me a choice and it was persuasive.

I did what we do when we are asked to be on panels that we're not experts about. I spent three weeks in between when he asked and when the panel was, trying to figure out some ideas. What I found out was that I had done to Lorraine Hansberry what so many people had done to Lorraine Hansberry. I had decided that she was one play and that was it. I knew what the play was about, what I thought the play was about, and I had interpretations. But there was so much more to her corpus even though she lived a relatively short life, and I just got a fire in me about thinking about her as a thinker.

What I discovered was that one of the things really philosophically significant about Lorraine Hansberry—at least for me as someone who wants to be a practical philosopher, a philosopher who writes for philosophers, who thinks about professional philosophy things, but also who does that in community with other folks—was that she was always an artist, a writer who was practicing her art and writing in a community of folks who were interested in issues of justice.

In some ways it's role modeling. I didn't know that that's the way she was operating. I only knew about this play. So in some ways, here was a woman who I think I just felt this kinship with, not only because of her sort of complex ideas, but also because of her desire to be a part of practical solutions. I sat on the panel. It went how things go. But after that I was always trying to figure out how I could give her some due, at least in the work that I was doing at the time.

MYISHA: So let's talk about Hansberry and black political illusions. Hansberry notes, "There is a desperate need in our time for the negro writer to assume a partisanship, and namely the war against illusions of one's time and culture." You also note that there are four illusions that she describes. But before we talk about these four illusions, why are they called "illusions" as opposed to "myths" or "falsehoods?"

DENISE: I thought about this for a long time when I really started to trace back through her work and think about her always using this term "illusion"; sometimes the word "delusion" but more often "illusion." I realized Hansberry was a writer and so she was really careful about her words. The choice in words, I think, signals what she thinks the illusion is doing.

See, an illusion is an oversimplification. You see, say, the illusionist, the magician performs the trick and what you see is the trick. Now, if you're attentive, careful, and you know what to watch for, you see that there are other things happening: that the coin doesn't really disappear, that the building actually didn't disappear, that he's not levitating. And it's this idea that she has that things are there but there's a way that we cover over them with illusions. There's these distortions of what is happening.

And it's not, I think, quite like myth or other sorts of falsehoods, because the illusion itself has its form, it takes on its own life. Let's say where I am right now it's thundering and raining and it's really dreary out. If I say it's sunny outside and you look out the window, I'm wrong. So if it was just something false, which this is an example of, there's something wrong about my interpretation. The illusion is something else. You look out the window and the illusion says it's raining and storming and it tells you things like "It is the best sort of day." Now, the interpretation of the fact of the matter, that it's raining and storming, is not what's at dispute for her. The illusion is not covering over a reality independent of the illusion, but it's making something seem a way that either oversimplifies or distorts multiple interpretations. I think she's saying it's a problem of perception.

When she's thinking about these political illusions, there are ways that our perceptions of things are crafted, distorted in certain ways. I think this is perhaps different from mythmaking. I think when people are engaged in myths, at least the way I understand them from Hansberry, there's a sort of story that is built, created, and told, and there are these popular tropes and ideas that get thrown in. Mythmaking may support the illusion, but you don't have to be invested in the whole myth to be subject to some of the illusion.

MYISHA: The first two of the four illusions are about how the writer should approach their craft, and the latter two are straightforwardly political. So let's first address those referring to the writer and then we can move onto the others. The first illusion for Hansberry is, "Art is not and should not be social." But on your reading of Hansberry, art is always social. So how is the former statement an illusion?

DENISE: Hansberry was writing at a time where one of the ways the mainstream art world, and also the mainstream world of critics for popular entertainment, disparaged what black artists were doing by calling it "political art," or "protest art." To do so was to say, "This is not really art," that if your art has a message, a sort of political voice or if it comes from some sort of values, then you're not actually producing what some folks thought of as art.

Now, Hansberry looked around and she said, "You know what, all these great playwrights, all these great novelists, the great American novel, all these people have deeply embedded social and political values in their art. We only normalize and say that it's not social and political because they're part of the dominant group." She really wanted to point out that even when the artist claims that this is not on behalf of some political ideology, the artist comes to the work with their views, their social values, and deeply held, sometimes conscious, sometimes not-so-conscious beliefs. She was just really, I think, trying to fight against the tide that said, "You know what? You can do art for art's sake and it doesn't matter how it appears in the social world. It doesn't matter what commentary you're making about society."

She was very keenly aware of how art, the use of art, the name of art in high and low was used to continue to segregate and disparage artists who were not from the mainstream. But she was also clear about pointing out the fact that all of these really sort of dominant canonical figures had social and political values that just had been assumed not to be value-laden art.

MYISHA: The second illusion, as it relates to the writer is, "people exist independent of the world around them." How did Hansberry see this illusion play out in art, and how do you see it play out in contemporary art?

DENISE: Hansberry was writing at the time when people were asking questions of existential anxiety—who am I, what am I in the world? It was a time when the Beatniks had come onto the scene and they were writing these deeply psychological, "inner life of man" works. She used the term "man" and I think she uses it on purpose. She's pointing out that this was a very gendered idea of art. It's all about the lone individual who is having these deep fits of conscience, and this is what was considered art at the time.

There was this desire for that art to somehow be art for art's sake, just like in the first illusion, and to be removed from the social world. And she was really against that. She thought that people were embedded in their social world; that we can't shake off society and somehow be a freestanding individual. This is not to say that she didn't have interesting ideas about individuality and agency, but she was just keenly aware that this idea that the artist produces a product outside of society could be problematic.

I think there are lots of different ways that this plays out in contemporary art. The most easily accessible to us is when, say, an artist makes some product, some work—whether it's a song or it's an exhibition of visual art—and people say it's offensive. And often what lots of artists say in response is, "Oh, but it's my art. It's a thing that I was thinking. It's my thing. It doesn't have a political form. I should be able to do whatever I like. Your offense is not a big deal for the sake of my art."

Whatever we think about those sorts of claims, Hansberry was suspicious. She thought that people would interpret her art in lots of different ways. She had some frustrations about how people interpreted her art, but she thought of art as a social product. She was an individual who created art which went into society, and society would have their judgments about it. What the artist has to realize is that they're a part of a larger social world, and artists can make things worse.

I think she thought that she was trying to make art in order to bring certain issues to light and in some ways to make some things better. But she also thought—and this is, I think, something that we don't talk much about, at least in my circles—that art can make things worse. You can use art in ways that hurt, damage, and harm people and call it art, entertainment—art for art's sake. What do we do in those circumstances? She was really keenly aware of that.

MYISHA: Now, let's turn to the political illusions. The third illusion is, "everyone in the country is middle class, with middle-class problems." I've noticed in the last few years the use of middle-class language in political rhetoric and it has rubbed me the wrong way. When politicians speak they say things like "We want tax breaks for the middle class," and I'm always wondering, "So what about the poor?" Give us more examples of this particular illusion.

DENISE: Hansberry is writing at a time when there's a growing mobilization of poor black folks in particular, but she's a socialist so she's also interested in labor mobilizing against capitalism. She's writing at a time where one of the refrains against that mobilizing is that the poor are somehow lazy; the reason why they don't have the sorts of things and social conditions that they need is because they don't work enough, or they're too concerned with silly things when they should be concerned with how they work and what sort of jobs they have.

In her time, part of middle-class values was buy-in to a system, capitalism for her, which said your material conditions were where you sought your value. So the goal was to get the best sort of single-family home, to have a job that paid you a steady paycheck, but not criticize what those values could also mean and lead to, which was class stratification, the estrangement of the worker from their work, etc. She was keenly aware that middle-class values actually didn't solve the problems of the poor, the people who were disenfranchised. Having a decent job in a factory and a single-family home at the time, especially for black folks, didn't mean that you were enfranchised.

Hansberry was keenly aware that with the middle class taking up these values of how you were supposed to speak and present yourself in public, they were actually leaving out and behind, one big ideological problem that she was having at the time. She thought that those sorts of middle-class values were really doing harm when it came to thinking about how we could better arrange our society.

MYISHA: You also think that these middle-class values are not only problematic domestically but also globally. How so?

DENISE: Hansberry was really a student of, and trying to process the growing independence movements in, Africa. She was part of the black intelligentsia in New York at a time where this was a thing to think about. What would an increase in nationalism in Africa, especially West Africa, mean for blacks in the diaspora? How would that help, or be similar to or different from freedom struggles in the US?

She was, I think, thinking about how people were criticizing the struggles for freedom abroad using the types of middle-class values that she thought were problematic in the US. If we're concerned, and the goal is something like freedom from poverty, freedom for self-expression, and increased awareness, that the world is not centered around what we now call "white supremacy" (she would say something like "white dominance"), she would say then that criticizing freedom movements because they're not generating factory jobs or the sorts of governments and ideas that we think of as dominant, is problematic.

MYISHA: So how do you wage war against this particular illusion? Do you promote the values of the poor, or is there another effective way to wage war against it?

DENISE: For Hansberry, and this is one of the things I've been thinking about a lot lately, the language of war and partisanship are really big for her. She's like "You know what? You choose a side. You choose the side that you think is the right side. You choose a side and then you got to figure out what sort of moves you can make."

She wasn't prescriptive in the sense that she proclaimed, "The way that we help out the disenfranchised and the black poor is this." That wasn't quite what she was about. I think her project was different. I think one of the ways that you wage the war is that you recognize, to use a very contemporary way that people talk about it, your first-world problems.

Like earlier this morning, I wanted to wear a particular shoe. I was real specific about which shoe I was going to wear. It's funny, I wear black all the time, so all my shoes are black too. But I wanted to wear this particular shoe. I searched my house high and low for this shoe as I passed by five other pairs of shoes that would have been just fine. And I mean, I was at the point of madness, like "Oh, I'm so mad I can't find my shoe. Today's going to be a horrible day. It's raining, and I can't find my shoe!"

Now, it was a big deal for me at 6:00 am when I was getting dressed. But in the scheme of things, I'm a person with multiple pairs of shoes, going to a very cushy job with people around that support me, in a vehicle that works. And I'm keen to think about that sometimes; that the things that sometimes occupy my understanding of what is a good thing or bad thing is based on my class status. If I'm not aware of them, if I'm not vigilant about that, I can sometimes multiply them into what everyone else is worried about. Like I'm worrying about my six-year-old—what the world is going to be like when she grows up. Part of that is where she will go to college, that sort of thing.

I know that there are other six-year-olds in the same city whose parents have to worry about other things. I think for Hansberry, one of the ways that she wages war is that you sort of continue to look at it. When the magician is performing his trick and you're watching and you don't know quite what's happening, she's saying, "No, no, you must pay attention to it, look at it. Figure out, are these first-world problems or are these problems that we should solve because they will help people in other ways?"

MYISHA: The fourth illusion is: "we have an inexhaustible period of time for justice." It's pretty apparent to me that this is an illusion. This seems to be in line with King's criticism of white liberals in his "Letter from a Birmingham Jail." Do you think—and this is just to put on our empathy caps—that a large majority of white liberals, the ones that Hansberry and King criticizes, believe that there's actually time? Do you think that they believe that patience is a virtue that will have some utility in the pursuit for justice?

DENISE: I have so many thoughts about that. I think we can be specific about which one of these folks we're talking about. I think there are a range of white liberal attitudes. And the funny thing is I don't think they're reserved for white liberal attitudes. I have friends of color who are sometimes well-meaning, well-intentioned, but are sort of on this spectrum.

Some folks think that there is time; time in the sense that now is never the time, to paraphrase King. There's always a wait; "If you wait now for a while, then we'll have better conditions, so if you wait for the new president, the new senator, if you wait until this happens." There are always the people who want to wait. I think the reasons why people want to wait put them on the spectrum. One of the parts of the spectrum are people who, frankly, know that we live in unjust conditions, especially folks who are poor and disenfranchised, and of color in the United States. And what those people want is not time; they don't want the pains of striving. This is something that Hansberry is really acutely aware of; that freedom struggles are difficult. You can't assert, "What we want is power for the poor, or what we want is different policing practices, or what we want is an end to racism in our institutions," and then not act on it. Or if you act on it, you can't act on it and it not hurt people. Not hurt in a sort of deep sense of harm; no, people's feelings get hurt. Folks wonder if you're calling them a racist, or folks are in their feelings because their day was disrupted because you had a protest.

For Hansberry, and I think I agree with this, there's this idea that the time for justice is slow not because we need to be patient, but because if it's not slow, it hurts, it's difficult, it's uncomfortable, and so we'd rather not do it. We'll put it off like we're putting off doing the dishes. You do the dishes, it sucks, but you got to go through the process. And I think that for a lot of liberal folks, people don't want the pains of justice.

I also think there's another end of that spectrum. Some folks, especially where we are now (I don't know that this was as true in Hansberry's time) think there aren't really any current freedom struggles. I think there are people who think that they're people who are mad about something that happened or particular issues, but they're not invested in the idea that some of us think that there are real persistent, current problems that stem from systemic oppression.

MYISHA: This makes me think about the reports by some white folks who claim that racism did not come about again until President Obama became president.

DENISE: People have all sorts of reasons why they have that view. But for lots of us, when someone says something like that, it strikes you as so odd, especially because of our social position. I'm a black woman who grew up poor and working class—more often poor than working. When someone says that there was no racism until 2008, sometimes I feel like we're on another planet, like she lives in a different world than I do, and it might be true in some ways. But I think there's something else going on with that sort of thing. I think about this when I read Hansberry too. There are a lot of people who, because of their own racism or classism, they want to say, "What you have is enough. It isn't what I got. You shouldn't have what I have." I think there are ways that they remind certain folk that they're always stepping out of place. And so we think about this when we claim that there was no racism until Obama. There was racism, but she felt like nobody had to call it out until there was a black man in the White House.

There's an interesting way that that gets turned back on people who say, "Something ain't right." I try not to be shocked, because I shouldn't be, because it's not an uncommon thing to hear. But every time someone says something like that, I'm just looking like "Where do you live, and how are we occupying the same world that we are?" That's a real, real problem. I'm not sure what the solution is, but it's a real problem that we could be in the same space and someone could be thinking racism returned with the election of Barack Obama.

MYISHA: So we've discussed the four illusions, but you think there's another one and this is pretty provocative. You think the idea that integration will solve our racial problems is an illusion. Why, Denise James?

DENISE: So you ask me that with the appropriate amount of "ooh." Here's the thing, and I started thinking this before: you ever have an intuition about something, but until you sort of sit with it, it's just in the background? I think I probably thought that integration was an illusion before I even had words to think about this. It recurred for me, and it has been recurring for me for several reasons—some professional, some personal.

I am a person who is recently middle class. I got a cushy job that I like in philosophy. I'm a tenured professor at a place that values me. I have a partner who is gainfully employed. We are suddenly the black middle class after not being middle class. That has posed lots of problems. I spend a lot of my time—and this was true of my schooling––as the sole person of color; just me, or one or two other folks, sometimes one or two other black folks, sometimes we get someone who is Latina. But mostly it's just me. I spent the majority of my professional time in those sorts of settings, but it also translates to my personal time, my family, where we live and what we do. Around me there are people who think that just the appearance, the presence of one black family or so, has suddenly integrated their community.

So it's a personal thing, but also a professional thing. Sometimes when we philosophers look at real-world problems, we come up with analytically neat solutions. One of the things to talk about, at least for a while there, was integration. It was like a recurrence in philosophy; although black thinkers who are not typically thought of as philosophers had been thinking about integration for a long time, including Lorraine Hansberry, whose family integrated a white neighborhood of Chicago. There was a big court case about it. It was a big deal in her formative life. So black people have been thinking about integration for a long time, but philosophers, I think, have taken it up recently.

I think integration is an illusion. Often what we're talking about when we're talking about integrating neighborhoods is we're not supporting and building up neighborhoods that had been racially segregated. The black side of town doesn't get integrated and doesn't get the sort of resources white neighborhoods have.

What we're thinking about is the "sprinkle-in" method of integration. Black folks get sprinkled in with white folks in better spaces. We look at data that says black people in poverty, living together, increases things like crime rates, and attrition when it comes to going to high school. And people say, "Well, what would be better is if we broke up racial segregation." What that means for the minority is the minority gets broken up and sprinkled into white communities.

There are lots of problems with that. One is a problem of values. Often we assume that everyone should be striving for the markers of success, markers of value that are white middle-class values. And frankly, I am not certain that those are the values that we all should be striving for.

There's this idea, at least in some of the literature, that the white middle-class values of single, not multigenerational, families who have people working certain jobs, and whose kids act in certain sorts of ways, and have certain sorts of activities, are the values we should strive for. I'm looking around and I think, "Who is being reflected in those types of values?" They're not the people that I grew up with who I think had some really good ideas. They're also not the people of the generation before, the two generations before I grew up—the people who raised us. They, in communities that were segregated, took great pride in cultural values that included community as central to well-being. Part of the thing that you strove for was to do good in, and for, your community, because you were a part of it. That's not necessarily what lots of people who are touting that "integration will solve our racial problems" are talking about. This increased, sort of capitalistic self-gain individuality is a big part of that integration illusion, and I worry about that. I worry about those values.

I worry, too, that black people have become a social experiment. People are interested in what happens when you integrate the school, when you integrate workspaces with one or two black people, because that's pretty much what we're talking about here. The thought is that black people will somehow get the social capital they need to be successful and that white people will learn because they are in close association with somebody's black child.

To me, that puts a lot of onus on the black child. I worry because I've been that person, the one person who is allowed into the party. The problem is the party wasn't meant for my black self to appear. The difficulty of that, and I think we don't actually want to talk about this, is not an equal share of growing pains when we integrate communities, but instead the real risks, real harms that can happen—I'm not saying they have to happen—when we integrate spaces as a minority.

I get really worried when philosophers get ahold of a problem and don't really think about the real-world impact, although it's a real-world problem. Philosophers take what they think is the best cognitive-science data about how people develop, then they rope them all together and say, "You know what we ought to do? We ought to do this thing to help the folk." The problem is the folk are actually folk. What seems like a line or two about emotional distress or problems with identity formation, all those sorts of things seem real neat on paper, but I don't think we understand that we might be participating in and championing ideas that could be seriously problematic. I'm not saying we should not think about these things. I'm not even saying we should not try to enact new racially desegregated communities. I'm just saying not enough folks are asking, "What is the cost of this?"

MYISHA: There was a profile in *The Washington Post* some time ago about a black middle-class family who decided to continue living in their working-class community for reasons of support. Going back to the question of how you wage war against these illusions, it seems like they are opting to stay in the black community as opposed to integrating. Have you thought about other ways to wage war against this illusion?

DENISE: One of the ways, and I think this is a really important way, is that you have to really examine the source. I think that's what I was saying before; this is a Hansberry sort of concept, that one of the ways that you wage war is by actually attending to what might be problematic. It is unpopular for me to say that I don't think most of, at least our theoretical ideas about integration, are helpful or working as solutions to racial problems. I just don't think they work. Part of what my battle is, is to examine the source. This is harder to do, and this is also really important. You stop saying, "Well, black people or poor people only do that because this." It's a way of sort of explaining away differences, but also it's a way of making neat and nice for the majority, things that perhaps aren't neat and nice. So that's an interesting practice.

I read that article that you mentioned really closely. The family chose to stay in their school district. When you are upwardly mobile, it is really tempting not to associate yourself with anything that has to do with your former poverty or distress. We get out of our neighborhoods; we send our kids to a better school. In fact, that is one of everybody's, or at least around the black families I know, refrains. You want your kids to live better than you did, so you try to give them other things. That family made a choice that I think is in many ways commendable. I think people question that choice. I had a great conversation with a friend who lives in that same area about that choice. She said, "I don't know if I want my children to wage my battles. Do I want to risk what I could give them in their mobility for what I think is, ideologically, a justice claim?"

That's real tough. That's something really to think about. It's something I think about all the time. We agonize about it. I live in Dayton, Ohio, where the city is racially segregated. There is not a big black middle class, and I'm being kind by saying there isn't a big one. I have to almost daily determine what sort of activities my child will participate in, because we're not thinking of a highly integrated place. Places are integrated because she shows up. This is a part of our everyday life. What struggle is a struggle to have? Am I going to make struggles for the kid, or I'm going to make struggles for me? Is this about institutional things or is it about personal experience?

You asked about another way to wage this war. I think the thing that I am really committed to is that Hansberry says we have to reclaim the past so we can look to our future. Part of my project recently has been being really attentive to sources, to information, to philosophically rich ideas that don't come from philosophers or professionally trained philosophers. That's really difficult because the question is: Do I then write in a way that's authentic? Do I translate them into a language that, because it's not their professional language, distorts the view? Those are all really sort of hard things.

When it comes to the on-the-ground stuff, when it comes to integration, I think the same thing happens when there are a few of us who say, "Some of the efforts we've put into trying to figure out how to integrate black folks into, say, white communities, should be efforts we put into strengthening historically black communities." It sounds really segregationist. There are people who tell me when I say things like that, that I have somehow missed the point. I say, "I worry that they don't see the value in those spaces, that they don't see the value in transferring resources to spaces where perhaps different cultural values, due to race and culture, prevail."

3

Lori Gruen on Prisons

MYISHA: So not only do you do work on animal rights, but you also teach in prisons. I want to talk about these two topics together. There are analogies often made between animals and black folks, and between the ways animals and prisoners are treated. What do you see as the dangers of such analogies?

LORI: I think there's an important way in which analogies themselves are always treacherous. Having said that, that doesn't mean that they can't be useful. But I think, drawing on the work of Frank Wilderson III, who talks about the ruse of analogy, the idea is that analogies have a way of flattening difference, and that's always a little bit dangerous.

I think that in the case of animals being analogized with black people, or with prisoners, there's a really long history of devaluation through analogy, dehumanization through analogy, and abjection through analogy. In my work on this, I'm always really specific about highlighting how dangerous these things are.

Now, part of the reason they're dangerous is because of the way the human itself has been constructed as white. I think that's another feature, and we get this in Sylvia Wynter. For example, whiteness and humanity are constructed as the same kind of thing. When you have the category of the animal, that's fundamentally the nonhuman. At least historically, and I think to this very day, we have blackness as sub-human. So the idea is that by putting black people or prisoners in the category of animal, it can reinforce the structure of the white human and all others. That's a big, big danger. The comparison *has* been used to reinforce that division.

Having said that, I think there are some important insights. Even though this is really treacherous, dangerous terrain, I think there are still important insights that we can get for working towards social justice by evaluating the ways that these categories are constructed.

MYISHA: When Cecil the Lion and Harambee the Gorilla were killed by humans, there was much public outcry. Many people showed concern for these animals but as a result some people criticized the outcry by noting that Americans seem to care more for animals than they care for black lives. I think they were pointing to the lack of public outcry at the death of black bodies by the hands of the police, for example.

We can take this concern to represent either an acceptance of the analogy or a resistance to the analogy. For instance, what some might have been saying was blacks are human, and therefore ought to be treated better than the way humans treat animals. Or we can read them as saying that animals should get respect, but blacks should at least get the same kind of respect we show to animals. What is your response to this?

LORI: It's a really, really important point. I'm actually taken by the work of black vegan activist Syl Ko, who's drawing on work of Sylvia Wynter. Wynter, highlighting police violence after the Rodney King beating, and the riots that occurred, notes that there's this acronym—NHI—which means "no humans involved." It actually means that there are no white people involved. Basically, it's about the way in which black people are not human. And the idea here, which is really I think forceful, is that this is still going on. What ends up happening is that for many black activists, the idea is that "Wait, wait, wait, we're human, we want to be sort of in that group and we don't want to be thought of in the animal group."

But I think the idea here is actually to recognize, as I was just suggesting, that the category of the human itself is not a category in a culture of anti-black racism that is ever going to be available in an un-critical way; the category itself is constructed as white. The category, necessarily, is going to preclude black people and preclude nonhuman animals.

I am drawing on the really interesting and important work of Claire Jean Kim, who has a book called *Dangerous Crossings*, which is, again, about questions of race and animality, and the ways in which these are really fraught and conflicted. So what Claire Jean Kim calls for is what she calls an "ethics of avowal." We don't have to throw lions or gorillas, as it were, under the bus; these aren't zero-sum issues. At the same time, it's a really important way of recognizing how these categories reinforce exclusions and abjection.

Having said that, there is something very serious about the way in which, at least most of the animal advocacy community, is unaware of their very deep anti-black racism and sexism as well. I don't want to suggest that this is a common view amongst those who advocate for animals, but I do think it's important to recognize that this is an important site of contestation; that we don't want to just accept the category of the human as one that's a biological category as opposed to a deeply political and social category.

MYISHA: So what do you say about this assumption, or at least this particular claim that certain kinds of activism, for example, animal rights and climate change, are issues for privileged folk?

LORI: I think that there's something that needs to be unpacked there, and I think that there are a lot of ways to think about what that means. On the one hand, if you look at those people who are the spokespeople for these particular movements, you'd see often that these are people of privilege. But if you look at the people who are doing on-the-ground work, or in the case of climate change, those people who are going to be most impacted most quickly, these are not privileged people. We're already looking at climate refugees all across the world; these are not privileged people. These are people from poor communities; these are people who are losing their livelihoods, losing their land; these are native peoples. So, I don't think that climate change is an issue of concern for only privileged folks.

What we see too, in the social-scientific literature, is that people of color are right on it. They're right on this problem of climate change. What I get from a group of really inspiring black animal activists, is that it's really upsetting to be ignored over and over and over again by other people of color who are saying that this is an issue for white people, because this is their issue. How do they get ignored?

Now, having said that, there is a problem of representation that I think a lot of people have been working on for a long time, in terms of who speaks about these issues and who speaks for these movements. I do agree that it's a problem. But I really don't think that these are issues necessarily for privileged people, or for white people only, because as I said, there are a lot of nonwhite activists for animals and there are certainly many, many, many different people who are working for climate justice.

MYISHA: So let's return back to the analogy concerns. Being careful with the analogy, you do suggest that there are some similarities, particularly between animals and prisoners, that have to do with captivity.

LORI: The idea of captivity is a really important idea that's been overlooked in philosophical literature. I've been trying to bring it to the attention of other philosophers and scholars. One thing that I think is really important for thinking about captivity is that it isn't just being confined or enclosed, it's also about being controlled.

The question of control is, I think, an important one. When you control another, you're actually denying them possibilities for expressing their freedom, or their autonomy, or their choice, however you want to describe that. I think that that's something that applies in both the case of captive prisoners, and also in the case of nonhuman animals.

It's really instructive and insightful to think about these things together. There's the question about control: If you look at these things together, you get a notion of domination, as well as the ways in which questions about the possibility of interest violation can occur in a captive environment.

I have to confess that when I first started working with incarcerated folks, I was really nervous about them finding out that I was interested in questions about our relationships with other animals. This was because of the abjection and dehumanization that's so much a part of a prisoners' experience, and because "criminals" are often stereotypically compared to animals who can't control their desires and need to be controlled. But it turns out that those whom I've been working with are really open to thinking about these issues in the same way. They are excited to think about how there are these institutions of captivity that operate with shocking parallels.

The idea of "lock the door and throw away the key" is really important to my thinking lately. It is the idea that these humans, and many animals, that are in captivity are disposable, that we don't have to think about them; they're out of our sight and we don't have to be concerned about their interests or their well-being. In some ways, that is already the norm with other animals. They're here to be used and discarded. That mentality of disposability seems to spill over into our general attitude towards those who are the victims of our current system of mass incarceration.

MYISHA: Are carceral spaces only limited to physical prisons?

LORI: I don't think so. I think it's really interesting to think about this notion of captivity as sort of a broader carceral space. Think about, for example, laboratories where they do research on other animals as a carceral space. There's interesting work that some critical geographers are doing right now to analyze these spaces. I think refugee camps can also be analyzed as a carceral space. They're an increasing problem, both given the kind of mass violence that's occurring in various parts of the world there and the state of climate refugees. Carceral spaces are canonically prison spaces, but I think we can think of other spaces that confine and control, both humans and other animals, as also being carceral spaces.

MYISHA: Let me try to prove to you that I've read some Foucault. Are schools carceral spaces?

LORI: This is a really interesting question. I think that what Foucault means by "carceral" and what I mean by "carceral" is a little bit different. The idea of the carceral for Foucault had to do very much with a certain sort of extension of governmentality throughout society. Dylan Rodríguez, for example, has written some really provocative and radical pieces on how university spaces are carceral in that Foucaultian vein.

I think it's really important that we do not blur the distinction between carceral in a strict sense and a looser notion of the carceral. Again, this is something that I think comes into some of the critical work that I've read on anti-black racism: the notion that there are actual prisoners, and other black people who are prisoners in waiting, and that the status of the prisoners and the prisoners in waiting is equivalent.

MYISHA: When you say "prisoners in waiting," what do you mean by that?

LORI: Other black folks.

MYISHA: Okay.

LORI: This is what an analysis might be: given a culture of anti-black racism, whether blacks are in prison now or not, they're prisoners in waiting and therefore the status between these two is the same. I think there's an important sense in which there are psychologically and statistically effective ways in which, one in three black men will be incarcerated at one point. So, there is that sort of prisoner-in-waiting thing.

But I think the idea that these are all the same is really important to push back against. There's a sense in which those who are currently ensnared in the many tentacles of the mass incarceration system are experiencing a certain kind of—I want to sort of draw on the work of one of my students—"triple consciousness," which is in some ways fundamentally different from a "double consciousness" that we have among other people. So I think there are parallels, but at the same time there are some things that are very different.

One of the key features of captivity is that not only are you confined and controlled, but your basic needs have to be satisfied by those who control you. Just think about that for a second. Your basic needs have to be satisfied by those who control you. That violation of your dignity, or your independence, your autonomy, your freedom—that is an injury that shouldn't be overlooked; it's a fundamentally different injury than the carceral space of the university, for example.

Sure, we're all limited in various ways. None of us have full freedoms, and those limitations track all sorts of lines: racial lines, gender lines, sexual-orientation lines, and class lines. But the idea of the carceral for me, is a sense in which your basic abilities to take care of yourself are stripped from you. So, I want to push back on this sort of expanded notion of the carceral. I don't want it to be limited to prisons, but I don't want it to expand to any place where there's a kind of governmentality happening.

MYISHA: You say that at the core of various functions of carceral systems, there is a carceral logic. What exactly is that logic, and what are its many types?

LORI: I have been thinking about what this logic does, and what it does is kind of complicated, so I want to go into it a little bit. Particularly, the carceral logic that underlies these mutual systems that perpetuate what Orlando Patterson calls "social death." Here I'm also drawing on insights that Lisa Guenther has shared in her work on solitary confinement.

The idea is that those who are subjected to the carceral logics are not just dominated, but that they're fundamentally denied a certain level of relationality, and they're exposed to a kind of excess violence. Saidiya Hartman argues that they are fungible: they can be owned, traded, and moved. The logic maps onto what Orlando Patterson describes as social death.

What this does is create an ontological category of "other." It's an "other" that's kept at odds with the center, the white center, the human center. This logic, the carceral logic, is what holds the center. It causes both a deep experiential and emotional distance; carceral logics perpetuate this distance, this "otherness."

Let me give you one example and a parallel example. Currently in European zoos, animals are allowed to reproduce and then the offspring are killed. That's just the standard practice. In the United States, they're usually given birth control. There are pros and cons here that we can get in a long talk about; I don't want to go there. The idea is that you move the animals around to breed and kill the offspring, all so you can continue to move animals around to breed. You continue this cycle, keeping the good ones, or the genetically valuable ones. This is to me a great example of a carceral logic because it's fundamentally about disposability.

Now, think about the parallel of taking mothers who have committed some serious, or not-so-serious crime, and ripping them from their families. This is part of the idea that either relations aren't going to matter, or they already don't even matter to those whom we keep as "other" or think of as "other." That's just one example of the effects of a carceral logic. There's no value; the animals in zoos or the people incarcerated are not even thought of as beings that are relational or worthy of having relations. One thing that happens in maximum security prisons, as you probably know, is if you end up becoming too relational, you're then moved to a new space. This is so reminiscent of ways in which animals, especially zoo animals, are not commodities in that people don't usually buy and sell them, yet they're still treated as fungible, transferable, and as beings whose social relations aren't really worthy of attention.

MYISHA: Those who are thinking about effecting some kind of social change in response to the carceral system and carceral logic may encounter a problem. How might the carceral logic itself get in the way of social change, and what can people do in response to that?

LORI: One of the most tricky things about thinking of carceral problems as akin to this notion of social death is that it seems there's no way of undoing it; it's part and parcel, it's integral to the system that we know. There's not going to be a whole lot of room for reforms in that system because the system requires both an insider and outsider, as it were. So this seems to suggest that this is going to be a problem for making social change or achieving social justice.

I am not probably the most hopeful at the moment, especially given the state of the world. But I do think, for example, that some of the notions about black study that Robin Kelley and Fred Moten have been talking about, and ways of autonomously and independently creating what Jared Sexton calls "the social life of social death," is to recognize these systems and to resist them from within one's own newly created form.

For me prison education work is a part of that. It's a way to try to generate or at least provide certain skills for imagining other ways that the world could be. In the same way, activism for other animals for some people is so weird to think about: "What? You're interested in animals? Why are you interested in animals?" Opening up that possibility means that we have to reimagine many different kinds of relationships.

So, part of it is imagining a different world. If you think about it in political-philosophical terms, for example, Marx called for an end of capitalism. That's pretty radical. I don't know if that's actually going to happen, and we can't quite imagine what the world will look like after that. Imagining the destruction of a carceral logic that fundamentally upholds a division between white humanity and black people and animal, I don't know what exactly that could look like. But I think that there are new ideas for thinking that through.

I also think, and this is in some of my other work, that what I call "entangled empathetic relationships" could take us in a whole different direction. I think it is fundamentally important to start with all of us recognizing that we're in relationships of all sorts, along different kinds of political, economic, racial, religious, gender, and class lines. Once we recognize these relationships as relationships, we could start to reflect on how we're individually implicated. There are ways that we might be able to imagine a way to make social change in light of these deeply problematic social constructs.

MYISHA: As we've been talking, some people when they think about a prisoner, imagine maybe a black prisoner, or I think most people have imagined an adult prisoner. So, I want to go back to the school question just a little bit.

I'm thinking about the school-to-prison pipeline. I'm thinking about the viral videos that we have been exposed to, where school police slam a young black girl in her desk, break a young boy's jaw, and arrest a five-year-old black boy for playing around with a female student. I know that you reject the notion that the school is itself a carceral space, but I wonder if you can provide some analysis about what is currently going on in the school system as it relates to incarceration and policing?

LORI: I don't want to make this sound like a silly semantic distinction, but I would think about that just as a problem of criminalization that's happening primarily for, but not exclusively black people, including black children. What's happening is that the educational spaces, the schools, the early-childhood centers, all the way up through high school, have become sites of criminalization. That is another part of the problem of this general idea.

So, in that sense, yes, schools are spaces in which the carceral logic is operating for sure. It's really dangerous because what ends up happening here is that children who in the past would maybe get detentions or community work for getting in trouble in school are now becoming criminalized and being put into the juvenile justice system. And we know that many people who are incarcerated as juveniles end up, if they get out of the system, which most of them do, in the adult populations in prisons.

I'm not an education expert, but part of what's happened, I think, is that increasingly teachers and administrators in schools, particularly in communities with less resources, are finding it easier to deal with problems by outsourcing. This is something that our society is doing in all sorts of ways. But outsourcing in this case is contributing to our terrible problem of mass incarceration.

MYISHA: Lori, are you a prison abolitionist?

LORI: I am a prison abolitionist.

MYISHA: Why?

LORI: Part of it is that I'm an abolitionist abolitionist.

MYISHA: What does that mean?

LORI: If we think about anti-black racism and the use of animals, the concept of abolition is necessary for imagining a different set of social, political, personal, and ethical relationships. For me, prison abolition means rethinking how we are going to solve social, economic, and political problems. I'm not denying there are problems; there are problems. But the current system, the criminal justice system as it exists right now, is not addressing those problems and in many ways it is actually the source of the problems.

An abolitionist perspective is one that says, "This system needs to be abolished." I think the system of anti-black racism needs to be abolished, and what we might call the *specieist* or *human-exceptionalist* system of animal treatment also needs to be abolished.

I'm in favor of the imaginative possibilities of what could happen if we were to end these systems of disposability and disregard, these systems of hate, and change the world so that we don't have systems that perpetuate such violence.

4

José Mendoza on Immigration

MYISHA: A lot of immigration rhetoric presently focuses on Mexican immigration. Why do you think this is the case? Is there such a thing as a Mexican immigration problem?

JOSÉ: Well, I think there's two answers to this. There's what I would call the short and myopic answer, which says: There are 11 million undocumented immigrants; about 80 percent of these undocumented immigrants are from Latin America. Of that 80 percent, approximately 75 percent of them are from Mexico, and a significant portion of the remaining 25 percent are from Central America. In most people's imagination, being Latin American is close enough to being Mexican, definitely Central American, and as I said, a significant percentage are from Mexico.

That's the simple answer. I call it the simple and myopic answer for a couple of reasons. For one thing, since around 2008, 2009 (and people are surprised to hear this), net migration from Mexico has been at zero. In other words, there are as many Mexican immigrants going back to Mexico as are coming into the United States. The other reason why it's myopic is that about 50 percent of undocumented immigrants don't unlawfully cross the border. What they typically do, almost 50 percent of them, is overstay their visas.

I think this obsession with the Mexican border is wrongheaded on two accounts. For one, at this point the people who are crossing the Mexican border aren't actually Mexican. Second, a lot of people who are undocumented don't arrive through unlawful channels; they simply overstay their visa. But I call this response myopic primarily because it ignores the history of Mexican immigrants, how the "undocumented Mexican worker" was actually a construction of US policy.

To the question of why people are particularly upset about Mexican immigration, why they see it as a huge problem, I think there is an existential answer. The United States is undergoing a major demographic shift. I've heard that by around 2050, the US is going to be a majority minority country. Immigration is seen as driving this demographic shift.

I think another way of phrasing the question you asked me, to use Ron Sundstrom's phrase, is: Why do people fear the browning of America? That's more of the existential answer to this question. I think it's two things. It's a loss of American culture, a loss of American identity. Many people would say this is a very xenophobic and racist view. But people also say this culture is the glue that holds a community together. It's what makes America great.

When you're part of the dominant culture, you'll notice it when traveling. You'll travel and it's almost like you don't understand what's going on in your surroundings; you don't feel very comfortable in a way. I think this is what a lot of white Americans are feeling. Things like "Press 1 for English, press 2 for Spanish" are not that big of a deal, but for them it's the beginning of not being comfortable in one's own country.

The second part of this larger existential answer is the loss of real material wealth, real opportunities, real advantages that for a long time white Americans enjoyed. Historically, if you were white and had a high school diploma, or not even the equivalent of it, there were always avenues for you to reach the middle class, either through manufacturing, meatpacking, and other service industries. Now when white Americans look around, they see that these jobs are either (a) gone or (b) being done by immigrants for below livable wages.

When a lot of these folks think about open borders, whether for trade, services, material, or for immigrants, they see them as the cause of why they can no longer move into the middle class. Before the 2016 election, Ann Coulter came out with a book called *Adios, America*, like "goodbye to America." The subtitle summarizes all I've been clumsily trying to say: she calls it the left's plan—by that she means people who are pro-immigrant—to turn America into a third-world hellhole. That's how they see immigration. I don't agree with it, but those are the worries, and this is why in particular Mexicans immigrants get the brunt of this fear.

MYISHA: Let's talk a little bit more about borders. Do states have a presumptive right to control immigration?

JOSÉ: Philosophically I'm in the camp that says they do not; I'm in the open-borders camp. But the problem with doing philosophy and trying to translate it to public policy, the problem with a position like mine is that I'm swimming upstream. Most people think that legitimate states have a presumptive right to restrict immigration. If you want to actually do public policy work, or influence public policy, sometimes you have to assume that. That's what I do in my work. I assume that and try to see what sort of immigrant rights I can derive from that.

I think individuals have a right to freedom of movement. I think borders perpetuate and create unjust global inequalities. That's what they do. Borders are the new way to keep feudal privilege: keeping certain groups of people in privilege and denying it to others.

MYISHA: You alluded to this before and I want to explore it further. How has immigration control in the US historically helped to construct what you call "whiteness," and how has it functioned to help maintain white supremacy?

JOSÉ: I've got a really long answer for this, so just jump in any time you want to interrupt me because I can just go. The first answer is very direct, and quite uncontroversial when you look at the history of the United States. A couple things happened in 1790. In 1790, if I'm not mistaken, all the states in the Union finally ratified the US Constitution. With the signing of the Constitution we went from being this loose confederation to now the United States of America.

One of the first acts the US passed was the Naturalization Act, and the Naturalization Act lays out the criteria for a path to citizenship in the nation. The first restriction was that only whites were eligible for naturalization. From then on, restrictions on admission and citizenship have been closely tied to whiteness. This doesn't just apply to immigrants; you see this in the 1857 Dred Scott ruling. That case said it doesn't matter how many generations you've been here, if you have African ancestry, you cannot be a citizen of the United States; you are not white. This continued on, even after the Civil War, and the passage of the Civil War amendments.

Beginning in 1875, you start getting these Chinese Exclusion Acts. The Page Act of 1875 is the first restrictive immigration act. Almost 100 years after the United States is founded you get the very first restriction on immigration, which is based on race. It's based on the desires of people who don't want Asian immigrants. These restrictions begin to expand.

By 1917 there's what's called the Asiatic Barred Zone. Now, you might wonder: Why did they start with an Asiatic Barred Zone? Part of the issue was that Japan was an imperial nation, which actually patted itself on the back and said, "Look, we defeated a white nation in a war!" Japan defeated the Russians at the turn of the twentieth century. So instead of having an exclusion act with Japan, the United States had a gentlemen's agreement; Japan would voluntarily restrict its immigrants from coming into the United States. But by 1917, this became a law. The whole Asiatic Barred Zone went about halfway through India. By 1924 the US had a national origins quota. They decided that people from Southern Europe, Eastern Europe were not white and so they faced immigration restrictions.

You see this in the Supreme Court cases concerning Takao Ozawa and Bhagat Singh Thind. In the first one, *Ozawa v. United States*, 260 US 178 (1922), the Supreme Court ruled that only Caucasians, people of the Caucus race or from the Caucas region, were eligible for immigration. In the second case, *United States v. Bhagat Singh Thind*, 261 US 204 (1923), the court ruled that since Thind was part of a high Hindi-speaking caste he was technically part of the Caucasian race. But the justice in that case looked at him and said, "But just by looking at you, we can tell that you've got the wrong culture." So race is not just biological or anthropological. It's also ethnicity that counts as making you nonwhite. So these immigration restrictions were linked to nonwhiteness.

This is very direct, it's in the law; the law is explicitly racist. Then we enter World War II where we're fighting Nazis. In addition, China, who we've had these exclusion acts with for about fifty to sixty years, is not an ally. This is really inconvenient, right? Imagine fighting a war against fascists, who have this view that there's certain groups of people who are inferior and need to be eliminated. Then people look at the United States immigration policy and say, "Well, in a way you guys aren't that different."

It's also inconvenient that for one of our allies, we had these very restrictive immigration policies. So, beginning in 1943, the restrictions on immigrants from Asia is lifted. By 1952, again, because of not wanting to be associated with the Nazis in Germany, the US got rid of the racial restriction in the Naturalization Act. By 1965 national origin quotas were abolished.

It's looking like we're making progress. But what ends up happening in 1965 is that for the first time in US history, there are immigration restrictions on the Western Hemisphere. People are surprised to learn about this. Before 1965 there were no immigration restrictions on countries in the Western Hemisphere; basically there were open borders with Mexico. In 1965 we get restrictions. This becomes a problem. During the war, we had the Bracero Program, which was an agreement with Mexico to send us workers. At the height of the Bracero Program, there were half a million Bracers coming to the United States yearly and working. When the national origin quota got abolished, they put a cap of about 20,000 immigrants per country. In the years leading up to 1965, on average, Mexico was sending about 250,000 migrant workers. So just imagine what happens if you try to cap 250,000 at 20,000?

The remaining 230,000 people don't just stop coming; they just become undocumented. So this is the history of how Mexican immigrants started becoming the face of undocumented immigration. Only ten years later, in 1975, a case goes before the Supreme Court, and it's basically a racial profiling case. It's called *United States vs. Brignoni-Ponce*. Border Patrol basically stopped this guy because he looks Mexican. That's the only reason. The court says, "Look, why'd you pull him over?," and they say, "We pulled him over because he looks Mexican." And what the Supreme Court says is, "Well, look, since 1965 we've had this dramatic increase in undocumented immigrants from Mexico, so it makes sense that we use your Mexicanness as a reason for pulling you over because of the dramatic increase in undocumented immigrants."

What you see is how the enforcement of a policy which doesn't adhere to social and historical circumstances creates what we talked about before, this close connection between being Mexican, being immigrant, and "illegal." These three things start to become synonymous.

It moves on from there to 1986, the first time that you have employer sanctions. Before 1986, if you employed an undocumented worker, there was nothing wrong with that. Someone might think it's morally wrong, but there was nothing legally wrong with knowingly employing somebody that's undocumented. After 1986 it was against the law; there was a fine and so forth. This was the beginning of the enforcement of immigration laws in the workplace. In 1994 there was a law called Proposition 187 in California. Now you see a state trying to enforce immigration law in the sphere of social services. What Prop 187 did, or would have done (the courts found it unconstitutional), was deny social services to undocumented immigrants and their children. Part of the reason this was found to be unconstitutional is because it affected citizens.

But notice what is happening. Immigration enforcement is creeping into the workplace and creeping into social services. By 1996 the US passed a law that's the federal version of laws like Arizona's Prop 187. They're called 287(g) agreements. The 1996 law introduced what most people who work on immigration and migration call "crimmigrations." It's the criminalization of immigration and has three parts. It started expanding. There were always one or two crimes, but it started expanding the list of crimes that would make you deportable.

It also made certain immigration violations into criminal offenses. Before, if you unlawfully crossed the border, you would get something equivalent to a parking ticket. But what they started doing is if you get deported and you come back again, you are subject to actual jail time. They started criminalizing migration. The 1996 law also used strategies that are normally used for criminal enforcement, like raids for example. They expanded these sorts of tactics into the enforcement of immigration. So that's why people call this "crimmigration."

What we've seen since then, especially at the local and state levels, in places like Arizona, Georgia, Arkansas, and South Carolina, is that the anti-immigrant laws they pass are all versions of this. They're expanding enforcement beyond the border into these different areas. The strategy is called attrition through enforcement: enforcing immigration laws in all these places such that you make the lives of immigrants so bad they want to self-deport. I think this is wrong on many different levels. Not in just the ways they treat "immigrants" or undocumented immigrants; these enforcement strategies and mechanisms also catch citizens. It's not that all citizens are subject to these sorts of enforcement laws. It's only particular citizens. In this way, if you go back to the story that I began with, you see how immigration restrictions and immigration enforcement do not so much create whiteness as much as they create nonwhiteness. So a group of people, Latino/Latinas, who are homogeneous (for within the Latino/Latina community you have a variety of races ranging from white to black and indigenous), in a sense become entirely nonwhite.

MYISHA: Earlier you talked about the fear of the eradication of whiteness. In some ways in the US, that could explain the xenophobia that is currently happening. But we know xenophobia is also happening in other parts of the world, where people that look alike are stopping people who look like them from entering into their particular country.

Is there any way that you can explain xenophobia beyond whiteness? What are some other things that are perhaps behind xenophobia? And for those who are currently experiencing it, how can they overcome it?

JOSÉ: When you focus on immigration justice the way I do, it's not clear that if we were ever able to get immigration justice that we would necessarily get rid of xenophobia. Because I think—and this might be part of what's behind your question—immigration injustice is more a symptom or result of xenophobia than actually the cause of xenophobia. So a lot of my work is like the doctors' Hippocratic Oath, "First, do no harm." I think that's almost where I am at this point. The way I look at it, things are so bad for immigrants that it's almost like we need to first "do no harm," prevent harm, and find principles, figure out how to argue against this kind of enforcement that perpetuates and, in a sense, creates xenophobia.

But I think xenophobia goes beyond immigration. It's definitely an issue of people's fear of insecurity, lack of safety. It could also be done for political gain through this fear of terrorism; fear of all these things can drive xenophobia. I assume the people who follow Le Pen and these xenophobic politicians aren't rich. They're usually poor people. So I think this feeling, "Well, we're poor and the opening of borders, which lets businesses leave and yet still bring back their products, and also allows immigrants to take these jobs" is also at the heart of things. Insecurity and inequality might be the causes. Those are definitely larger issues than we can solve in immigration justice. There are things that happen in immigration policy and immigration enforcement that perpetuate and create xenophobia. Dealing with xenophobia itself is a much larger topic than immigration justice.

MYISHA: Can you tell us what is problematic about using "illegals" or "aliens" to refer to immigrants?

JOSÉ: For one thing, it's grammatically weird. We can always start with that. There are actions that are illegal. It's weird to say that people themselves are illegal. But it's problematic in a couple ways. One way in particular is it hides a lot of the history that I tried very quickly to explain. If people are interested in a really good historical account, Aviva Chomsky has this great book called *Undocumented*, in which she traces out in more detail the history I have tried to get at. The term "illegal" hides all that. It's very shorthand. It makes it seem as though the world began yesterday and these people just decided that they were going to not obey the law. It takes people who I think have been victimized by bad immigration policy and transforms them into lawbreakers. It's not that the current law is doing an injustice; the current law is doing an injustice to them. That would be the legal political philosopher in me answering that question.

But the critical race theorist in me thinks that there's something else happening here too. Ian Haney López calls this "dog-whistle politics," and you see it in a lot of different communities. You see this when President Reagan said, "You have young bucks who are using their food stamps to buy steaks" and talked about welfare queens in their Cadillacs. He never used racial language, but he was able to use certain code words that made the imagination of white Americans light up with images of black men and black women.

"Illegal" functions in a similar way. You don't need to say a racial or ethnic slur, but when you say "illegal," you know who you're talking about. So it's problematic in that respect. It's not just that it's used as a legal term; it's being used as a kind of code word that denigrates a particular community. What's even worse, places like California, Arizona, and New Mexico are places where Mexicans were living before those places were part of the United States. This idea that these people are somehow not true Americans is what gets encapsulated in the term "illegal."

MYISHA: The nerve of settlers to call natives "illegals" or "aliens"! That's who they are.

JOSÉ: I think this is just part of the imagination of white America, that there's a particular thing, a particular identity that is America. The part that's true is that it is changing, but for them it's changed and it's bad. When the 45th President says, "Let's make America great again," he's using dog-whistle politics. You and I might not hear exactly what he's saying and it might feel weird, but for other people, they know exactly what he's saying. There's a particular kind of America and it's disappearing.

MYISHA: When people hear the word "undocumented," they usually think about people who have illegally crossed the border, so I'm very glad that you cleared that up. Just to clarify once again, would you say that most people have just overstayed their visas and have not necessarily illegally crossed the border?

JOSÉ: To get a clear number, it depends on basically the study you look at. It's somewhere between 40 percent and a little over 50 percent, so close to half. What is interesting about that is that even if you get "the wall," and you are somehow able to seal off any sort of unlawful crossing, all that would actually do is increase visa overstays.

Some people can't even get a visa. My dad unlawfully crossed four times. He was deported three times and he unlawfully crossed four.

My mom never crossed the border unlawfully; she crossed with visas, she would come and work. She had a tourist visa, to come and do some shopping, but she would cross over on Sunday night, work Monday through Friday as a live-in nanny/maid, and then on Friday nights she would cross back. They didn't have any way to really check, so they just thought she was coming and shopping. Then when she fell in love with my dad, she crossed and didn't cross back for ten years. So actually, my mom technically never crossed the border unlawfully; she just overstayed a visa.

MYISHA: Cesar Millan, the former host of *Dog Whisperer*, has openly talked about his experience of crossing the border. He crossed it illegally and it was very interesting to hear his story. Can you describe for us, or put us in the shoes of a Mexican migrant who crosses the border? Why are people willing to risk their lives to come to the US? And what are their experiences upon arriving in the States?

JOSÉ: There are some really good documentaries out there like *Far from Home* that describe these experiences. Those who cross the border aren't a homogeneous group. You get a lot of children and you also get a lot of people who are wanting to reunite with their spouses.

One of the things that happened in the early '90s is that law enforcement ran a strategy at the border called "prevention through deterrence." The idea was fairly simple. This is what they told themselves: "We have limited resources. Instead of spreading all out everywhere, let's focus on really easy points of entry, double up, triple up the wall, get people up there with guns, get helicopters, drones, all kinds of technology. And then the most inhospitable parts—the deserts, the rivers, these sorts of areas where it's very, very, very difficult to cross—we'll leave those open."

I mentioned my father crossed four times. He never went through anything like this, because when he was crossing "prevention through deterrence" hadn't gone into effect. For him it was like, maybe half a day's walk. Some of these journeys now can take anywhere between three days to a week to complete. Many migrants don't carry enough water or food with them, and a lot of them don't make the passage. So this has increased the deaths.

The thinking was, "Well, once word gets out, people are going to stop trying to cross," and they haven't. They haven't because one of the other things we did was sign free-trade agreements with Mexico, but those free-trade agreements weren't really free trade. The United States still subsidizes a lot of corn farmers. US corn can be sold in Mexico without any tariffs and it's actually cheaper than corn grown in Mexico. Mexico is the original source of corn, and now Mexico imports its corn. It has made the corn farmer's life basically unsustainable. What's driving people to not just the United States but to the border region is a need for jobs.

Mexico's birth rate has stabilized a little bit, and its economy is doing a bit better. A lot of the immigrants that we see now come from Central America, and these immigrants are a little bit different than the displaced farmworkers of Mexico. A lot of these immigrants are fleeing violence. There's been a lot of violence in Central America. In 2009 when Hillary Clinton was Secretary of State, the United States helped dispose of President Zelaya in Honduras. Since then Honduras has become kind of a hub for the narcotics trade. All the drugs that come from Colombia and in South America, they land in Honduras before they come to the US. Honduras right now is one of the most violent places on Earth. The kids there, all of them, either have to join gangs or risk getting killed and so forth. This was behind the surge that we saw a couple years ago. The people were fleeing violence. If you think about it, we are responsible for it. We consume these drugs, and our policies towards Central America destabilized that region such that drug cartels now basically control the region. So when you ask, "Why are people willing to risk their lives to cross in these ways," it's because there really is no alternative. It's starvation or a violent death for a lot of these folks.

MYISHA: What do you think is our ethical obligation towards undocumented immigrants?

JOSÉ: I think that at the very least we shouldn't get in undocumented immigrants' ways. This is what I mean by negative rights. Most undocumented immigrants can find jobs for themselves and do things for themselves. It's the current policy that we have that really undermines their ability to succeed. I think my position is actually very close to a libertarian position: Just leave them alone, don't get in immigrants' ways. Don't restrict immigration. We have undocumented immigrants in the United States and we have in-state tuition; let them have in-state tuition and driver's licenses, these sorts of things.

What I mean is that you don't necessarily have to give entitlements to undocumented immigrants, but there are certain things that we owe them. I think everyone could agree that what we owe immigrants is pretty basic. By denying them these things, we are denying them the opportunity to have a decent life. I'm not talking about a very extravagant life, but just a decent life.

I think, ethically, we owe a lot to the global poor in general, but especially to people who are unprotected by the laws, as most undocumented immigrants currently are.

5

Wendy Salkin on Informal Political Representation

MYISHA: Your current project in political philosophy is on representation. I'm wondering if you can tell us what the difference is between formal and informal representation.

WENDY: I think that there are these key differences between formal and informal representation. Formal representation is what many of us are familiar with. Our congresspersons are paradigmatic examples of formal representatives. They're people who speak for us, express what they take our interests to be in these fora where we can't be. They're elected, or they're selected, in these formal or organized procedures; Senators, for instance, by election. Or they might be selected for us in other ways, appointed by someone else we elected. This is what happens often in judicial contexts.

I also include among formal representatives, people who are elected or selected in these ways to serve as heads of nongovernmental organizations or advocacy groups like the ACLU or the NAACP. They're the formal representatives of people who are members of those organizations.

By contrast, the informal representative is someone who speaks for me or you, or both of us, or a whole group of us, even though they weren't elected or selected to do so. Paradigmatic examples of this include celebrities; others are public figures like Malala or Martin Luther King Jr., or Malcolm X. Depending on whether you think I have it right, I happen to think it can be just about anyone who's taken by an audience to speak or act for some group in a politically salient context.

MYISHA: How did you get interested in informal representation? Is there a lot of literature in political science, political theory, or political philosophy about the latter? We hear a lot about formal representation, but how did you get interested in informal representation?

WENDY: There's not a lot in philosophy on this. There are a few key texts that touch on it. There are political theorists who think about this, and I think in political science there's a lot of work on this. But I don't know that we've put our philosophical tools to work on this project.

I first became interested in it after reading this paper by Linda Martín Alcoff (see Chapter 19, this volume), who is this fantastic philosopher at CUNY. The paper's called "The Problem of Speaking for Others." I read it in my first year of graduate school and I thought, "Yeah, that is a problem. How can people justifiably or legitimately do that, speak in the voice of another person?"

This idea was bouncing around in my head, and I met with Tommie Shelby (Chapter 22, this volume) for the first time. He encouraged me to do two things. One was to pursue this as a philosophical question; and the second was to read W. E. B. Du Bois's *The Souls of Black Folk*, which is one of the most important philosophical texts I've read. It's really shaped what I think philosophy can look like and what sorts of questions count as philosophical questions.

The third chapter of the book is called "Of Mr. Booker T. Washington and Others."

MYISHA: That's probably one of my favorite chapters in *The Souls of Black Folk*. I mean, Du Bois throws major shade at Booker T., in the most philosophical way. But go right ahead.

WENDY: No, it's such a good chapter. It's interesting because he is pointing out Booker T. Washington, but he's also using him as an example of a phenomenon. He's directing our attention toward this phenomenon—people speaking for other people. Du Bois is concerned about Booker T. Washington speaking for black Americans, but his points can be generalized. He's worried about how people come into this position and the sorts of responsibilities that somebody has once they're in that position.

From there I realized, "Look, this is a really ubiquitous phenomenon," and I think even more than most scholars take it to be. For me it's like this, "If you're a hammer, everything's a nail." Now I see informal representation everywhere in our contemporary interpersonal and political relationships. I think it's all over the place, and I don't think we quite know how to think about it.

MYISHA: You already know about my current project that's concerned with reporters asking black victims of racial violence, police brutality, to forgive. While they're in that particular space, in some ways I think the reporter takes the victim to be representing black people. At least in some sense, victims also feel that burden too.

So, I want you to describe for us a little bit more in detail the phenomenon of informal representation, and tell us what you think is the promising side of it.

WENDY: I think informal representation is good for one of the same things formal representation is good for: ensuring that a person or groups of voices are heard even if they're not in the room. Iris Young has this great thing she says about representation. She says, "Representation is necessary because the web of modern social life often ties the actions of some people and institutions in one place to consequences in many other places and institutions." She makes this point like, "We all can't be present at all the decisions or in all the decision-making bodies whose actions affect our lives." So she says, "Look, even when we're not there, we would hope that somebody would say what we want or represent our perspectives to the issue forum, whatever that issue forum is." I think there's something really crucial to that. I think it's not just whether we can be present. It's whether we're going to be invited to speak, it's whether we'd know how to say for ourselves what we want or what our perspective is if we were invited to speak.

I think informal representation can be beneficial because it allows for efficiency in communicating ideas to a broad public or in private meetings, it can allow for coalition-building, and it can allow this one individual, the representative, to crystalize ideas for people who, in Du Bois's terms, "only at first dimly perceive" what they might want, value, prefer, or what their options are. I think a representative can serve that role of trying to crystalize those ideas that we can't quite see as our own yet.

MYISHA: There has to be a flip side to this. What do you take to be problematic about informal representation?

WENDY: So many things. There are so many perils. A representative can harm a group, even wrong a representative group. They can do things like knowingly or unknowingly misinform or mislead an audience about what a group's expressed interests are.

So in the cases you're talking about in your work, where a journalist is taking someone to be speaking for a community, they might not realize that that's what's being done to them. They might speak very particularly about the situation as they see it. But it's then translated by the journalist or by the audience as something that they are saying on behalf of a community, and that statement might not be true for all of the members of the community. In addition, it could be that the representative keeps the group hidden from view or occludes the group. If the group at issue is a marginalized group, it can be the case that an informal representative wittingly or unwittingly contributes to a group's further marginalization. This tension is at the heart of that relationship between the informal representative and the represented group, even if the representation is very badly needed, and even if it's done in good faith.

MYISHA: Elaborate on the latter point about contributing to the group's further marginalization. How so? Can you provide an example, if possible?

WENDY: I've written a little bit about the Montgomery bus boycott as an example. You might think, "Look, King is speaking for black Montgomerians about this issue of exclusion from the means of public transport, disrespect of space, and doing this sort of as a microcosm of the many issues that were being faced by black Montgomerians." But focusing attention on one issue, the bus boycott or some other particular issue that affects one member of a community, or a set of members from a community, can occlude other things. It can place the focus on one set of issues.

You might think, "Oh, well, black Montgomerians had a huge set of needs that required focus. And if you place focus on one particular area, you can draw attention from other considerations." That's the idea.

MYISHA: What would you say to the objection that in informal representation, the representative lacks agency. For example, you suggest that someone is taken to be a representative, but that implies that they did not sign up or proclaim themselves to be. If a reporter or anyone takes me to be a representative for black folk or black women but I didn't sign up for that, am I (1) still a representative and (2) have I lost some agency as a result of such representation?

WENDY: I think it's not unique that people make demands of us. So sometimes quite unreasonably, sometimes quite reasonably, we spend so much of our time in the world responding to demands of us that we comport ourselves in certain ways when we respond to others. People make these demands of us. This is, I think, just one type of way that a person can be asked to respond to a demand.

Now, one response is "no." Sometimes the response can be, "No, I reject this role." In the case of informal representation, sometimes I want to say, "Well, look, you might have a reason, or really good reasons, to remain in the role even if you didn't want to be in it because you stand in relationships of solidarity with a group, or you have a duty of mutual aid to a group by virtue of independent reasons."

So you didn't want to be called upon to serve in this role, but I wouldn't say that it diminishes your agential capacity. You get to respond in the way that you want to, but you might have duties with respect to a group that would suggest that you ought to take up the role even if you don't want it; or if it's really hard to shape the role, there are going to be questions about how it would be best to serve in it.

MYISHA: Before we get to duties, let's talk a little bit about power. You talked about the promising side of informal representation, but you also say that there are normative and political powers that the informal representative can have with respect to the represented. What are these powers?

WENDY: These are features that are intrinsic to the relationship between the representative and the represented. I frame them as normative and political powers that the informal representative has with respect to the represented by virtue of being specially situated to affect the represented group and its members' circumstances.

There's a wide range of these powers, some of which come up in some contexts, others of which come up in others. I'll tell you about a few that I've thought about a lot. Informal representatives tend to have at least some of these powers. I think it's by virtue of having these powers with respect to the represented that the representatives end up having corresponding duties to the represented.

There's the power to create epistemic entitlements in an audience. Audience members might come to the entitled to receive certain conclusions about the represented group or its members based solely or partly on the representatives' statements or actions about that group. These entitlements might make it such that audience members don't feel the need to consult members of the group directly on matters about which the representative has spoken. They might reasonably assume that the representative's statements or actions are properly ascribable to the group.

Because of this, you might think, "Well, this answers the question about why somebody should serve as a representative in a certain way," because it turns out that an audience might take their views to be true of a whole bunch of different people. It might also be the case that the informal representative has the power to make promises or give assurances on the group's behalf. We can imagine a case where the representative says to an audience, "Look, if you agree to change this policy in the way I'm proposing, I can assure you that the people I'm representing will be on board."

It's not that the representative has the power to bind the group. If the group isn't on board or doesn't go along with a proposal, its members can't be said to have done something wrong. It's not that the members could be held accountable for breaching something. But the representative can give this assurance that's not merely like a prediction about what the group or its members are likely to do. The representative won't be open to criticism for providing the assurance, and the group members might be criticized for not going along with the offer even if they didn't wrong anyone by not following.

Similarly, the informal representative might have the power to determine or change a group's negotiating position by offering commitments or concessions on the group members' behalf.

There's this other really interesting power, which is the power of group formation. A would-be informal representative can bring a group into being, or help people realize that there is already a group there, by speaking about the values, interests, or preferences of some individuals in a certain way.

MYISHA: Give us an example of that.

WENDY: You might think there's a plurality of individuals. What they all have in common is that they are working for very low wages. Somebody comes along and says, "Hey, you people are all not being paid enough for your work. And you're subject to these common sets of social forces; the boss is never going to raise your wages. You guys have something in common by virtue of which you should think about yourselves as a group; you should think about yourselves as workers, as people who should be able to form unions."

Once the representative does this, those individuals might come to feel themselves bound together in a way that creates greater social cohesion than the individuals might otherwise have had without the representatives' interventions; or it could be that the representative instead creates the group by communicating in that same way to an audience. So that's what I have in mind by the "power of group formation."

MYISHA: You note that given these powers, these normative political powers, the informal representative has a duty to the represented. Tell us more about this duty.

WENDY: It's in virtue of having, or being in a position to gain, one of the types of powers that I just described that the representative has responsibilities to the represented. And it's not just one duty but a few different types of duties.

The background aim that these duties serve is this: To promote social equality for the represented group or its members, both in their relationship to the representative themselves and in the represented group's relationship to the society that is, for instance, marginalizing or oppressing them.

That's the aim. I propose that with this aim in mind, there are two sets of duties—what I call "democracy within duties" and "justice without duties"—that should guide the informal representative in their action. The duties I refer to as these *justice without duties*, they concern what guides the representative when they're in the process of speaking or acting for the represented to an audience; they are outward-facing responsibilities. They concern the norms that ought to guide the representative in his or her relationship to an audience.

One duty the informal representative has in representing the group is to promote or not obstruct the promotion of the group's circumstances so that the group members will come to have equal status with other members of society. If I want to know as a representative what I should do, the kinds of questions I might ask myself to know what my justice without duties are, "What should I say or do when I'm speaking to this particular audience, or how should I say or do this when I'm representing before this audience, and should I even be the person to speak?" So sometimes it could be that the justice without duties point towards stepping aside.

The other side is the *democracy within duties*. Those are the duties that guide the representative in their immediate relationship to the represented. One way to think of them is as inward-looking duties. "Democracy within duties" arise out of a commitment to promoting or maintaining a society of equals. To do that, the informal representative should, insofar as it's compatible with those "justice without duties," promote democracy which I conceive of as a set of social practices, conventions, norms, and rules within the representative's relationship to the represented group.

What does that look like? I think that for an informal representative to promote social equality in their immediate relationship to the represented group, they have to show the represented recognition respect. I think that recognition respect (which is regard due to others because they are persons) is shown in representative contexts by the informal representative promoting transparency, publicity, being open to the criticism of the represented, and tolerating dissent.

A big criticism that Du Bois had of Booker T. Washington is that he was always trying to quash dissent. Any sort of dissent against the way that he approached representation he would try to silence—not any, but much of it. I follow Du Bois in thinking that a duty of a representative is to be present for the dissent of those you speak for.

MYISHA: The Booker T. Washington example is very clear to me. It's more the ordinary citizen, whether they're a black victim of police brutality or some other example, that's more puzzling. We can imagine you as a woman in an interview taken to be speaking for other women, which is not necessarily the case for majority groups. Unlike those in majority groups, members of minority groups are usually taken to be representing their particular group. In the case of an ordinary citizen, not necessarily a celebrity or famous leader, what is their duty?

WENDY: First of all, I limit it to cases where people know that they're being taken to speak for others. Regarding the case you mention, I refer to these as the unwilling and unwitting representative. I'm sure that people often take us to be speaking for other women, but we never find out that that's happening. In that case I think no duties are in question. You can't be held accountable or responsible in those cases. The case you're describing is someone who is unwilling. I want to point out that lots of times the people who are taken to be representative are willing. They want to be in these roles; often people want to be in the role of speaking for others.

I think there are two questions here, and I think it's better to keep them separate.

One is: Did somebody wrong or harm me by taking me to be speaking for women or speaking for philosophers? Then it's on them, and we can say, "Look, that audience wasn't acting epistemically virtuous in doing that." But we're here. We're in this nonideal space where it turns out that somebody's taking me to speak for women, and I want to get it right or I ought to want to get it right and I ought to try to think about "Well, what is it going to look like if I say that women want x but what they really want is y; or if I try to reject the role when there's no one else who can speak?"

I think it's important to think of this as a responsibility in line with lots of other responsibilities we have to our fellow citizens. It's not much different from other duties we have to help out other people; duties we owe to other people, even though we haven't voluntarily taken them up. They're just responsibilities we have in virtue of living in a community with others.

MYISHA: If a person takes someone to be an informal representative, for example, does that person have any powers and therefore any duties in regards to that?

WENDY: I have this paper I'm working on called "The Virtuous Audience," where I'm trying to claim that they have powers. Taking someone as a representative is a power. That's the triggering condition for the whole set of questions we've been discussing. I do think that because they have that power, duties arise. There are ways of being a good listener, there are ways of being attuned to the fact that you can put somebody in this position.

So, in the case you're talking about, between the journalist and the victim, or between the journalist and anybody taken by a journalist to be speaking for a community, the journalist or whoever is asking the questions has to check themselves and say, "Hey, am I putting on this person a particular role that they didn't take up?"

Writer Ta-Nehisi Coates has an interesting interview with Robin Young on WBUR's *Here & Now* talk show. In the interview he says, "I don't mind people calling me to ask me about current events. I wish there was more space though. There is an uncomfortable tradition in this dialogue of 'race relations' in this country where people are selected at various moments to be spokespeople for what right now is a community of 40 million people. Obviously, I write and I write for the public and I want my thoughts considered, I want my writing considered, but I didn't ask for a crown."[1]

I think that's crucial. He goes on. "And that's kind of what has happened, honestly, to be straight with you. Because with that comes assumptions about what you're saying and what you're supposed to do, you lose some of your freedoms as a writer, you lose your ability to be curious in public because you have a crown on now. You're supposed to have the answers; probably the most regrettable development personally for me out of the past eight years."

So maybe my virtuous audience piece should be called "Wearing the Crown" because it's the idea of having a crown placed on you. I do

[1] Young, Robin. *Here and Now talk show*. September 28, 2017. www.wbur.org/hereandnow/2017/09/28/ta-nehisi-coates-eight-years-in-power.

think that there's a duty to be a good listener, a good audience member, etc. One thing I want to do with this work is to try to bring to light that we're all doing this all the time, that we're all in these relationships of representativeness, being represented and putting people into the role of representatives. I want to see how to ameliorate those tensions by thinking about what our responsibilities are.

Section 2

LANGUAGE, KNOWLEDGE, AND POWER

6

Rachel Ann McKinney on
Police and Language

MYISHA: What does the phrase "words have power" mean to you?

RACHEL: Words allow us to do things in the world in a really fundamental way. It's not like we only use language to express ourselves,
convey information, or pool information with others. We also use it to
get things done. Anyone who's ever had the experience of being unable
to use their words to do something that they ought to be able to use
them to do, like to refuse or to contest, or to ask or to disagree, knows
the frustration from that kind of misfiring. Philosophers have focused
in particular on a few phenomena related to the fact that words have
power; the phenomena of being silent, for instance, which is what I was
just describing.

I think there are a lot of other interesting phenomena in the neighborhood. I think the phenomena of being willfully misunderstood,
especially willfully misunderstood by those in power, is a really important one. I think the phenomena of finding out that you don't have
the words you need, having your language sort of give out underneath
your feet when you're trying to articulate something, I think that's another important phenomena to figure out.

So I think it's definitely the case that words have power in a really concrete, material sense. They allow us to do things in the world, to get around and meet our needs.

MYISHA: What is extracted speech, and what are some examples of it that we use in our everyday lives?

RACHEL: Extracted speech is this category of speech that I'm trying to figure out. It is speech that someone sort of makes you produce. One way of thinking about it is in terms of speech that might be a response to practices of coercion, deception, manipulation or intimidation. But more generally, I think it is speech that one utters in response to having one's communicative agency undermined or bypassed in some way.

MYISHA: Okay, that's a big word! What does "communicative agency" mean?

RACHEL: We usually think that when we speak, what we mean is some sort of function of our intentions in speaking, what we want our words to do. When I ask you, "Have you gone to the store yet," I'm requesting—I intend to get some information from you. So "communicative agency" is a way of encapsulating this idea that we typically have some wiggle room and some choice in the words we use, in what we want those words to do, and that speech is typically the result of a decision-making procedure. That's what I mean by "communicative agency," the choice and decision involved with the speech that we make.

I actually think that extracted speech is pretty ubiquitous. It's really easy to see it with cases where we haven't been coerced or manipulated, or anything like that necessarily, but our decision making has been sort of bypassed in some way. Think about terms-of-service agreements. When you update iTunes, the little box pops up with a lot of text that you don't read, but you just click that you agree to the terms of service. Think about other sorts of bureaucratic forms. You are applying for a job and there's the form on the application that says something like "Have you ever been convicted of a crime?" You have to fill out that space and truthfully in order to hand in the form.

I don't think these are cases necessarily of being coerced or manipulated. You can opt out, you don't have to update iTunes, and you don't have to apply for that job. But you do have to do those things if there's some other end that you're trying to reach that's meaningful to you. And even if there is a choice in the matter, maybe you don't experience it as a choice; maybe it's really automatic, or unwilled in a sense for you to check that mark or to click the button.

MYISHA: Do we also see this in any form on social media? I know the stakes may be a little lower, but sometimes it's a little higher.

RACHEL: Oh, for sure. I think a lot of social media interaction is this sort of automatic stimulus-response-type thing that we do. I do it too. We click the "like" button when somebody posts a joke that we like or our new favorite song. We're not being coerced into doing it, we're not being deceived or intimidated, nobody's holding a gun to our heads. But it is this sort of automatic response that we have. Those are behaviors that get collected by the folks at Facebook to figure out what our preferences are, to figure out what strikes our attention, and then to sell us different types of things. So it's not as though those choices are inert. They have consequences for our future lives.

MYISHA: How did you get interested in language and police interactions?

RACHEL: One thing that you see when you look at contemporary philosophy of language is this focus on a particular kind of conversational context; a focus on a conversational context that is cooperative, where interlocutors share their goals, their beliefs, and their presuppositions. You also get a focus on conversational contexts that are abstracted from power, as though all speakers are able to do the same things in the conversation.

I was particularly interested in conversational contexts where neither of those things is true; where speakers don't agree on the nature of the language game, or the interaction, they don't share presuppositions or beliefs, they don't share goals, and where the interaction is risky or difficult, or dangerous for some of those interlocutors.

I began thinking and reading about police interrogations in the context of sociolinguistics and forensic linguistics. There's some really great work that linguists have been doing on these sorts of contexts. There were other contexts that I was interested in, but the police-interaction stuff grabbed me because it's such an important context to figure out. It's something that a lot of people deal with and it ruins lives; sometimes it ends people's lives. So it's a really pressing thing to figure out, and I think it's something that philosophers can maybe lend some resources to helping figure out.

MYISHA: I've seen lots of police interrogations—I mean, not because I've been at the police stations but through TV. I think the most heartbreaking police interrogations I've ever seen were those conducted and shown in the documentary *Central Park Five*. The police interrogate those teenage boys and ultimately get them to confess to a beating and a rape that they had no part in whatsoever.

RACHEL: Right!

MYISHA: What are some of the linguistic strategies that police use?

RACHEL: I'm glad you brought up the *Central Park Five* case, because I think this is a case that really brings to the foreground something that might at first glance seem really puzzling. It might be really puzzling why somebody would confess to a crime that they didn't commit. Lots of times in these cases, people seem to make decisions against their best interests. They will "choose" to "consent" to a search, confess to crimes, wave their right to an attorney, or admit testimony.

It would be irrational or imprudent, or ill advised for them to do any of these things. So why would anyone voluntarily expose themselves to criminal prosecution and punishment?

First of all, people don't do this because they're stupid. It's not something that only happens sometimes. These aren't isolated incidents. It's not like people only rarely make these mistakes. These things happen all the time. They happen systematically. We can make predictions about when and where people will make these sorts of mistakes, and really smart people make these mistakes. So we need an explanation for why people seem to do things with their words that are completely against their own interests.

The *Central Park Five* case is one where I think it's really clear that there were a lot of different factors. One was that these were kids, teenagers between the ages of, I think, thirteen and sixteen. They were held in police detention for twelve or eighteen hours. There were a lot of times, instances where they were straightforwardly lied to about the conditions under which they would be let go. They and their parents were straightforwardly deceived. They were operating under conditions of low information, conditions of deception, and that seem really clearly to amount to duress.

There are less extreme cases as well, where it doesn't quite get to the level of duress but I still think that something has gone wrong. Take an interaction like getting pulled over. When you get pulled over, there is some ambiguity in how to interpret what a cop says to you. When they say something like "Can I see your driver's license" or "Can you get out of the car, please," they probably intend this as a command or an order; you're being detained. He's telling you to give him your license, he's telling you to get out of the car, and you have to do it.

But the way it's phrased is really ambiguous. It's phrased like a question that you might use as an indirect request. It's phrased like saying something like "Can you pass the salt" at the dinner table. Somebody who asks you, "Can you pass the salt" isn't literally asking if you're able to and they're not commanding you to. But "Can I see your driver's license" is different because the cop has the authority to order you to show it to him. It's not like the "Can you pass the salt" case. It is closer to something like a sergeant saying to a soldier, "Don't you think it would be a good idea to shine those shoes, Private?" It's a command that's phrased as an indirect request. You take it to be a command, so you get out of the car, you show him your license, but then he says something else.

He produces another utterance that's phrased similarly. He says something like "Can you open the trunk," or "Can I look in the trunk," or "Do you mind if I search the car?" This is again an utterance that could be interpreted as either a command or a request. But given the nature of the interaction, it's only natural for the driver to assume that they're being ordered to open the trunk and that the cop is telling them that they're going to search.

Now the thing is police don't usually have the authority to search your car without your consent. In these interactions, they leverage you into providing "consent" because you don't think you have a choice in the matter. The question "Can I look in the trunk" is a request. It is the sort of thing you can refuse, but because the police officer has already exercised his authority in stopping the car, ordering you to get out of the car, ordering you to hand over your license, you interpret "Can I look in the trunk" as an order or a command. And you say, "Yes."

Then that "yes" is taken to be an act of consent to the search, even though it's not genuine consent. If you take a cop to be ordering you to let him search your car, I don't think that counts as genuine consent. Because in order to genuinely consent to an action, you have to be able to not consent, and you have to know that you're able to not consent. You could not consent as well. But in this case, you don't know that you have that option.

These are cases of extracted speech. You have an act of "consenting" extracted from you. Given the conversational context, given the relations of authority, and given the fact that you are in detention—you're in police detention—I don't think it's surprising at all that people would do things with their speech that are against their interests. I don't think that's surprising at all. I don't think it's something that people do because they don't know any better. It's because they have had their decision making undermined or bypassed, or overridden and they're not able to make decisions or deliberate in ways that they otherwise would.

MYISHA: I don't want you to give any law advice, but philosophically speaking, if I am a young black male living in Bed-Stuy, Brooklyn and I have a police encounter, what are some tools, some strategies, some useful advice that philosophy of language can give to me?

RACHEL: I'm glad that you said "not law advice" because I am not a lawyer. I am not an attorney. One thing I will say is that there are regular know-your-rights trainings that are put on by people like the National Lawyers Guild that I think are really valuable. I think this is one of those cases where the recommendations for what is prudential to do, what is safe to do, might trump what is totally legitimate: to ask whether an utterance was a request or an order. But I think, prudentially, it's important to say it as sweetly as possible. Police really like compliance. They don't like even the suggestion that you don't take them seriously. I've had interactions with police that have turned really ugly, and I'm very white and middle class. As far as I know, it's within your rights to ask whether an utterance was a request or an order, and that will give you a little bit more information about what you can do at that point.

Another thing that I would say is don't talk to police unless you have to. Ask whether you're being detained. If you know that you are being detained, just don't speak. I think the edict "Don't talk to the police" is actually, again, just speaking in terms of what is in your best interest, a pretty good suggestion.

I think this can turn really quickly into a know-your-rights thing. You don't want to get into an argument with the cop about what your rights are, because he's going to arrest you anyway. Then if it turns out later that the case goes to trial, then maybe you can have a conversation with your lawyer and the judge about whether proper criminal procedure was followed. But it's not going to matter for the twelve hours that you're in Central Booking. Police routinely violate people's rights in this regard. And they hate it when you suggest that you know the law better than they do, even if you do. I guess my recommendations are pretty prudential more than philosophical.

7

Cassie Herbert on Risky Speech

MYISHA: You have developed an account of two different kinds of speech acts: accusations and reports. What are accusations and reports? Why are they often mistaken for each other?

CASSIE: As you identified, these are speech acts. We do things with our language. Language is itself an action and these are two different kinds of actions that we can perform with our language. Reports are one of the things that make up the fabric of our daily interactions. They're truth claims. They are reporting on things that are going on in the world, so they're declaratives. They're declaring something to be true.

But more than that, they're declaratives about something that the speaker has this particular standing to talk about; something that the speaker has either investigated or experienced. You could give a report about how your morning went. If you say, "Yeah, I overslept and missed the bus and it was just an awful day," that's a report on how your day went because it's something that you personally have experienced. Or if a botanist is issuing a report about the growth patterns of trees; they have investigated this. They have personally looked into it. They have a particular standing to issue truth claims about what's going on with those trees.

What's interesting about reports is that they're doing two things. One, they're an invitation to trust. They're an invitation to trust that the speaker is a trustworthy, epistemic agent in the world. More than that, they call for trust that the speaker in fact knows the content of what they're talking about, that they have this particular connection to it either through investigation or experience. They're connected in a way that you wouldn't get from reading a book on the growth patterns of trees. You could give a report on that book, but you couldn't actually report on the trees themselves yet.

On the other hand, we have accusations. Accusations are a way to hold a person to account for their wrongdoing. It's a way of trying to get a person to feel the weight of the norms that they have violated. It's a deontic move. It's a way, again, to try and hold someone accountable.

Now, what's important about these two kinds of speech acts are that they call for really different responses from the audience. For reports, the proper response is to start off believing what the person has said. And if you find conflicting evidence, if you find some reason to be a little bit skeptical of what they've said, then you start looking into it. But you start off from this position of default belief. On the other hand, you're doing accusations wrong if you start off from default belief. Accusations call for a kind of suspended belief—not necessarily disbelief, but not yet getting on board with what someone has said. They call for us to find evidence, something to corroborate what the person has said. Often, we're given evidence at the same time as someone issues a report; "You didn't empty the trash and that was your chore," as you're pointing to that overflowing trashcan. So, then it's an accusation with the evidence all bundled in right at the same moment.

But the point is that in order to believe an accusation properly, you need to have some sort of corroborating evidence. If you don't find it, then you don't end up believing it. Whereas on the other hand, reports start off from this position of default belief that you can always reevaluate. Accusations and reports are really different in terms of the sorts of responses that they call for. What gets tricky is that they can be exactly identical to each other in terms of the words a person uses. So, if I say (going again to that overflowing trashcan), "You didn't empty the trash and it was your chore this week," I might also just be reporting on "This was your chore, you didn't do it." I'm not trying to hold you to account. I'm just trying to alert you to this.

There are times when it gets really, really unclear what it is that a person is doing with their speech. If they say, "I was sexually assaulted," they might in fact be trying to issue a report. They might simply be calling for belief in what they said, or they might in fact be issuing an accusation. They might be trying to hold the person accountable for what it is that they did. There are really significant effects from how we take up what sort of action a person is doing with their words here.

MYISHA: Someone is making an utterance about being sexually assaulted. How do we figure out if it is a report or an accusation?

CASSIE: I think this is genuinely tricky, and I'm not sure that I have a hard-and-fast rule that we can follow here. One thing that we can do is try and figure out, from context and from the speaker themselves, what it is that they're trying to do. If we ask them in the right context, properly supportive, "What do you want to have happen?" oftentimes someone will tell us through that answer what it is that they're looking for. Are they looking for belief? That's huge, especially when a person is reporting on a serious injustice that was done to them, because those things are so often glossed over, so often disbelieved. Just looking for belief often is in and of itself incredibly significant.

Other times one might say, "No, I want them held to account for what they did, they have to pay, or they have to learn that this isn't okay." And then we can get a cue that "Okay, maybe what's going on here is an accusation." Often these things get really, really blurred together. So I think it often is difficult to separate out what it is that a speaker is trying to do.

MYISHA: What is risky speech? Can you provide some examples of it?

CASSIE: Risky speech is, as it sounds like, speech that is risky to the speaker. I'm drawing on Kristie Dotson's notion of risky speech here. She thinks of risky speech as being speech that is somehow unintelligible, so incomprehensible to the audience that it brings risks to the speaker, especially risks about whether or not the speaker is going to be properly recognized as a knower. If someone says something that's just utterly mind-blowing or incomprehensible to an audience, the speaker often risks having the audience think that she is the one who is incompetent.

I'm thinking about risky speech in this way and also a little bit more broadly. I'm also interested and especially want to be attentive to the risks that speech can bring, beyond just epistemic risks, such as physical and social risks. Things like being ostracized and being opened up to physical attack. This is especially the case for speech that pushes against the status quo. Speech that challenges our established systems of power is especially the example that I have in mind; things like accounts of racism, accounts of sexism, and reporting on or issuing speech about experiencing sexual violence. I'm calling attention to and asking to hold people accountable for even just beliefs in actions that violate our established systems of power.

MYISHA: Why, in your view, should risky speech be seen as a report and not just as an accusation?

CASSIE: One of the things I'm worried about is that we have this default tendency to take risky speech always as an accusation. I do want to acknowledge that sometimes risky speech is in fact an accusation and that is how it should be taken up, but not always. That's not always what a speaker is trying to do. I worry a lot that we're blocking off this avenue of speech, this avenue of action to folks who are issuing risky speech. But more than that, I have this worry that taking risky speech always or by default as an accusation, serves as a really subtle way of delegitimizing this speech. This kind of response is what I call the "objective response." The objective response is when we say, "Hold on, slow down, we have to be objective, we have to be careful, we have to really treat this seriously. Where is your evidence? How do you know that that storekeeper was racist? How do you know this really was sexual assault? How do we know that's what happened?"

The worry here is that this kind of response looks a whole lot like taking risky speech very serious. It specifically is calling for more evidence. But in calling for more evidence, it places that speech in a position of distrust. It's sort of paradigmatically not taking it as a report, and instead is treating it as an accusation whether or not the speaker was trying to do that. My worry is that when we always treat risky speech as an accusation, it puts the speaker in a position where they have to find evidence in order to be believed about things often from their own experience. It calls into question whether or not the speaker is trustworthy about their own lived experiences, about their life.

MYISHA: How would you respond to people—and this may be part of the objective response—who after hearing this would say, "Well, it seems like reports conflict with the notion that a person is innocent until proven guilty?" You note that we ought to believe a person who's making a report, but a worry may be, "Well, what about the person that they're reporting on? Don't we have an obligation towards that individual?"

CASSIE: I think it gets genuinely complicated so I don't have good, easy answers to this. I don't want to say that we should always, no matter what, never, ever, ever disbelieve a person's report. I think that's far too strong, especially given that we know that there are some pretty horrific ways things go wrong. For example, white women issuing reports against black men about sexual violence. That's a place where believing these reports goes wrong in ways that are really serious. As far as I can tell, it's one of the only times when people default to believing that sexual violence has happened, and often women haven't been telling the truth.

What to do about this I'm not sure. I think a first step that we can make is to carve out this distinction between reports and accusations, to figure out what it is that the speaker is trying to do and how we're taking it up. And that might give us some clues about how to go about sorting this out.

If we take a speaker's report as reason to believe that something has happened, well, then we may have reason to believe the accused as well if they say, "No, I didn't do that. The difference here is that this sets it up as a position between equals. One says, "Yes, they did that"; the other says, "No, I didn't." We have reasons to believe both of them, which is really different from innocent until proven guilty, where the speaker has to automatically find a whole bunch of evidence in order to establish them as a person who could be believed.

That matters, again, especially when pushing back against the status quo, when pushing back against entrenched systems of power. That's the other thing that I think we can start to take into consideration: What is the social standing of the person who is issuing this speech? What are they trying to bring about, and what is our history in terms of taking up this speech? If there's a whole history of disbelieving it or disregarding it, well, then that might give us more reason to be very careful in how we go about responding to it. That might give us more reason to err on the side of taking it as a report, to err on the side of believing the person. That doesn't always mean, again, that they're telling the truth. But it means that we should be more careful with our responses.

MYISHA: Do you think the response to risky speech that you highlight here is one of the main reasons why people are hesitant about engaging in the process? We know that victims are less prone to report assault because of a fear of not being believed. What you're suggesting here is that it's not just about being believed but the extra burden of having to prove it.

CASSIE: Yes. I think that often one of the things that block people from coming forward, especially when we're talking about things that are in a sense intangible, is how do you prove it was really nonconsensual? How do you prove that they were really motivated by racism or sexism, ableism, homophobia? Proving these things is difficult. It's not an easy thing to do.

So when a person is faced with the option of either talking about and recounting their experiences, and they know that they're going to be placed with this position of having to defend, having to take on this extra burden of proof, or just staying quiet, well, it seems like it's a whole lot easier to just not get into it; especially when what counts as proof is often extraordinarily high. This is, again, forcing someone to take on this extra burden just for talking about what's going on in their life.

MYISHA: So give us some normativity. What are some ways that we can resist defaulting to the objective response?

CASSIE: Something that we can do—and I'm thinking especially of the sorts of reasons that we see on social media because this is a place where this plays out all the time—is to hold off on those "Well, what's your proof?" statements. Oftentimes people will take to social media just to get trust that this happened. Oftentimes it's a move of "This is something that exists, this is a thing that happened, this is something that we should be attending to." Sometimes it takes the additional move of "And we need to hold someone to account for it." But overwhelmingly, that doesn't quite end up happening in part because of the responses of "Well, where's your proof?"

So we can slow down with the where's-your-proof responses. If it is the case that someone issues statements of "we need to hold someone to account," then we can switch over into taking it as an accusation. We can say, "Okay, where's the proof, let's amass it, let's see if it's there, what can we do to hold someone to account, and hold people to these norms that they have violated?"

But again, we need to slow down and figure out what a person is doing, especially given that we live in a world that so systematically denies the reality of these forms of oppression. If someone is specifically talking about something horrific that they've experienced, we can start off with saying, "Okay, by default I'm going to believe you that this happened." If we find conflicting evidence, we might re-evaluate that default belief. But slowing down and resisting the automatic move to asking for proof is, I think, an amazing first step.

8

Luvell Anderson on Slurs and Racial Humor

MYISHA: What makes a word a slur? Should slurs be prohibited? If so, on what grounds?

LUVELL: Ernie Lepore and I wrote a paper that was published in 2012, and the answer we gave to that question was a slur is basically a prohibited word; a prohibited word that a particular social group deems a slur.

The prohibitionist, of course, is doing a lot of work in our account and we think that once you look at the kinds of features that slurs exhibit, a prohibitionist view explains those things better than alternative views. You have to explain things like, for example, why we can't unilaterally detach the affect, hatred, and negative connotations tied to most slurs and use them interchangeably with their neutral counterparts. What I'm saying is that there are these slurs. You know who they refer to when people use them; we know who they're supposed to pick out. There are these other expressions that refer to the same group but lack the negative connotation of slurs, so those are the neutral counterparts.

We also have to explain why occurrences of the slurs within things like definitions or within quotations can still provoke offense. We also need to explain why it's difficult to avoid slurring people when we're using someone else's term, indirectly quoting them, for example. Saying that slurs are prohibited expressions and that the prohibition is on their occurrence explains why you can't quote someone indirectly and not provoke offense. The one who uses the slur to quote someone else is still using the slur, and that's a violation of the prohibition against its use. Even in direct quotations, you get this too, which is why newscasters often employ mechanisms like "the n-word" or something like that to cloak the word, not expressly use the expression themselves.

MYISHA: If I quote an American president and all the derogatory things that he says about certain groups, you're suggesting that even though I don't hold the same negative attitude as the person who said it, it is still prohibited for me to say it?

LUVELL: Yes, kinda.

MYISHA: Why is that so?

LUVELL: There are a couple of possible explanations one can give as to why that's so. For some people, they want to ground that prohibition in a moral principle or something like that, where calling someone a slur inflicts a certain kind of moral harm in them, or even mentioning the slur might raise the negative associations that that word brings to mind or brings to bear. Doing so is itself a morally inappropriate action.

I'm not wedded to that kind of view. I think that probably a more general explanation about the prohibition of slurs is grounded in something like a group's right to determine important aspects of their own identity. Presumably, what name a group is called is an important aspect of their identity. Violations of the prohibitions of names that the group explicitly prohibits in some sort of way, either is explicitly saying that this is the name that they don't want to be called, or it's more likely that you observe linguistic practices and observe members of that group's response to being called such names. Those things are violations of the social norm, the norm of a right to self-determination which grounds the prohibition in the first place.

MYISHA: There are other philosophers also writing about slurs. You all have to write papers and so the slurs are written in the work. I've read your work. Are you and other philosophers also participating in something that one ought not to do, or is it different when one writes in a technical way as opposed to quoting someone directly?

LUVELL: That's a great question. I think it's not always clear whether or not there's a simple, straightforward answer to it. Actually, I think that even in what I'll call "pedagogical uses," you run the risk of provoking offense. To be clear, I think the view that Ernie and I were pushing in the paper is that violations of prohibitions explain the offense response to the expressions.

One thing we did not do in the paper is give a view about when such offensive provokings are themselves problematic or racist. I think it's possible to do something that's offensive yet not racist if we're talking about a racial slur, for example. You might think that there's a weighing that takes place in these pedagogical contexts where we're trying to gain knowledge of the mechanisms and nature of these kinds of expressions. Perhaps the potential for offense might be outweighed by the epistemological gains from doing so, or maybe there's something about the power of expression that necessitates mentioning the expression in the text to illuminate the broader point.

MYISHA: I wonder, is it possible for me tonight to call another one of my friends and we create a slur to refer to a particular group? Or is it the case that in order for a slur to be a slur, it must be popular and it must be known not only by those who use it but by those it's being used to reference?

LUVELL: This is where a distinction between what I might call a "slurring speech act" and an expression that goes into the category of slur comes in handy. I think that if you and your friend were to try to coin an expression tonight, what you would succeed in doing when you target the group of your choice would be to perform a slurring speech act towards that group, but in doing so, you weren't creating a slur, as it were. I think the word itself would have to be recognized by the group or relevant caretakers of the group as an expression that's deemed prohibited. It's not until the group prohibits the expression that it becomes a member of the category slur.

MYISHA: Let's talk about the n-word. Is there a difference between the n-word with a soft "a" and the n-word with a hard "er"? What arguments have been given that prohibit or allow their uses?

LUVELL: I don't know if you want the FCC down your back.

MYISHA: No FCC. We can do whatever we want.

LUVELL: All right, I'm going to be real then.

I think many people see a difference between the n-word with a hard "er" and the n-word with a soft "a." They believe the ending indicates whether we're dealing with a slur or with a term of endearment. For instance, comedian Lisa Lampanelli, who's a white woman, tweeted a pic of herself and a friend, Lena Dunham, a few years ago. It had the following caption: "Me with my nigga @LenaDunham of @

HBOGirls—I love this beyotch!!" When she ultimately had to answer for her shenanigans, she made the infamous "I used the 'a' and not the 'er' ending. It just means friend." Then for added clarity, she of course cross-referenced Urban Dictionary. You get a similar appeal from the Kentucky high school English teacher who was flamed in an episode of *The Boondocks*. After telling a black student to "Sit down, nigga," he insisted that he used the soft "a" rather than the hard "er," which again is supposed to be the friendly version.

These two people, of course, are appealing to a distinction between the "er" and "a" endings. But at the end of the day, I think that the n-word with a soft "a" is really just a contemporary stylistic variant that captures the way that black folks have been pronouncing it for years. It's more likely that it's just a way of explicitly signaling the difference in what speech act is being performed and not necessarily two different words.

As far as arguments against nonblack use go, some argue that since nonblacks haven't suffered the experiences of black folks in this country, they don't really have a right to appropriate abusive terms that target black people. It's a kind of, to borrow some Radicant Bourriaud language, "You-weren't-with-me-shooting-in-the-gym" objection. You might develop this kind of argument in the following way: that black folks were left abandoned in the social wasteland with only scraps out of which to make a life, to build a community, and against all odds we managed to do that. You, white folks, gave us leftover pig intestines, we made chitlins; you left us sticks and rocks, we made stickball; you hit us with "nigger" and we made it "nigga"; on top of that, we managed to build community and experience joy. Then you, white person, see us experiencing joy and now want to get in on that action, but it's too late. You weren't invited to the party and we don't take kindly to crashers.

I'm not unsympathetic to this kind of argument—that there's something about experiencing the venom, the vitriol of the expression that licenses one to do with it what you will, to use it in certain kinds of ways. If you haven't been under that experience, then you don't really have a right to it because it's kind of a cheap intrusion.

MYISHA: Is this why blacks are able to produce what you call "nonderogatory elocutions" with the n-word?

LUVELL: Yeah, I mean, basically. To flesh it out a bit more, we can borrow this notion of a community of practice that was first developed by anthropologists and then later applied to language and gender. It's this notion of an aggregate of people who come together around a mutual endeavor and then in the pursuit of that endeavor, they build up certain practices, ways of talking, beliefs, and values and such.

You could think that, well, one of the practices (and you might call it a discursive practice) that emerged within a community of practice or communities of practice within the African American community had to deal with addressing oppressive speech. Of course, one way of addressing that oppressive speech was to take the speech itself and try to disarm it or flip it on its head. What explains black usage, or at least the production of nonderogatory uses of the n-word in these black communities of practice, is that they belong to a community of practice in which this emerged.

MYISHA: This forces me to ask: What if I'm a white person and I was raised in a black family? Does that get me closer to being able to use it?

I remember watching the film *Dope*. And if you notice in the movie, the white kid, the white friend of the group of black kids, is constantly trying to get a pass to say the n-word with an "a." There is another minority, a nonblack minority in the group, who's able to get away with it. And the white kid is wondering, "Why does he get to say it? I'm white and I'm raised in an all-black family? That's all I know."

And what if I am a member of another minority group who's also oppressed and I have this kind of familiarity, not with the exact black experience but experience with oppression. Am I able to use the n-word with an "a"?

LUVELL: I think we can start with empirical data. We see this already. We see situations in which we have nonblack speakers who are for all intents and purposes part of a particular community of practice for which this nonderogatory use of the n-word occurs. They are somehow adopted into the community and given a pass by members of that community to use the expression in its nonderogatory way.

It's not just a theoretical claim, it's an empirical claim that this is actually happening. I think what explains those occurrences is this appeal to a community of practice which is largely a localized kind of notion. That local license that the nonblack person gets in that particular community doesn't travel to all communities of practice. I think we saw this several years ago, for example, where this white rapper, V-Nasty, in Oakland got in all sorts of trouble for using the n-word in one of her songs. V-Nasty's crew, her black friends, came to her defense saying, "No, she's cool, she's one of us, she can use it." Then, of course, you had black folk in other places like "No, we don't know her. And who are you to be giving her a pass?" At the level of the everyday, what she knew was that in her localized community with her localized group of friends, they shared this practice in which she was able to produce these nonderogatory utterances. So that's what happens there.

We also see a kind of slippage with respect to other communities who have also experienced oppression in the US. There's always been a murkiness around the n-word being used by Dominican and Puerto Rican communities in New York, for example. We also see variations that arise due to gender; J.Lo is Puerto Rican and she gets flack for using the n-word in songs, but nonetheless Fat Joe is able to use it all day long without any issue and he's also Puerto Rican. It's complicated there.

MYISHA: What are the rules for appropriating slurs? I have a friend who is adamant that no matter how we women use the word "bitch," it always has a strand of misogyny in it.

LUVELL: I think there aren't really any hard and fast rules for doing so. There might be some rules of thumb. One might say, "Well, only attempt to appropriate slurs that 'belong to you,'" which is kind of a funny phrase because there's a real sense in which it doesn't really belong to the targeted group but the targeting speakers. This is the kind of sentiment that James Baldwin, for example, talks about when he says that Nigger is a caricature that really belongs to white people. It's their fiction, a fiction that white people have concocted to cope with their own psychological fallout over the kinds of atrocities that they've either been a party to or have committed themselves. But nonetheless there's still a psychological fallout or backlash for black folks too, and that fallout is going to be present for slurs that belong to their own group but not really for someone else's. So only attempt to appropriate slurs that belong to you. Secondly, you can't do it alone. It's something that's a communal shared practice. Appropriation is successful only in the midst of a community of practitioners who share and recognize the use.

Addressing the charge of participation in one's own degradation— I think this is an interesting departure from what we might think of as the "linguistic mechanisms of appropriation." We can explain just on a social linguistic level why appropriation happens when it happens. But then there's a further question about whether or not a group should do so. You might share a Cosby type of view where you're just deceiving yourself if you think that uses of the n-word, for example, are doing anything other than reinforcing negative stereotypes about your own group. It's not clear to me that there's a consensus on this issue. So of course, people come down differently on this question.

I often wonder about what someone's mental state/attitude has to be like in order to make use of the n-word in a purportedly nonderogatory way and nonetheless be slandering themselves or slurring themselves. I think you would have to have some kind of self-hatred or some kind of negative self-evaluation. It's just not clear to me that, for example, the uses of the n-word that often come across internally and inside the black community have that kind of attitude.

MYISHA: Let's transition now to racial humor. Related to the community of practice point that you made earlier, what is it about humor where one's group membership affects one's ability to make a certain joke?

LUVELL: I do think that the communities-of-practice notion applies here as well. Humor is also a kind of cultural production that has a particular social role. Again, if we're dealing with vulnerable groups, there's going to be something similar to the practices that emerge out of n-word use; perhaps it serves as a mechanism for building solidarity or maybe even a cathartic practice in certain instances.

If you are a member of the community of practice, that licenses you in a certain way to make these kinds of jokes. Whereas if you're not a member of the community, it makes it difficult for you to do so.

MYISHA: Does this also apply to the permissibility of an audience to laugh or not laugh at certain jokes?

LUVELL: I think so. Let's say if we're looking at a comedian who is telling racial jokes. It's important to see that comedian as a member of a shared community of practice because, I think, that affects how we interpret what's going on, how we interpret the comedian's jokes.

Of course, humor is intricate in some instances, and if you don't have the relevant background experience, you might miss out on all sorts of cultural cues—that is, you missed a joke and perhaps are laughing at the wrong thing. Then what you're laughing at might in itself be problematic. It might not be a person's being white per se that's the problem, but it's their lack of cultural familiarity, lack of familiarity with certain kinds of experiences that might pose a hermeneutical barrier to understanding the humor.

MYISHA: Why do swears/curse words have the power that they do? When I hear a Brit use British curse words, as an American, I do not feel the power of the words. I wonder if my membership or lack of membership in a practicing community has a lot to do with me not feeling their effects. Is it that I'm just not familiar with the taboo surrounding the words?

LUVELL: Yeah, that's right! The particular taboos are going to be, I think, society relative. We're acculturated in certain kinds of ways in our particular social, cultural locations, our situations. We pick up on the gravitas, the feelings of our own sort of taboos, but not so much on others. So when I hear "wanker," for example, or something like that, I'm not particularly moved because I haven't grown up with that particular type of word.

9

Jason Stanley on Satire and Public Philosophy

MYISHA: You were in Paris in 2015 giving a series of lectures. On the day you arrived, the offices of Charlie Hebdo, a satirical magazine, were the target of a terrorist attack. You would later go on to write a *New York Times* piece about it. What is your opinion about what happened in Paris, particularly how it relates to speech?

JASON: Well, I'm no expert on French society. My piece was really about liberalism, and I think it's not controversial to say that French society is at least self-consciously governed by the ideals of liberalism—*Laïcité* (French term for secularism), for example.

I came to Paris to give a series of talks about liberalism, and then an illiberal moment occurred where an ideal of liberalism, free speech, was challenged. We can for the moment take liberalism to be the political philosophy according to which freedom and equality are the two ideals. But of course, there are many senses of freedom and equality. France does have some hate-speech laws that are more restrictive than the First Amendment. Nevertheless, despite the existence of those laws, there's a pervasive culture of challenging the sacred that is at the very heart of liberal democracy, an ideal liberal democracy. So, it was a moment where free speech, that ideal, was being literally murdered before our eyes.

On the other hand, there's another ideal of liberalism, which is equality. In moments or cultures that are deeply devoted to equality and freedom, equality and freedom can blind you, or can prevent you from seeing (to avoid the Ableist language) that there are inequalities in society. This is, for example, the point of the subtitle of Michelle Alexander's book, *The New Jim Crow: Mass Incarceration in the Age of Colorblindness*. She's drawing our attention to the fact that in the 1960s there were 200,000 prisoners; now we have over 2.2 million, almost a million whom are African American, and yet we think we are governed in a post–civil rights era by the liberal ideal of colorblindness, a form of equality.

In my article, I was drawing attention to the fact that there is a difference when criticizing a religion that represents a group, a minority group in society. I think many people in that minority group are not religious. But nevertheless, when you're attacking icons of Islam, it can be taken as an attack on those people: religious and atheist alike. I was drawing attention to the fact that there really is a difference between criticizing Islam and criticizing Christianity, even in a secular, atheist society where most people of North African descent or Middle Eastern descent are atheists, and almost everyone of French, European descent, originally Catholic, are atheists as well. There still is a difference between criticizing the religion associated historically with one, and the religion associated historically with the other. It's similar to, in the American body politic, lampooning Frederick Douglass and lampooning icons of white society, such as James Madison. Those would be very different because of the power relations.

At the end of my article, I relayed an anecdote about coming back from a demonstration commemorating the satirists who were brutally murdered. I came by a synagogue on Rue de la Roquette that was guarded by a number of highly militarized French policemen. There was one man in particular standing in front of the gates who was North African. I think it would be fair to take him as being in a group whose ancestors were Muslim, and yet here he is protecting a synagogue. The point of the ending of the article was to say that while liberalism leads us to be blind to or fail to recognize these differences in power, it nevertheless can result in a society in which a North African, presumably non-Jewish North African, can guard a synagogue.

MYISHA: I want to talk about that a little bit more, particularly as we begin to rethink the place and limits of satire in popular culture. There was controversy about releasing the 2014 movie *The Interview* in theatres. The movie is a satire on North Korean leader Kin Jong Un.

I remember debating with some kinfolk about it and saying something like "I believe in freedom of speech; they have a right to release the movie. I just think that it was done in bad taste and they shouldn't have done it." Some people disagreed with me. Their reasoning, their justification was, "Well, it's satire, it's just satire."

You say in the *New York Times* article, "Satire is the alternate method by which reason can address power. The use of satire, even by those without control of resources can, with merely the use of a pen, bring figures of authority down to earth." It seems as if you're suggesting that satire has positive power depending on if the satirical subject has authority or not.

JASON: That's right. It's meant to be this leveler. You can think it doesn't matter, you can think that you can satirize everything. But for it to have the positive impact that it's intended to have in a liberal democracy, it should be wielded against those with power.

I think it's important to note that, as I say clearly in my article, the satirists of *Charlie Hebdo* were aware of this. If you look over time at what they focused on satirizing, it was generally structures of power. Satirizing fundamentalist Islam, or Boko Haram, was meant to be a satire of the French who were not from that background. However, I think it didn't really work. The subjects of the cartoons were minorities. As you say, the point of satire is so the powerless can address the powerful on their terms and equalize. When the addressers have more power than those they satirize, it becomes somewhat problematic.

MYISHA: I see this a lot in comedy clubs. Nowadays we're just used to black comedians talking about white people.

JASON: Right.

MYISHA: It's hilarious when they talk about white people. It's strange and probably unheard of, or the ratio is pretty small, for a white comedian to make their whole act about black people. We would look at that differently.

In writing the article you reference here, you allowed your thoughts on current events and your philosophical knowledge to converge in the public sphere. As a philosopher, I would like to see more philosophers in the public domain. This is not to say that every philosopher should take this on. But I would like to see more. Why do you think there is a lack of philosophers serving as public intellectuals in America?

JASON: Well, because we have economists. That's our public culture. Our public culture is one where if you have policymakers, they're going to valorize economics. I think it's actually an anti-democratic feature of American public culture. It has to do with the desire for experts to give us some kind of scientific judgment. You find in the American public culture a constant valorization of anything that's presented in the language of science.

Psychologists tend to play the public role of philosophers on philosophical questions. Actually knowing Adam Smith's work on empathy is not important, but doing a psychology experiment that might be less informed by political philosophy, or the history of political philosophy, well, that's going to be recorded in the public culture as science and it's not going to matter that it's not informed by what those notions are, and the roles they play in the history of philosophy.

I think that in general, there's an overall bias against anything that's qualitative in the sense that any "real knowledge" must be packaged with the use of science, with the use of statistics, with the use of experiments. I think we've had in our public culture horrendous problems as a result because there's no quantitative way to investigate ideology and bias. We have science being used in incredibly ideological ways. I think Carl Hart's book, *High Price*, brings this out with the drug war, and Khalil Muhammad's book, *The Condemnation of Blackness*, brings this out with the use of social science in criminalizing black Americans.

We don't have a place in public discourse for qualitative reflection or narrative. You can present to me everything you want, every statistic you want about, for example, the black-white wealth gap, but you can't understand the black-white wealth gap. You can't understand what it means in human terms unless you have someone explaining what it's like to be poor. Forget the black-white wealth gap and think about poverty versus wealth. You can't understand what it's like to be in Appalachia, to be in the repeated, incredible poverty in Appalachia that is immovable generation after generation, without a narrative story of what Appalachia is like and what it's like to grow up in that environment. We're presented with all these facts about methamphetamine and the newest wave of the drug war, but we can't understand why people are drawn to such a terrible drug unless we understand how miserable living conditions are in those communities. That requires something other than science. It requires narrative. Philosophy, I think, is the victim of an overly "scientistic," statistical, and "technicist" (as my father called it in his work) public discourse.

MYISHA: So how can things change, or should we want things to change? How can we mix philosophy and politics? It is my assumption that in France, for example, philosophers have a place at the policy table. Philosophers are public intellectuals there. Students take philosophy classes before attending university. This shows that they recognize that there is value in what philosophy can do and what we can do with philosophy.

JASON: I think it's going to come with a general reaction to the "technicist" public culture, and I think it's going to bring with it not just philosophy in the public realm but also creative writers, fiction writers; in general, reflective, narrative, and conceptual engagement with the problems of the day. What we have to do is somehow get people to understand that you can gain insight via that method, that not all knowledge must be packaged in this "technicist" form.

Americans are conditioned to see anything in the vocabulary of science as objective, real, and true. But even a true statistic, or a true experiment that only gives you one piece of information is going to lead to a skewed sense of reality if you don't have the rest of the information. Somehow, we need to get that message across, that elucidation and understanding is not just being provided with factoid by factoid. Even those who are providing us with correct facts are often ideologically biased or maybe invariably ideologically biased in which facts they think are important to draw to our attention.

MYISHA: As we talk about seeing more philosophers in the public sphere, I think it is apt to explore the title itself. I am really into the bio sections of social media accounts. I'm intrigued by how people describe themselves. Sometimes I'll see a bio, for example, that says: John Doe, "Lover of life, sports fanatic, and philosopher." It's pretty clear that this person is not what we call a professional philosopher, but he or she identifies as a philosopher. Do you think in order to call oneself a "philosopher," one must be trained in philosophy and do philosophy for a living, or is being a philosopher a way of thinking?

JASON: Ah, that's a fantastic question. I think that "philosopher" carries with it a suggestion that one enjoys reflection. I think that that's an extremely important sense of the term. I often describe myself as teaching philosophy, or working in philosophy, rather than as a philosopher. First of all, I don't want to distinguish myself from others who reflect but do so without teaching in a professional setting. Secondly, I also don't describe myself as a philosopher because there's a kind of authoritative connotation with "philosopher" that I don't want to abuse.

My general reaction is that I hope everyone's a philosopher. Everyone should so self-describe, although there are definitely some people out there who really, really should not. It would be highly misleading.

MYISHA: Can you name a rapper, past or present, who you would describe as a philosopher?

JASON: I guess the first person that comes to mind is Ice Cube. Take his song "A Bird in the Hand" and compare it to Tommie Shelby's 2007 "Dark Ghettos" paper, which draws our attention to the nonideal conditions in the American inner city that lead to economic crimes by drug dealers. What Shelby says is that there's a failure of reciprocity in American society. People are born into great poverty and there are large wealth gaps between races. In those conditions, some of the issues about punishment become irrelevant. Ice Cube's "A Bird in the Hand" song is about that very topic. It's about the forced economic choice that would lead one to become a drug dealer. Given the structure of society, Ice Cube claims that it's unreasonable to punish someone for that choice.

10

Winston Thompson on Educational Justice

MYISHA: You make a distinction between what we call "topics of educational justice" and the "concept of educational justice." What is the difference between the two?

WINSTON: A lot of the educational research and scholarship often invokes the idea of justice in trying to make sense of some topics that the scholar thinks deserve our attention. The different types of discussions of educational justice, to my mind, are both rather political. The first invocation of the concept of educational justice is as though educational systems are either just or unjust when they're pursuing their educational goals. This is because they either honor or fail to honor a traditionally political standard of justice. The work that I do on understanding this first type of educational justice is towards understanding the ways in which this type engages the topic of educational justice without doing very much work on the concept itself. To my mind, the second type of educational justice is related in that it's also political in nature. But rather than thinking of educational goals as honoring some traditionally political standard of justice, under the second type, we might think of the educational goal as being almost identical or synonymous with political standards of justice.

Both of these types of educational justice get invoked often as educational scholars are talking about topics of educational justice. There's not really much attention given to the fact that there are these two different types of educational justice described, nor is there much attention given to what this typology overlooks or the ways in which it limits the scope of the discussion that we might have about the very concept of educational justice itself.

MYISHA: You invoke terms such as "potential" and "formation" in your work. How might we understand educational justice in ways that take potential and formation seriously?

WINSTON: If we're thinking of discussions of educational justice as being primarily political in nature, I think that the two types that I've just given you a sense of do a lot of really good work. But I think if we press the concept of educational justice and ask ourselves, "What sort of things might be owed to one as an educational matter rather than as a political matter in the context of education," I think we might begin by asking questions of one's potential and how one comes to be formed relative to that potential.

So again, if we think about justice as making sure that one gets what one is owed, educational justice, in my view—I might begin asking questions about what one is owed in light of one's potentials; one's potentials to become or to be formed in one way or another. It is often the case that we might recognize that there are going to be some limitations, some tradeoffs that have to be made under conditions of finitude. We've got only a finite amount of time, energy, et cetera.

In this work I've been drawing on some of the work of Robbie McClintock. McClintock gives a really nice articulation of the degree to which questions of human potential are at the very core of what we might mean when we're discussing educational justice from this educational perspective rather than only the political perspective. In my view, these two perspectives certainly overlap in practice and conceptually lean on one another in ways that will call us to ask, of course, questions of distributive justice. It will also call us to answer those questions as they feed into this more educationally focused approach that I'm outlining here.

MYISHA: Give us an example of how this looks on the ground.

WINSTON: It might be the case that we find ourselves in a situation in which we check all the boxes relative to political justice. Whatever the sort of approach to political justice is that we've got, we can check all the boxes according to a particular theory or theories of political justice.

We're sure that in an educational environment, we're not distributing resources in such a way that we're overlooking the rights or maligning the intentions of persons. We're recognizing people as they are in the moment and so forth. But what my work would pose is the observation that even if we're meeting all those standards, it might be the case that there is still some sense of an injustice, an educational injustice, under certain conditions. And that educational injustice might, again, not be linked only to those political standards that we hope to endorse, but instead are linked to the observation that one or another particularly valuable potential is being overlooked or underattended. It is overlooked to such a degree that a third party might observe that a situation is a real shame or real injustice or it falls short in some ways because it fails to give to the individual what they are owed relative to their potentials.

MYISHA: Let's go into a high school in the United States. Let's make it more specific. Let's go to an East Coast high school, let's say an urban community where a large population of black and Latino folks attend. Let's say that you become the official Educational Injustice Inspector. What would you see in classrooms that would indicate to you that, based on your view, an educational injustice is taking place?

WINSTON: If we think about the ways in which a person is not given their due relative to their status as a knower, I'd like to extend that towards thinking about the way in which a person might not be given their due and their status as one who is coming to know themselves or the world around them. So in some ways this points to some of the work that Miranda Fricker has done on epistemic injustice.

In the context that you're presenting here, we might imagine all sorts of ways in which a black Latino student comes to recognize themselves and recognize the world in a way that diminishes their sense of what is possible in that world and what they're capable of doing relative to facts of the matter. If it's the case that the educational experience is somehow suggesting to these students that there's either possibility A or option A is necessarily more realistic than possibility B, I think we might be witnessing an educational injustice. And you are witnessing an injustice if it's the case that that educational experience is one that diminishes an individual's capacity to realize their elements of their potential that they would have some cause to value.

MYISHA: The account would suggest that in these education environments that I'm referring to, they ought to create spaces in which young people or knowers can flourish in ways that will actualize their potential.

WINSTON: That's right. The question of discovering or deliberating about which potentials we're going to pursue is in some sense a question of justice, it's a question of educational justice. It's a question of educational justice for the school and for the educator working with the student. But it's also a question for the student herself to begin thinking about which of her potentials she wishes to elevate, especially given, as I mentioned before, conditions of finitude in which there have to be some choices made about which parts of one's self one will actually pursue developing.

MYISHA: You say in your work that "politics, especially in a democratic context, can be understood as an essentially educational project." What do you mean by this?

WINSTON: What I've been attempting to do is to show that the relationship between politics and education, as I alluded to earlier, is often presumed to operate in one direction in which educational concerns are subsumed under larger political concerns.

Under my view, it's the case that we might also think of that relationship as operating in an inverted fashion in which political concerns can be understood as falling under the umbrella of education. That line that you referenced there is a statement about that. What I mean by this is that there's a way of thinking about politics, especially in a democracy, as the interchange of ideas, the sort of expression of positions and values that individuals hold. We can think of politics as being an activity that is educational in the sense that it is an activity in which individuals are making the case toward another, attempting to teach one another about the experiences of those who are unlike oneself. It's the case that one way of thinking about politics is as an act of continual self-study. A community, a polity, and a society are engaged in an act of self-study about its problems, about the solutions to its problems, about the solutions to those problems, and the ways to pursue those solutions.

John Dewey in *Democracy and Education* gives an account of democracy as being essentially educational. He's not talking about democracy only as a system of government. He's not only talking about politics; he's talking about democracy as a way of life. I do think that there's a foundation there. There's a core that we can pursue that allows us to recognize that the actions and the systems of politics are in some sense about communication and about recognition of shared problems and shared attention towards inquiry. And we can figure out how to address those problems.

MYISHA: Given your view of educational justice, how might you respond to the following educational issues? The first issue is charter schools.

WINSTON: Given the account that I've given you now about educational justice, I'm going to want to focus primarily on the person and what the person can achieve and accomplish relative to their potentials. On the second order, I think I might want to talk about what a society, a polity, and a group of people can achieve and accomplish.

It's entirely possible that charter schools can pursue educational justice by tailoring the types of educational experiences that individuals have, especially in communities in which certain individuals and members of particular identity groups have been historically and presently underserved. Charter schools represent a change, and with that change they represent some possibilities. I certainly think that it's the case that on the individual level, a certain type of educational justice could be pursued with greater freedom under charter conditions. Now, given the ways that charter schools actually tend to operate in the world around us presently, I think that there is a larger question about what a society can pursue as a matter of educational justice via charter schools. I think that charter schools ultimately erode some of our abilities to engage in some of the shared processes of life lived amongst others.

Without getting into all of the details about how charter schools operate and how they select or retain certain types of students and the ways in which they visit upon certain communities, certain burdens, I would say that I think it's more difficult to make the case for charter schools when we're looking at things from a systemic level than when we're looking at things from the individual level. This might explain why many parents and individuals might be in favor of charter schools for their students, for their children, for the people around them, whereas by and large, most educational scholars are either antagonistic toward charter schools or agnostic and somewhat ambivalent about the relative or the reported successes of charter schools at that systemic level.

MYISHA: The second issue is free tuition in higher education.

WINSTON: That issue is one that I think becomes tricky as we start thinking about the history of higher education in this country and what higher education historically has represented and represents in the present moment. Given the degree to which higher education is almost a requirement for access to a livable wage in this society, it seems as though things are getting worse, although perhaps I might be speaking from my own particular positions as someone who went to the university and took out student loans and is still living with those loans.

MYISHA: Tell me about it.

WINSTON: I'm sure that readers know this experience well. Let me just pull back slightly and say subsidized tuition is a way to better realize educational justice as it makes access to the experiences of the educational institution available for a larger selection of persons. Now, whether or not free tuition or subsidized tuition would result in a further bifurcation of your upper echelon or more desirable educational experiences relative to less desirable educational experiences, I've got no strong view of what would likely happen. But I do think that free tuition would certainly increase access while potentially also visiting burdens upon persons who receive that tuition, as they're likely, given the history of higher education in this country, are going to be recipients of a subpar educational experience relative to those who likely would be able to pay for it.

MYISHA: Here is the last controversial issue. What do you think of decolonizing the curriculum?

WINSTON: Calls to decolonize the curriculum are calls to recognize the degree to which the curriculum, the subject matter taught draws upon particular traditions, cultures, and prioritizes those cultures and traditions over the cultures and traditions of those individuals who are the recipients of the subject matter. So a very easy way of thinking about it is that people aren't taught about themselves in the subject matter that's presented to them.

This is a great issue to think about under the lens that I'm suggesting. The view that I have is certainly one that would be in favor of reviewing and revisiting the curriculum in attempts to understand the ways in which the curriculum might be reifying certain social structures but also certain conceptual or intellectual and interpersonal relationships to what it means to know and to be an educated person.

Section 3

SOCIAL GROUPS AND ACTIVISM

11

Serene Khader on Cross-Border Feminist Solidarity

MYISHA: What is feminism and what is transnational feminism?

SERENE: This is a big question. It's a bigger question than it seems, but the definition of feminism that I like to use comes from bell hooks. She said in her early work that feminism was opposition to sexist oppression. She later revised her definition to say that feminism was opposition to all intersecting oppressions. My view is that we should use both of those definitions, but use different ones in different contexts. I think that we should use the sexist-oppression one in transnational contexts for reasons that I can explain.

But before I get ahead of myself, I should say a little bit about what oppression is. Oppression, on Marilyn Frye's classic definition, occurs when you have practices that systematically target members of certain social groups and disadvantage them relative to other groups. Feminism if it's opposition to sexist oppression, it's opposition to the form of opposition that happens when members of certain genders are systematically subordinated.

In terms of the question of what transnational feminism is, a lot of readers might have heard of Global feminism. That was kind of a phrase that people used in the 1980s and a little bit in the 1990s. The idea of Global feminism was the idea that women are facing the same struggles everywhere, the same struggle against patriarchy, and all women need to unite around their shared struggle against patriarchy. Transnational feminism is one of the approaches to international feminism that questions that framing. It basically says that in order to think about feminist solidarity, we need to constantly think about the history of imperialism and also the ways that ongoing neoliberal, capitalist exploitation and ongoing northern-driven, in particular but not exclusively, militarism affect the opportunities for women to organize across borders.

It's not as simple as "Oh, women everywhere experience the same form of oppression because they're all oppressed by men," even though I do think that most or all women are oppressed by sexism. The fact is that because women in the Global North or in the West benefit or have benefitted from the subjugation of other women, sometimes it's important for women in positions of privilege over other women and who are actively promoting exploitation and domination of other women, to take those things into account when they're trying to determine what their moral and political responsibilities to those women are.

MYISHA: What do you see as the role of solidarity in feminism? Is solidarity a necessary or sufficient condition for feminism? Is solidarity always the goal? Is solidarity in service to a greater goal?

SERENE: What it means to be a feminist is to be committed to opposing sexist oppression. In that sense, if you believe that sexist oppression is a genuine moral problem and that it exists in various places around the world, then you think in general, yeah, it's a good thing to take political stances that will work against ending women's oppression or ending sexist oppression. But I think it's really important to say in that same breath that given the fact of historical and ongoing imperialism, some of the acts that are solidaristic to other women may not be the ones that seem like the obvious right ones to people in the Global North or to women in the West. Alison Jaggar, in her important article, "Saving Amina," for example, talks about how the most solidaristic thing to do in some cases for Western women will be to stop contributing to the domination of women in the Global South by opposing economic policies of the countries in the Global North.

If you're a feminist, probably, you have to believe in and support some kind of solidarity. But the form that solidarity has to take does not mean, and in most cases probably shouldn't mean, directly intervening. In fact, directly intervening to take over other people's oppositions to their own oppression, I would say, is not even really solidarity. Solidarity says that you're standing with another person as an equal. Saying, "I'm going to offer an analysis of your world for you and decide what kind of political action should happen in your context" is not treating someone as an equal. It's treating someone more like somebody who is subordinate to you, whose own kind of evaluations of their own situation you don't take seriously.

MYISHA: What are some of the "hot-topic" issues that Western feminism seems to be most concerned about when it comes to the struggle of women in the Global South? Is it even proper to call them "struggles"?

SERENE: I love this question. I guess part of why I love it is that you used the word "struggle," and I want to think a little bit about what the word "struggle" means because there's two different things that it could mean; one that we hear a lot about and another that we hear almost nothing about.

"Struggle" could mean the political activism that women in the Global South are engaged in, and that's real. That's happening every day and we don't tend to hear that much about it in the Global North and especially in philosophy. There's actually almost no literature that talks seriously about third-world women's movements, transnational women's movements, and women's movements from the Global South.

On the other hand, I guess, "struggle" could mean the travails and horrible lives of women in the Global South. I think that's how we're used to hearing struggles talked about. In her famous essay in the 1990s, "Under Western Eyes," Chandra Mohanty says that Westerners have this image of the single third-world woman. The features of her life are that she's ignorant, poor, uneducated, tradition bound, domestic, family oriented, and victimized. "Struggle" could mean that. When people in the West think about struggles of women in the Global South, I think they often are imagining women facing these horrible life conditions.

Any time I talk about my work, the first two things people want to talk to me about are female-genital cutting and women being forced to engage in various forms of Islamic dress. Then also, of course, there's domestic violence. Those are the kinds of topics that we hear being talked about a lot by feminists and audiences in the Global North. Of course, those things are real and are genuine moral problems, but I think there's a couple different important things to recognize about them. One is just that they don't expose the whole truth about what other women's lives are like. There's no single truth about what other "women's lives" are like. There isn't a real answer to the question, "What are the needs of these other women" because they are not this preconstituted group. They're a diverse group that have diverse needs and diverse strategies.

But the other problem, which gets talked a lot about in the transnational and postcolonial literature, is that the reason why people love to talk about issues like female-genital cutting is that these are harms to other women that are easy to attribute to their cultures. There's a racist element toward men in the Global South here too. The harms are easy to be attributed to being caused by barbaric brown and black men. They're easy to attribute to religions, and so on. If those are the issues we focus on, it's very convenient for the West and the North because we get to absolve ourselves of moral responsibility for causing any harms that women in the Global South might be facing.

Another problem with framing the struggles of women in the Global South that way is that we hear a lot about third-world women and women in the Global South as victims of these practices, and we don't hear very much about the things that they are doing to stop these practices. We don't hear about the other feminist things that they're doing because sometimes they have other priorities both because of the way that sexist oppression manifests in their lives and because sometimes, tragically, opposing other oppressions may have to take priority and may be the rational thing to do given the fact that they have to agitate against multiple oppressions in order to improve their own well-being. The other kind of danger of focusing on these issues is that it really causes us to overlook the ways in which women in the Global South are agents. And they use that agency often to come up with political strategies that are actually more effective and smarter at overcoming the manifestations of sexist opposition in their communities.

MYISHA: You note that a problematic response from women in the West to the struggle of women in the Global South has been a promotion of universal values. Give us some examples of this.

SERENE: I am in favor of promoting universal values. I think you have to believe in universal values to be a feminist. I also think you have to believe in universal values to be anti-imperialist. At the end of the day, what we're saying is that imperialist oppression is bad and sexist oppression is bad, and that is just morally true.

I actually think that believing in those universal values is not the cause of the problematic things and the oppressive things that have become commonplace in Western feminism. Nor do I think that postcolonial and transnational feminists are actually arguing against universalism of the moral type. What most postcolonial, decolonial, and transnational feminists are really arguing against, I think, are two things. One is they are sometimes arguing against claims that are descriptive universalism. By that, I mean they're arguing against claims that certain facts about the world are universally true. For example, there's a big literature in transnational feminisms about the idea that earning an income will liberate women. To make it into a factual claim, it says earning an income will increase women's well-being. Well, that's something that is mostly just a fact about the world. It varies from context to context. One of the reasons that harmful interventions that increase women's work burdens and decrease their negotiating power have happened is partly because of people just getting the facts wrong about how relationships work and the effect of income in different contexts. Sometimes the universalism that's wrong is just a universalism about what the facts are, not a universalism about what values we should endorse.

Saying that the debate between Western or what I call "missionary feminists" and transnational feminists or postcolonial or decolonial feminists is a debate about universalism and relativism is a convenient move that a lot of people in the Western, liberal, missionary position take in order to avoid having to engage with the other literatures. What is really going on is that the transnational, postcolonial, and decolonial feminist literatures are saying, "No, there are universal values. Westerners are just wrong about what they are. There are universal values, they just aren't the ones that are expressed in Western culture." It's really convenient for people of the Western and liberal position to say, "Oh, we need to oppose relativism," because what that does is propose a question-begging response from a philosophical perspective. It doesn't prevent you from talking about the issue at hand, which is: Which are the right universal values to have? Instead it says, "Well, the only possible universal values are the values that have been adopted by the West. And if you don't believe in these, then you are a moral relativist." And clearly, we can't have that as the solution.

I really want to reject that way of thinking and say, "No, let's have a universalism, but let's have a real conversation about what the values of that universalism should be. And let's specifically talk about whether the values that transnational feminists have accused of being vehicles for imperialism are the actual values that feminists need to endorse."

MYISHA: What is the connection between these universal values and exploitation?

SERENE: One thing that is happening in the world right now that I think we should be concerned about is the rise of neoliberalism that has been documented to have really adverse economic impacts on women and on the poor in general.

Neoliberalism is an approach to making economic policy that says that the solution or the right way to make economic policy is to reduce restrictions on trade and to cut social services. You want to have freer markets and lesser availability of social services. One way to think about both of those things is a narrowing of the role of the state. Often people who are in favor of neoliberalism, although not all of them, believe that freer markets and less state involvement will result in some kind of greater freedom for people. This economic agenda that we call "neoliberalism" has been driving Northern-led financial and development policy for some time now. Northern governments have dramatically shaped the policies that poorer countries are implementing in their own countries in ways that cut social spending and in ways that liberalize markets.

One way that a universal value that has been claimed to be necessary for feminism can promote exploitation has to do with the idea that liberating women from the household, which is operationalized as getting women to earn an income, is going to liberate them from sexist oppression. So all over the world, we have these development policies that are organized around the idea, "Oh, it's feminist to liberate women from being controlled by the men in their household. So what should we do about that? Oh, we should make it possible for women to earn an income."

Sylvia Chant has done a lot of really good work about a phenomenon that she calls the "feminization of responsibility." What she basically finds through a bunch of cross-cultural empirical studies is that in many cases what's happening when women are encouraged to earn incomes is that the amount of household labor that they're doing doesn't decrease. Women in the West have experience with this. We know that in the West, women still do the vast majority of the housework and care work even if they are the main breadwinner for their household. There's a study I cite in the book where researchers find that these women in India, once they put together their housework and their income work, are working eighteen hours a day. Then the study concludes that they need to use their spare time to think about how to economically better themselves.

MYISHA: Oh my goodness. Wow!

SERENE: Yeah. In terms of connecting it to universal values, one part of what's going on here is that people have in their mind, the correct idea, that relationships of certain sorts and household labor can be part of the things that cause oppression to women. I think they also have wrongly in their head, what I call "enlightenment liberal narrative" or the "enlightenment teleological narrative." This says that the oppression of women is caused by tradition, and capitalism will liberate them from tradition. I think this idea—that universally what we need is to make women into economic individuals who will be capable of earning their own incomes, and that along with that, the idea that somehow it's magically going to cause women not to be oppressed by men—is causing interventions that don't improve people's lives. In some cases, it seems to be worsening sexist oppression. If we had better values, we would be less likely to think that this thing that is actually harming women looks like it's a benefit to women.

MYISHA: So let's talk about tradition a little bit more. You claim that people in the West have a tendency to see other people's ways of life as a tradition, but they don't look at their own way of life as such. How so? What is the problem with this?

SERENE: My view is that Westerners often think of themselves as having modernity and have been sold a story about a history of their own countries and a history of the world that's about modernity. My view is a common view in postcolonial and decolonial literature.

Part of that story about modernity says, "Look, tradition was this backward thing that oppressed everyone. Everyone began in this traditional or barbaric kind of structure. And then because of a series of developments that, according to this narrative, were caused by endogenous factors, meaning internal factors to the West—it made the West step away from tradition, and it became modern." Part of what I just want to really emphasize is that the word "modern" is not a morally neutral word. If you say that you're "modern," usually, what you are saying is that you have achieved a certain level of moral progress.

I think the West is already telling itself this story. The West story says "we are modern. What that means is that we have liberated ourselves from tradition, and tradition is the source of all of these bad things that happen to people, including sexist oppression." What's the problem with that? Well, I think there's two answers to it.

One is, it's false. That narrative is false because it overlooks the history of colonialism. It says that the reason that the West is supposedly modern or developed and other people aren't has to do with the internal features of those societies and not Western imperialist domination. That's part of why the narrative is false. But, also, the view that Westerners don't have traditions is simply false. We can play a lot with how we define the word "tradition." Part of what it means to be a human being that's socialized is that you inherit certain beliefs and practices before an age where you are really in a place to separate yourself from or question them. You could try to separate yourself from them latter, but you would already have been constituted by them. It's just false that people in the West don't have traditions. There's a joke in one of the responses to Susan Okin's *Is Multiculturalism Bad for Women?* which I think is "Liberalism's Sacred Cow" by Homi Bhabha. I think he's trying to point to that idea: of course, people in the West have traditions.

The second problem, and this is where I think the moral and political danger really is, is that it makes it look like what are really requests for cultural others to adopt Western culture, are actually requests for people to become free or to start making your own choices or asking questions. The danger is if you think that freedom from tradition is good and then you also think Westerners don't have tradition, what it lets you do is ask people to adopt Western traditions and not see that you're doing that. You think instead, "Oh, I'm just asking you to be free and ask questions" or "I'm just asking you to become modern."

I started reflecting about that a lot. And what led me to write about that particular topic was that I was living in France in the years after the ban on the hijab in public schools was happening. I was paying a lot of attention to the French coverage. It was actually surprising to live in France and to see that most of the people I interacted with who identified as feminists really believed that this was the feminist solution: to ban wearing headscarves in public schools.

You would ask, "Why do you think it's a feminist and important thing to not be allowed to wear a headscarf to school?" And you would constantly get answers that were about freedom coupled with an unwillingness to question whether any French gender protocols were patriarchal. Anytime you questioned whether any mainstream French gender protocols were patriarchal, you would be laughed out of the room a little bit. Once I was like "Isn't wearing high heels patriarchal?" Some of them would acknowledge that, but then they would say, "Oh, but it's a choice." Anything that was part of the French gender protocol got painted as a choice; anything that was part of the gender protocol that they associated with Islam got painted as something that people were coerced into doing. In Joan Scott's book about this, which I think is really good, she actually cites a story where a French official is complaining in public about the tragedy of "young girls covering up their beautiful faces." It's kind of funny. It's also terrible. But it's funny in a bunch of ways. One of them, which is totally not quite on this point, is I don't really know what hijabs have to do with covering people's faces.

MYISHA: Exactly!

SERENE: Everything associated with Islam has been bundled into this ball for them. I think more germane to the point I'm trying to make now is just that the idea that women should be available to be sexually objectified in public for him was like "Oh, this is modernity. And obviously, it is just a good thing, when you are young, to have your beauty on display for people." To me that seemed like it's a case where "No, what you're really asking is for people to adopt your own culturally specific and patriarchal conception of how gender should be lived, and yet you keep saying that all you're doing is asking people to abandon their traditions, asking people to be free, and make choices."

MYISHA: Is it possible to be a traditionalist and a feminist?

SERENE: I think the answer is yes, absolutely, it's possible to be a traditionalist and be a feminist. But here's the qualifying remark: it depends on what the content of your tradition is.

A nice thing about thinking about feminism as opposition to sexist oppression is that it actually moves the language about freedom and choice and modernity off center stage, and moves instead to asking the question, "Well, what do you believe about whether gender should be hierarchically arranged to each other?" My point is, it doesn't matter where you believe that belief came from. If you believe that sexist oppression is wrong, if you believe that one gender should not have more power and resources than another, you believe in feminism, and it doesn't matter where you think that belief came from. You can think that belief came from your reason and maybe some kind of anti-traditionalist. But you absolutely can think that that belief came from God or that that belief came from the tradition of your people.

When you look at the activism and work of a lot of feminists working in the Global South, you see that lots of people in the world are saying, "I oppose sexism because it is part of the dictates of my tradition. I oppose sexism because gender equality just is the spirit of the Quran." Some of the people who are doing that kind of work are Islamic feminists—that term is controversial in itself. But they include people like Amina Wadud. An example of activism based on that is an organization in Morocco and North Africa called Collectif Maghreb-Égalité 95. That group said, "We're going to appeal to both Islamic and secular justifications to explain why we think gender equality is important. Why should we only appeal to secular justifications?"

Some people don't want to appeal to secular justifications at all. Part of why I talk about Amina Wadud a bit in the work is that she really says, "Part of what it means to me to be a Muslim is just that I do not get to question the Quran. What the Quran says is just something that I accept. I am a believer, so I have to submit to it." But then in the same breath, she's saying, "Good thing that the Quran clearly says that sexist oppression is a bad thing." So my view about this is, of course, you can be a traditionalist and a feminist. You just have to believe that your tradition says that gender inequality or sexist oppression are bad things.

MYISHA: So this leads us to where we began in a way. What do you imagine cross-border feminist solidarity to look like?

SERENE: Solidarity has to look different from what it has looked like historically and from the way that philosophers and theorists often have imagined it in the past, in order to take seriously the facts of imperialism. I spend a lot of time talking about the ways in which imperialism interferes with the possibility for solidarity. But I want to be really clear that I'm not actually pessimistic about it. I think real solidarity is happening every day. I just think that the solidarity requires taking certain things seriously.

First, it requires realizing that feminism is opposition to sexist oppression. And what that means is that feminism doesn't have to require adopting the norms of any particular culture. You can have your own cultural set of practices. The real question for feminism is not "What should your cultural practices be?" It's "How can your practices be organized in a way that doesn't subordinate women?" One thing that is necessary for solidarity is recognizing that feminism doesn't require the adoption of any specific cultural form, even if does require universal opposition to sexist oppression.

Second, it's really important for especially Western and Northern feminists, when they engage in activism, to recognize the ways in which their activism could actually worsen the problems of the women's lives that they are trying to help. I mean, some of that worsening can happen concretely. You can literally make a person's material life worse. But another way that Westerners can make other people's lives worse is by engaging in activism whose main effect is to reproduce the view that Western intervention is the solution to everything and that other countries and cultures are barbaric.

The third thing is that solidarity from women in the West and North or from people in the West and North needs to move away from the idea that Western intervention is the solution to other women's problems. That doesn't mean that Western intervention is never appropriate, but Umana Ryan helpfully talked about the idea that Western feminists are caught up in something that she called the "missionary position."

The idea was that Westerners often think and have set up their understanding of the world in a way where they think that the only thing that can be done about practices that oppress women in other societies is for Westerners to name them, because supposedly, people in other countries think that the oppression of women is fine, according to this view. So Westerners are the only ones who can recognize the wrongness, and then Westerners are the only ones who can fix it. Feminist solidarity needs to move away from the intervention obsession. When it does do interventions, do them—and I don't mean military interventions. I mean supporting development projects that are run by local women. When it does do them, it needs to do them more attentively and take local people's voices very, very seriously and to have them leading. They also need to realize that sometimes the right thing for Western feminists to do is to change the behavior of their own governments.

The last thing that I think is really important for solidarity now is just for Westerners and people in the North to recognize that there are really strong universalist reasons to amplify and pay attention to women in the Global South's own beliefs about what should happen to change the conditions that they live under. People's own perspectives about what's happening to them are extremely important. Because there's no one way, no single strategy for ending sexist oppression in any particular context, we really need to know what the people who are in the context see as the tradeoffs that they might face with any strategy for change, and what they think their priorities are. Every situation about what we should actually do politically will be different. I would say that feminist solidarity requires acknowledging these four things.

In my book, one of the examples that I talk about as a successful example of solidarity is the activism of a group called the Freedom Without Fear Platform in the UK. That was a solidarity movement formed in the UK largely by South Asian and black women in response to the gang rape and eventual death of Jyoti Singh Pandey, who later became known as Nirbhaya, in Delhi. Without going into a ton of detail about the case, this young woman had been very brutally raped and murdered on a bus in Delhi. This was a real catalyzing moment for anti-sexual-assault work in India and it really did successfully result in changes to the legal structure in India. It especially placed focus on honor and victim-blaming in the legal conversations around sexual assault.

Thousands of people marched in the streets in the weeks after. This UK movement was saying, "Well, how can we support the activism of the women and the people that are marching in India without either engaging in activities that worsen it, but also without reinforcing the view that rape is something that only happens in India?" Kavita Krishnan, who was one of the activists in India, said that she got called over and over again. When Western newspapers interviewed her, they always wanted to say, "Oh, things are so bad in India. It must be so bad to have to deal with so much rape in India." One of the things that the Freedom Without Fear Platform in the UK did was really try to put out a lot of material that was designed to showcase the ways in which the UK Government and multinational corporations were involved in helping promote rape culture and the presence of rape in India. For example, they showcased the ways in which multinational mining corporations were using rape as a tool to silence indigenous women in one region of India. They also talked about how within the UK, resources for domestic violence and violence against women that had been allocated to local women-run organizations had actually been removed, and that funding even within the UK had been removed from organizations that were community-led to stop violence against women. It had focused on forced marriage and criminalizing and incarcerating men instead of doing something to actually stop violence against women.

One of the most interesting things that they did was organize against Narendra Modi, who was the prime minister of India and who is a supporter of the kind of religious fundamentalism that the Indian activists were trying to fight against and that they saw as promoting rape culture. These activists in the UK said, "Okay, what can we do to stand in solidarity with the women in India? Well, one thing we can do is say that we in the UK don't support the fundamentalist leader that is promoting these very harmful and sexist responses to rape." They then organized protests of Modi's visit to the UK and tied the UK support for him to support for the prevalence of sexual assault in India.

People often want to know, "What can we do?" I thought that this activism was a really good example of what can be done that's still an example of solidarity but that refuses to fall into the narrative that says, "Other cultures are backward and harbor sexual assault and violence. And that Northerners are modern. They don't do that. They bear no causal relationship to the harm that other women experience."

MYISHA: I think that was an excellent example.

12

Joel Michael Reynolds on Disability

MYISHA: My mother—she is no longer with us—was confined to a wheelchair all of her life. She was born with spina bifida. Her spine was not fully developed. Therefore, I have my own experiences of and my own history with loving a person who lived with a disability. Tell me more about your mother and brother's experiences with their disability. Can you also describe some of the stigmas and oppressions of their disability?

JOEL: My brother was born with muscular dystrophy, cerebral palsy, and hydrocephalus among a couple of other things. Doctors said there was a 95 percent chance he wouldn't live to be one year old. My mother was his primary caretaker for the majority of his life. Through a combination of the physical labor that that required and other random things, she is now disabled through chronic pain, fibromyalgia, severe temporomandibular joint (TMJ) syndrome, degenerative disc disease, et cetera. I have spent so much time in hospitals or doctor's appointments over the course of my life. I knew more types of doctors by the age of probably six or seven than anyone around me, both inside the medical establishment and outside.

The older I got, the more I witnessed all the various levels of disability stigma. There were very obvious examples. For example, we took

Jason (my brother) to my school for the very first time. A number of the kids were kind of sweet or indifferent, and one kid, who was my arch nemesis at the time said, "He drools just like his brother." He was clearly trying to not only insult me but he was also tying drooling to some kind of negative state, which didn't make any sense to me. I was thinking, "That is just part of what Jason did." It made no sense to me why that would be negative.

Or in my mother's case, there has been three times where my dad has had to show up to appointments so that what she was saying could be taken seriously. The level of disregard she gets as a female, which was actually exacerbated by her being a female with a son with a disability, is heart-wrenching to watch. As I became more aware of disability-rights activism and disability studies, I was like "Okay, well, how can I be involved in changing these things?" That's one of the things that led me into my work today.

MYISHA: You make a distinction between impairment and disability. What is the difference between the two? And how is it that, as you say, "disability is everywhere"?

JOEL: This distinction between impairment and disability is at the heart of what is known as the social model of disability. This model has provided the theoretical foundation for the disability-rights movements of the last half of the twentieth century and also the institutional rise of disability studies within multiple academic fields.

In a nutshell, "impairment" names a person's embodied condition, whereas "disability" names the social problems and social stigmas that result from a given impairment. The social and political point here is very simple: Let's focus on altering conditions, not people. Or if put in the first person, "I'm not the problem. The conditions under which I'm oppressed are."

One of the clearest examples is one would say, "I'm not disabled if I use a wheelchair to get around. Ambulation or nonambulation is not what causes the problem. I'm only disabled when there aren't curb cuts or ramps, or when people assume that by using a wheelchair I can't speak or hear and then I'm socially ignored or mistreated." These are facts about the social environment. The social environment is also built to a degree. And for the majority of history, the social environment has been intentionally built with a standard, able body as the norm. Looking at architecture is the easiest example there. This is why ideas like universal design in architecture and digital design is so brilliant and simple. They say, "Why don't we design things for the widest range of use possible?"

This, I think, is one of the connection points to that last question you asked me about the idea that disability is everywhere. This is another disability-studies slogan, though the full version is: "Disability is everywhere once you know how to look for it." In the United States, Americans with disabilities constitute the largest and most inclusive minority. It's also the largest minority in the world. Even if we're thinking of it outside of the terms of identity politics or a minority model, the deeper truth is that disability is constitutive of the course of any given human life. When we understand disability in that widest sense, as anything that falls outside ablest norms, norms of that healthy, youngish able body, then in this sense disability is also the only position everyone has already been in through infancy and childhood, and the only identity position into which everyone will find themselves if they live long enough. This is why disability is everywhere, which, to be clear, is not to say "everyone is disabled."

Each day we all face ability troubles of all sorts, and the trick is precisely that we don't all experience these in the same way. The reason the idea that disability is everywhere is so powerful is because it undermines and problematizes any strong ontological distinction between disability and ability. No abilities exist without appropriate supports. From oxygen, to sustenance, to sleep, to forms of shared communication and interaction, we can't do anything without these things. We don't have abilities. We enter into and we're claimed by relations of affordance. When we say, "I can do x," we're making a kind of philosophical error.

MYISHA: This is very connected to the term "transability"; is that correct?

JOEL: Yeah. There's also another sense of transability. Whereas my use of the term "ontological" is describing a way of being of the human, this other, more narrow sense of the term usually refers to people who are medically diagnosed as having some form of BIID, or body integrity identity disorder. These are people who desire or need to move from their current state of able-bodiedness to a comparative state of impairment. This might mean the amputation of a limb or it might mean the severing of a spinal column.

The history of this designation is itself revealing. It began in psychological literature in the 1970s as a type of fetish. In the last decade or so, neuroscientists are now saying it's a body-mapping issue along the same lines of phantom-limb pain. For people who want to learn about this, Chloe Jennings-White is one of the more famous people who identifies as having BIID, or identifies as transabled. She went on

Anderson Cooper's 360 show on CNN, I believe. At one point, the audience actually applauded when Cooper said that her understanding of her body was "completely inappropriate." Not only do people with BIID experience disability stigma from able-bodied people, but they also experience it from within disability communities and also from trans communities for the use of that prefix.

Part of what makes transability in the sense of BIID so controversial is that it expresses the most transgressive thought from the vantage point of ableism, namely the desire for disability. One can today at least imagine a desire for many things: being a different race, gender, et cetera. But a desire for disability is too transgressive. There's some disability-studies scholars like Fiona Kumari Campbell, Bethany Stevens, and Alexander Berill who have done some fantastic work untangling all of the hostility that people who are transabled in the sense of BIID have to go through.

MYISHA: One of the things that you mentioned was that disability makes up the largest minority. Philosophy has existed for thousands of years. However, you're working within a subfield that is not that popular in professional philosophy. Why do you think disability has not been given much attention in philosophy?

JOEL: If questions are understood as responses to one's situation, then one answer might be that disability hasn't become a question for philosophy historically because too many philosophers in the Western canon, at least, have responded to the situation of being mortal through either an avoidance or denigration of the body. The body has always been an issue in philosophy. It's the way in which it has been an issue that is the issue.

Disability historians have been exposing so brilliantly that disability has always been at the center of Western intellectual history, just under other names. So for example, what if we interpret Cartesian doubt as a form of intellectual disability relating to anxiety? Or what if we interpret Spinoza's theory of affects in book IV of *The Ethics* as a form of psychological repression in his emphasis of overpowering negative affects by positive ones? I think we've barely scratched the surface of reading the philosophical canon through a disability lens. As more and more of that work comes out, I think we'll find that disability has always been a central question in the history of Western thought.

MYISHA: You made me think about this notion of terror management, which in this case, refers to not dealing with issues that relate to our own mortality. It makes me think about some current technologies that are out now that could be read as helping others deal with terror management as it relates to disability. I recently saw a video that highlighted a stand-up Segway for persons confined to a wheelchair. It allows them to move uprightly as opposed to seated. I also saw a documentary about a deaf family a few years ago. One of the things that were offered to one of the children was a hearing implant. The teenager refused it and noted that he would be fine without it. What do you think about technologies that seek to make those who are disabled, less disabled?

JOEL: Disability, again, meant in the broadest sense of anything that falls outside of ablest norms, is not going anywhere. Contrary to the misguided aspirations of transhumanists and posthumanists, we're not going to be immortal, we're not going to stop aging, and honestly, I don't know why we would desire to. As far as I'm concerned, part of the beauty of the human condition is its finitude. I think hell is actually eternity.

Now, having said that, using assistive technology is also part of the human condition; we're toolmakers. The unbelievable abilities at our fingertips with smartphones, I think of speech technology as one example, increase access for all sorts of people in really positive ways. But there are certain forms of technology that are trying to make people "less disabled." I think those technologies are really, really misguided. Why would we spend millions of dollars on exoskeletons when most of the United States' basic architecture is still inaccessible? There's a perverse misallocation of resources and goals in those types of technologies. Now, this is not an either/or situation. Project-RAY's smartphone, the world's first completely vision-free smartphone designed for the blind, sounds great. But I also think we need to make sure that crosswalks have signal sounds. We need both of these things going on here.

MYISHA: Allow me to return to my mother as an example. My mother didn't have an electric wheelchair. She had the old-school one where you used your hands. I always wondered why she never used an electric wheelchair. But that just wasn't what she wanted. I remember her also telling me that there were opportunities for her to get prosthetics, but she was not down for that. Now that I look back on it, I think my mother liked "her normal." She did not want to become anything else but what she was. Do you think that the technologies are a way to make those who are "disabled" become "normal?" What do you think of the rejection of such technologies by the community?

JOEL: I think you hit on a very, very real issue there. "We" in the largest "we" are uncomfortable with the variability of our bodies. It's not just a fear of death, as Heidegger was convinced. It's the pervasive inertia of our ability expectations. We expect and we want to expect that the conditions of our purposive action are going to stay the same even though, again, aging, if nothing else, proves that that's just not going to happen. But because we fear and act against change almost instinctually to a degree, when we are forced to undergo drastic ability transitions, we deal with it really poorly initially.

This is where I think social scientific and psychological literature is very revealing. There's this term called "psycho-social adjustment." Let's say you get a life-altering diagnosis. It's going to be really bad for the first six months to a year or two. But what will happen is, assuming there's a certain level of stability, one creates new normals; we adjust. We will often live flourishing lives that, beforehand, would have seemed restrictive. The way I think of this is that ability expectations overdetermine our interpretation of ability transitions. This is where the phrase "I'd rather be dead than disabled" comes from. I've heard it so many times. I've heard it in front of my family with Jason right next to us. It's horrific and offensive on so many levels but it's also empirically misguided. The data says that, no, actually, most people would not rather be dead than have some relative state of impairment. On the contrary, they would want to live and they would roll with whatever that condition brings about with it.

The question "Would I choose x" is a completely different question from "If I end up in situation x, what would I do?" Again, this is what disability studies, I think, points out so well. Saying, "Look, disability is everywhere, disability is constitutive of a human life." There are particular difficulties that may match with certain types of disabilities. But on the whole those are because of the way we set up the world, and we've got to change that.

MYISHA: Like I mentioned before, I recently saw a documentary about a deaf family. The mother and father are deaf. They have two children who are also deaf and one child who is not deaf. I remember the mother saying that when she had the first child and recognized that he was deaf, she felt that she had given him the greatest gift. What do you say in response to that?

JOEL: There is a distinction between lowercase and uppercase "d" in deafness. Deafness with a lowercase "d" refers to some form of audiological loss relative to whatever speech is typical. Deafness with a capital "D" refers to being culturally deaf, part of a community of signers, whether it's American Sign Language or some other form. I think this is a very powerful example to show the way in which what someone

might assume is "Oh, that's a disability in a negative sense" is actually–
–when you talk with people—"No, this is just a difference and it's a difference that I actually value."

For example, you have some in the Deaf community with a capital "D" saying, "Deafness is no more a disability than if I as an English speaker go into a Spanish-speaking place in the world. That's not a disability. That's just I don't speak the language." I think that that captures something powerful about the way in which, in the public imaginary, we assume that disabilities are negative.

This goes back to the forms of what's called "inspiration porn" that can be seen in ads and viral videos online. The message of inspiration porn says, "Look at this person with a disability. They overcame it and now they're doing all these things." That's so unbelievably offensive and stigmatizing! It reduces a person with a disability not just to their disability but to their ability to overcome it. It's a misunderstanding of human variability and human difference. It requires some integrity and some research on the side of people to not judge the disabled in that way. There needs to be more disability-studies classes—let me put it that way—so that people start learning about these things.

MYISHA: What do you say to people who sincerely are inspired by inspiration porn?

JOEL: When I teach about inspiration porn, I show my students this satirical image. It shows this middle-aged woman lying in a field where there are flowers and it's a sunny day. And then there's a big title over the image that says, "This woman is strong, sexy, and brave, even if she does have both legs." Everyone immediately gets the punchline, which is we don't valorize the able body for doing anything normal and it's only the disabled body that gets such praise. Even though someone might think, "Look, my feeling of inspiration is not meant to denigrate the person in question. It's a positive thought. Why can't I enjoy this?" The reality is that the logic of that inspiration is assuming that the disability in question is a negative state. That's part of the logic.

I would just ask people to critically reflect upon why they find it inspiring. Once they critically reflect upon it, they'll go, "Maybe I shouldn't find that inspiring. Maybe it's problematic and I should look for inspiration in other forms of representation." Adorno has this amazing line and it's quoted a lot for good reason. He says, "The need to let suffering speak is a condition of all truth." I think he's right, but the problem is then how is that suffering heard. And if, in the case of disability, all one hears is, "Look at my tragic life" or "Look at what I've had to overcome," it's possible that one will just pity the other person or just be inspired.

But Aristotle in the *Poetics* says that a tragedy fails if you aren't shocked into identifying with the hero or heroine. To identify with another is not simply to imagine oneself in their shoes. It's also to experience their situation as an aporia, as an impasse. In other words, I don't think one can simply ask the question, "Why do they suffer as they do?" You have to experience that question as one that demands an answer. I would amend Adorno to say something like "The condition of truth is to let suffering speak, such that one seeks to alter the conditions of its emergence." On that type of logic, inspiration porn is unjust. It does not lead one to seek to alter the conditions of the actual societal ramifications of disability stigma. That's why I think it's quite problematic.

MYISHA: What are three myths of disability that you would like to debunk?

JOEL: One is that disability is negative. That is a myth that is still very much a part of the cultural imaginary of the West. Another myth would be—and this is one where I have learned much about from people like Bethany Stevens and other academics in the disability-studies community—that people with disabilities, especially intellectual disabilities, are not fully fledged, sexual, loving, caring, emoting beings. The infantilization of certain sets of people with disabilities still goes on today. The third myth is that variation entails degradation. If the conditions of my life changed substantially, I will automatically be worse off. I think it is just false in the vast majority of cases.

MYISHA: Let's talk about the second myth a little more. My mother was disabled, but she had two children, so you can imagine how that happened. I think my mother had a very healthy sex life. The thought that because she or whoever is in a particular physical condition, they have no sexual desires is false. I think my mother was a testament to this.

JOEL: There's an amazing documentary called *When I Walk* by Jason DaSilva. He was a filmmaker and at twenty-five he got diagnosed with degenerative multiple sclerosis. One of the things that he deals with very well in the film are conversations with his girlfriend about their sex life and having children. And of course, one of the things that you see is that it's just like any other conversation in some respects between two loving partners—do you like this, that, and the next.

MYISHA: On one end, there's this perception of those who are disabled as asexual beings. But I also see judgments of people who are attracted to those who are disabled. People may be surprised that a person finds a disabled person sexually attractive. This just shows the things we need to learn, the stigmas we need to get rid of, and the prejudices we have. That is why I'm excited that you are doing this work, Joel.

Let me end with one last question. How can we change the world so that we create less disability?

JOEL: I don't think we should change the world to create less disability. I think we should change the world so that it affords the full, always-variable range of human supportive conditions for flourishing.

MYISHA: One of the things that you mention in your TED Talk on disability is that those who were seated in their seats in the balcony were able to get upstairs because there were stairs. I took that as you saying, "Someone built stairs and that made the audience less disabled." You mentioned the ramp that's on the street as an example of the kind of social structures in place that makes life livable. Absent of those things, it makes life difficult for those who need the structures. Years ago before all buses came equipped with handicap lifts, my mother and I used to just wait and wait and wait until that one bus with a lift arrived. That's how tough it was commuting when I was younger. Sometimes my mother would just decide to get on any bus, but this meant she would have to crawl up the stairs to get on. If all city buses had lifts on them, we would have had no problem getting around. And my mother being in a wheelchair would not have been a huge barrier to that.

JOEL: I think that that story happens all the time to people. Just think about the lawsuits against some ride share companies because they didn't work to have accessible cars. Supposedly, in some cities they have tried to address this. But hailing a taxi in New York City, for example, if you're using a powered wheelchair is difficult. You're usually out of luck.

But I will add one thing here. A few years back, there was uproar by the public because the airlines had left a person who used a wheelchair on the tarmac and that person had to crawl all the way to the terminal. What I love is that a disability-studies scholar named Gregor Wolbring, who himself uses a wheelchair, made a comment on social media, and he's like "Yeah, this is a problem, but I wish they would stop demonizing crawling." He's like "I crawl all over the place because I like it. It's a great way to get around" or something like that.

What I like are both levels going on there. One, absolutely, we need to make the physical environment more accessible. But at the exact same time, we need to work on the social and psychological stigmas we have like, for example, thinking crawling is bad. I always think of Wolbring's comment because I think it pushes the level of internalized disability stigmatization to another level.

13

Elizabeth Barnes on the Minority Body

MYISHA: What are some theories of disabilities? What is your account? And how does it differ from those other theories?

ELIZABETH: My book focuses on physical disability, to start with. I want to be super clear that I don't mean to, by focusing on physical disabilities, say that other forms of disability aren't important to talk about. What I just wanted to be really careful about is avoiding a certain type of imperialism that I think sometimes happens in conversations about disability, where we talk about physical disability and then we just assume that other forms of disability are kind of the same. Sort of like "All right, so this will go for physical disability, and then we can just extend that to psychosocial disability or cognitive disability" or that kind of thing.

The arguments that I really wanted to explore did apply directly to the case of physical disability. So I wanted to start small and see if we could build up a conversation. Disability is a many-splendored thing. I think conversations about disability have got to be a big tent. So that's what I'm focused on and that's what I'm looking at.

So in terms of other theories of physical disability, I think there's pretty much two main camps. The first one is probably what you might say is the commonsense view of disability. I think it's how most people think about physical disability, which is basically just more or less a medical view of it, where it's like you've got a normally functioning body and then you've got bodies that are a little bit busted, broken in some way, have some sort of defect that we can understand in medical terms.

And if a defect is sort of significant enough, it'll count as a disability. So you probably don't count as having a disability if you're a little bit nearsighted.

MYISHA: Which I am.

ELIZABETH: Yeah. I am too, and it doesn't have that profound effect on my life. It's like if you have one of these defects seriously enough, if you lack a sensory modality or if you need some sort of equipment to get around, or if you're in a large amount of chronic pain or something like that, then you're going to count as having a disability and can understand these in just sort of like purely physical or medical terms.

I think within academic conversations about disability and also just within social movements surrounding disability and the disability rights movement, there's been a thought that this kind of view is too reductive because it just talks about what's going on with a person's body. And it doesn't understand that disability is the sort of complicated relationship between a person's body and their social environment.

There are views of disability that broadly get this label called the "social model" of disability, which basically says that there are ways that your body can be, and let's call those "impairments." But disability is the disadvantage that's created by having an impairment in a world that's not designed for people who have bodies like that. So disability is created by prejudice against disabled people, disability is created by lack of access, disability is created by lack of accessibility and accommodation and that kind of thing.

So disability is the disadvantage that's created by certain types of inequality. And the idea behind the social model is that the impairment isn't the thing that we should focus on. The impairments—sort of by themselves—are not what disability is. Impairments by themselves just wouldn't be a very big deal in the absence of this sort of structural prejudice. What we need to focus on is the structural prejudice. On this view, society is what disables people. That is what people often say when we're talking about the social model.

I think there's a lot that's good about the social model. I think they're absolutely right that we need to think about disability as a relationship between a person's body and their environment, and that we need to think about the social dimensions of disability and how much a lot of the bad effects of disability aren't just a matter of what a person's body is like.

But I think the social model goes a little bit too far. So what I was trying to do is sort of develop a view that would in a way be a social view of disability, a social-constructionist view of disability that sort of steers a middle ground between the medical model and the social model. Because there's a way in which disability on the social model becomes a little bit disembodied. It's just this thing that society does to you; disability is the structural disadvantage.

I think disability, though I reject the purely medical view, in many ways is a matter of what your body is like. I also think that for a lot of people and for a lot of types of disabilities, especially disabilities that require ongoing complex medical care, are painful, are progressive or things like that. It's not really that plausible that in the absence of these kind of structural prejudices these impairments would be nothing more than a nuisance or wouldn't really have a profound effect on you. I think there are ways that your body can be what we label "disabilities" and it is going to have a profound effect on you even in a much more accommodating society.

So I wanted a theory of disability that recognized the social dimensions of disabilities, but also acknowledges that disability is complicated and it is a matter of what your body is like and not just a matter of how people treat you.

Therefore, disability in a way is a fact about what your body is like, the physical state of your body. But the reason that we label certain physical states of your body "disabilities" has more to do with how we think about people, what's normal, what's acceptable, and what's broken or defective, than it does anything like biological commonality that you might have between all the disabled people forming a natural kind or something like that.

MYISHA: Someone may pick up the book, read the title and then the subtitle, and come away with a disconnect of sorts. Why call your book *The Minority Body*?

ELIZABETH: Partly because it's kind of a pun, and I love bad puns. But I guess partly because I was influenced by this amazing book by the feminist philosopher Susan Wendell called *The Rejected Body*, which is her book on disability.

I wanted a spin on that that was a little bit less value-laden. And one of the ways that I was trying to sort of think about and conceptualize the way that I want to think about disability was in terms of disabled bodies. Yeah, they're different, they're statistically atypical. If you have a disability, you have a body that sort of marks you out as different in some way, and also that means that you're going to navigate the world differently than most people do. You're going to experience some things differently than most people do.

But that doesn't mean automatically that you're worse off. That doesn't mean automatically that you're at a deficit. We can't understand disability simply in terms of loss or lack or something like that. I think that's an impoverished view of disability.

I wanted to focus on this idea of physical difference in a way that's not as value-laden as we tend to think about disability in everyday terms. So I thought there's all sorts of ways that you can be statistically atypical. You can be statistically atypical when it comes to sexuality. You can be statistically atypical when it comes to gender. You can be statistically atypical when it comes to ethnicity. There's all these ways that you can just be a little bit set apart from what's considered normal.

I think one of the things that the experience of disability shows us is that you can be statistically atypical and be something other than what people consider normal when it comes to your physical body. So I wanted to explore that idea without laying on the extra baggage that we tend to have when we think about disability as having a body that's not just different, it's to have a body that's broken, it's to have a body that's defective in some way.

MYISHA: Usually, when people think about that which is normal, they associate something that's good with normality; and they associate something that's bad with abnormality. What do you see is the connection between disability and well-being?

ELIZABETH: So that is really complicated, really, really complicated. Because one of the things that I want to be really careful about is not to downplay or not to undermine the way in which having a disability in the world as it is now, especially our currently political and socioeconomic situation, can be awful. Having a disability can be something that can absolutely ruin your life.

I think one of the things though that people often move from is this idea that disability is in fact something that can be bad for you, to this idea that there's this necessary connection between disability and reduction of well-being. So we look around us in America and we see in this culture where it's really hard for disabled people to get adequate accessibility and health care, where disabled people are constantly worried that they're going to lose their insurance, go bankrupt, and/ or not have the money to pay for their assistive devices or their health needs. These are all the ways in which disability incurs extra financial burdens. Then there's all the shame put on disabled people that you have a body that's wrong in some way or you're defective or you're this—all these sort of complicated cultural stereotypes that are put on disabled people.

So no wonder that people who have those kinds of experiences might have a hard time. But we move from that to the idea that what we need to make the world better is to get rid of disabilities. And it's pretty far from obvious, I think, that what's causing the reduction in well-being is the physical condition of people's bodies rather than the social environment in which we live.

The other thing about well-being is that given the sort of empirical evidence that we have about self-reported happiness or self-reported quality of life, it would be pretty surprising to nondisabled people. Disabled people by and large don't self-report lower quality of life than nondisabled people. Disabled people by and large tend to report good quality of life. Now, that doesn't, of course, mean that it wouldn't be better if they had better access to accommodation and better access to health care, but they do tend to report pretty good quality of life.

Then the other thing that we at least have pretty good empirical evidence for at this point (you don't know how much you can rely on these kind of studies) is that well-being for disabled people doesn't seem to track what nondisabled people think it's going to track. It often doesn't track what you might think of as the objective severity of a physical disability. Instead, it tracks social support. It tracks things like positive disability identity or sense of acceptance of disability.

So the relationship between disability and well-being, on the ground, doesn't look like what a lot of nondisabled people expect it to look like. Some other interesting research that we have suggests that nondisabled people expect disabled people to say that they're very unhappy and to say that they would give up years of their life to get rid of their disability and things like this. Nondisabled people are really bad at predicting these claims about well-being in disabled people.

We're pretty familiar with the idea that people's lives can be worse for things that are only contingently connected to some social fact about themselves. Look at the suicide rate for gay teenagers. We hopefully don't look at the suicide rate for gay teenagers and say, "Oh gosh, it's terrible to be gay, so you need to find a way to fix the gay people." I mean, there's some people in the world who say that, but they shouldn't.

I think it's been really striking that people are so confident that there is this close connection between disability and reduction of well-being; that even if the world was much more accepting of disabled people, even if the world was a much more accessible place, disability would still be perceived to very likely reduce people's quality of life. I mean, that's a really distant possible world that we're thinking about. And I don't know about you; I find it really hard to have strong intuitions about pretty distant possible worlds.

People are really confident about this and they think it's commonsense, and I think that that's really striking because it seems like a thing that probably shouldn't be commonsense.

MYISHA: So let me push you a little bit. Well, not necessarily push, but I wonder what the empirical data has to say about this. While I was reading the book particularly on this point, several examples popped in my head. So I began to think about my mother who is now deceased but lived her whole life in a wheelchair; she had a birth defect. And I've discussed this before in my interview with Joel Reynolds. My mother was perfectly fine with who she was, and no way in the world did she want any type of cure, she didn't want prosthetics, she didn't even want an electronic wheelchair. She was okay with what she had. Then you take my sister who is in her early forties but has lupus. It's having a tremendous effect on her body. She's constantly in pain. And then you take, let's say, a fictitious example, Lieutenant Dans from *Forrest Gump* who's very upset when he becomes disabled. So you take these three different individuals who all have different perspectives about what their well-being is given their disability; and it makes you wonder: What does the empirical data say about these kinds of cases?

ELIZABETH: So one thing we definitely know—or I mean, insofar as we know anything from social science research— is that it is a hell of a thing to become disabled. Being disabled, not so bad; becoming disabled, wow, that is rough. And typically, what we see for people who become disabled is they're sort of going along at a steady state of happiness, they become disabled, their happiness kind of falls off a cliff, then their happiness adapts.

One thing to emphasize though is this is just what happens in general. Human beings are complicated and it doesn't happen for everyone. So some disabled people—their happiness doesn't really go off a cliff ever if they become disabled. Other people—their happiness doesn't adapt. And one thing that I think is really important: sometimes when you read this literature on happiness adaptation, hedonic psychology, and that kind of thing, it then gets spun into this sort of positive psychology. "Oh, we just need to focus on resilience" or that kind of thing.

One thing I want to be really clear about is that there should be absolutely no blame or stigma attached to the person who just really hates being disabled and that is just not their thing, that is not their life, that is not the life that they wanted, and it was not the life that they chose. For some people it's a tragedy and it doesn't get better.

And I think, for one thing, we have to recognize that it's really hard to be disabled in the current world. It's just really, really hard and there's so much—especially, I think, perhaps for women, especially of a certain age—shame that gets put on you about your body not meeting certain standards. I think for men it can be extraordinarily emasculating if you have to rely on help; if people have to help you, that's a threat to your masculinity.

There's so much stigma about being a person who needs things, who's dependent. We have this ideal of the person who is independent and we valorize independence, which is kind of a fiction; we're all dependent on each other.

For some people, you had a thing that you were doing and then you acquired a disability and disability has just got in the way of that thing. And that is sad and that is tragic. I think we need to focus on the ways in which it is really hard, regardless of the fact that lots of disabled people are happy, it's really hard to be disabled in the actual world. And probably even if we lived in a perfect world, there would be some people who just did not want to be disabled, and that's okay.

MYISHA: You mentioned this notion of becoming disabled, and because you've been public with this, I want to bring up your life as an example. I'll let you tell the story, but it seems as if you didn't get a precise diagnosis about what was happening to your body until later on in life.

ELIZABETH: Right.

MYISHA: Did you become disabled at the time in which there was a name for it, or do you think you were always disabled?

ELIZABETH: I have a genetic disability that I was born with. I had weird stuff happen to me in childhood, but it was nothing that you really would have noticed. It wasn't really until I went through adolescence that I began to develop significant health conditions. It would have been when I was about fourteen or fifteen that I began to have really significant health issues. I had to have my first surgery when I was fifteen, second surgery when I was seventeen, and things like that. I think I was diagnosed with five or six different things during the course of that time. And it wasn't until I was twenty-two, when I got sent to a geneticist, that I finally figured out what was going on.

I think I definitely had the experience of a person who was disabled from the age of about fourteen or fifteen. My experience was very medicalized in part just because I kept getting diagnosed with different things. I had fibromyalgia, I had rheumatoid arthritis, I had lupus. I had really sort of vague, nonspecific things that they give people. So I bounced around between different doctors and different diagnoses. And it wasn't until I was, twenty-two, that I understood what my disability was. But I had had the experience of a person who was disabled from the age of about fifteen.

MYISHA: If a person doesn't from the outside look disabled, whatever that looks like, we have these assumptions. You describe yourself as having an invisible disability. Tell us more about that.

ELIZABETH: Up until three and a half years, maybe four years ago, I would have been completely invisibly disabled. Now I suppose I'm quite visibly disabled because I walk with a mobility aid, but I'm only visibly disabled if I stand up, which is very interesting. If I'm sitting down and my cane is folded and it's under my chair, nobody notices. And then I stand up and people are like "Woah, what?" But that was a really, really striking transition for me just socially, the difference between being mostly invisibly disabled and now mostly visibly disabled, partly because it didn't represent a particularly large shift in my health condition, but it represented a radical shift in my social experience, which was interesting along many dimensions.

I think in a lot of ways, I, as an invisibly disabled person, didn't meet people's expectations of what a disabled person looks like. I think a lot of people think you can instantly be able to tell when a person is disabled. And now people are quite confused, because I think they think I don't look like someone who they associate with needing a mobility aid because they associate mobility aids with age and frailty. I'm thirty-three and I'm very fit, I do a lot of exercise, but I have to have this mobility aid to get around. So people are just continually baffled, and I think it's very interesting for me just sort of sociologically to see many stereotypes, baggage, and perceptions of these kinds of things.

MYISHA: You said earlier that we shouldn't judge those who don't "value" their disability in some kind of way. What does it mean to value disability?

ELIZABETH: I think this is the kind of thing that can mean different things for different people. I think a lot of what gets talked about in disability communities when we talk about valuing disability is partly this idea that disability is a part of human diversity, the human spectrum, and the human condition and not necessarily a part of the human condition to be feared or to be freaked out about in general.

If you're a straight person, you can think about being gay and think about the dimensions, but you don't have to worry that like one day you're going to wake up and become gay. That's not something that actively has to be on your radar. You don't have to worry about "Oh, but how would I feel if I caught gayness?"

MYISHA: It doesn't happen.

ELIZABETH: That's not how it works.

But people do have to worry about that for disability, and this is something that people actively worry about. Most people, if they live long enough, will be disabled before they die. I think this is something that people worry about and they're afraid of for themselves. It represents a certain type of frailty. I think it is associated with mortality. It represents something that they worry about for their children where they worry about their ability to do things that they want to do.

I think partly when we talk about valuing disability, it's just accepting that this isn't necessarily the bogeyman that it's made out to be in our lives. This is a part of human diversity, and people live rich, wonderful lives with these physical conditions that a lot of people are very afraid of. I think on top of that, it's a rejection of a certain type of narrative about disabled people's lives that says the way that disabled people can be happy or have good lives is this sort of idea of the tragic overcomer; that you can have a good life as a disabled person by having overcome your struggles with your body, by being very inspirational, by being all this sort of Tiny Tim stuff.

I think when we talk about valuing disability, it's a rejection of that idea. It's saying, "No, you can just live a good life as a disabled person in a different kind of body, and you haven't overcome something dramatic, you're not inspirational. You're just a person living a good life in a different kind of body." Are there bad things about being disabled? Sure, yeah, absolutely.

When we talk about valuing disability, we want to emphasize though that there are good things. There can be good and wonderful and unexpected little joys, and that's the part of the story that we don't tell, that I think a lot of nondisabled people don't know. They think that disability is just lack or loss. So it's like you take all the abilities of a normal, functioning person and then you just subtract and that's what disability is. Then it's hard to imagine what it would be to value that.

The narrative that a lot of people are pushing when they want to talk about valuing disability, and certainly the narrative that I want to push, is this idea that it's not just lack, it's not just loss. Is there loss? Yeah, there's loss. There's also gain; there's gain in other places such that you can have this rich life that is different but is not less.

MYISHA: Let's transition from the valuing question to the pride question. What is disability pride?

ELIZABETH: For me I think it's important to talk about disability pride, mostly just as an epistemological resource to help people think about what it might be for disability to be something that by itself doesn't make you better or worse off; by itself it's just neutral. It doesn't make you better, it doesn't make you worse, it just makes you a person. It's just one of these things where you can't infer anything about a person's overall well-being by understanding that they're disabled.

That's the kind of model about the value of disability that I like, but I also think it makes sense in the current cultural context to celebrate disability, to say, "Disability by itself is something that is totally neutral, yet disability is something that we personally value." I think you see people say very similar things about things like sexuality. If you know that someone is gay, that by itself doesn't make them worse, it doesn't make them better. It's just kind of neutral. And I think something similar about disability.

I think that gay pride is extraordinarily important because sometimes it's not enough to just say, "Okay, here's this thing and it's not bad, it's fine." Because in a context where something is so stigmatized and we have such deeply normative understandings of what it was like to be gay and currently what it's like to be disabled, you've got to do a little bit more. I think what "disability pride" means is not this sort of what I call the Magneto view of disability pride, where it's like, "Actually, we're the better humans. Disability somehow makes us better." That is not my view.

MYISHA: Right, it's not like white pride; a pride that stems from a view of oneself as superior because of a feature like white skin.

ELIZABETH: Yeah, exactly! It's not that kind of pride. I think it makes sense to take pride in things that you don't actually think make you in any way better off; they're just important to you. You can take pride in some weird fact about yourself. You can take pride in how fast you can run a marathon just because you've worked hard at it; or you can take pride in your enormous comic book collection; or you can take pride in how good you are at some video game. This is something about yourself that you celebrate. It doesn't make you better than other people, but it's something that is permissible to celebrate.

I think the idea of disability pride is people getting together and saying, "All right, this thing that people say makes you less than, makes you broken, makes you deeply, fundamentally unlucky in some way is something that you can celebrate, something that you can embrace." You don't have to say, "I will overcome this, I will move past this, I will find a way to struggle through." You can be happy as a flourishing, delighted, disabled person who wouldn't want to be any other way. You can embrace this thing about yourself that everyone else is telling you is wrong with you. I think that is the core idea of disability pride. And again, it goes back to this idea of disability being a part of human diversity.

MYISHA: I have a friend who is doing a PhD in religion who has found interest in queer studies and disability studies and is using them as invaluable resources in his religious project. People are reading your book who may not be directly interested in disability studies but are still finding value in it. I think this speaks to the field of disability studies as a whole. What do you think it is about disability studies that is interesting for people and why now?

ELIZABETH: I mean, that's a fantastic question. For the first question, "What might be of interest for people who aren't sort of intrinsically interested in disability studies," I think—I mean, my hope for the book—and I don't know if it's successful in this regard, but this is certainly how I think about it—is that sometimes thinking about what it is to be disabled and what it means to think that disability is neutral, what it might mean for it to be permissible to value disability and these kind of things, I think part of it is just a reflection on the human condition and what it is to be a human being. We all have bodies. We all have bodies that sometimes don't do what we want them to do. We all have limitations. We are all fundamentally limited, especially by our bodies in some ways. We're all going to age, our bodies are going to change, and we're all going to die.

I think this may play a part in why we pathologize disabled bodies so much. It is because they represent something about the human condition that I think a lot of us maybe don't like to acknowledge and are a little bit fearful of. But I think even if disability isn't something that personally affects you, your family, or something like that, there is just something very basic about trying to think about limitations and the connection between limitations and well-being and the connections between having a body that's gross. Bodies are gross sometimes. Sometimes they do weird things, sometimes they don't do what you want them to. What's the connection between that and well-being?

How do we think about well-being? How do we think about what's commonsense for well-being?

I also think that anybody who's interested in social kinds then disability is kind of interesting as a social kind. I think it has some similarities to other social kinds, like gender and race and sexuality, but also some significant differences. So I think those questions are interesting.

Why now? I really don't know. I hazard some guesses, but I think there's an increasing sense within philosophy that maybe these questions of social kinds and social experiences are worth taking seriously and worth investigating. Hopefully, maybe an increasing understanding that a priori reflection on some of these things has a tendency to lead us astray doesn't produce knowledge.

I think one of the things you often see when disability gets talked about in, say, just standard moral philosophy, is people forget that you can't have disability without a disabled person. Disability is attached to people. You can't just talk about disability in the abstract and theorize about it in the abstract and use your a priori intuitions. You might get it wrong.

I think maybe there's an increasing sense that we do need to take more seriously the reports of people's lived experiences. Hopefully, there's also an increasing awareness that philosophy has more to learn from the rest of the humanities than we might have been open to. This certainly applies to me as somebody who loves disability studies in the abstract, but who's heart is with analytic philosophy. Analytic philosophy is the discipline that I was trained in, that's what I love, that's how my brain works. So this book is kind of my love letter to analytic philosophy.

I think that the kind of views that I'm interested in are often defended in a methodology that's not the methodology of the discipline I love. So part of what I wanted to do is just say, "Look, actually, these kind of views can be given arguments for in the style and in the tradition that we as analytic philosophers are familiar with."

14

Douglas Ficek on Frantz Fanon and Black Lives Matter

MYISHA: Who was Frantz Fanon?

DOUGLAS: Frantz Fanon is someone I was familiar with for a while, but I will admit that for a time I was a bit intimidated by Fanon primarily I think by his writing style, which can be difficult, ironic, and poetic. I really started to appreciate Fanon once I started reading more and more of Lewis Gordon's work.

Frantz Fanon was a Martinican psychiatrist, political thinker, activist, and revolutionary. He joined the Free French Forces during World War II. After the war, he studied medicine and he became a psychiatrist. During his medical studies, he actually wrote what became his first book, *Black Skin, White Masks*, which is very much a classic work. Many people teach that book alongside, for example, *The Souls of Black Folk* by W. E. B. Du Bois.

After finishing with his medical education—and by the way, he was actually a student of Aimé Césaire, one of the founders of the Négritude movement when he was a younger man in Martinique. But when he was done with his medical studies, he ultimately became the head of the psychiatric hospital in Blida, Algeria. Shortly thereafter, the Algerian War broke out and Fanon found himself very much so siding with the Algerians against the French. There are lots of very interesting and compelling stories about what he did as a psychiatrist in that hospital with a revolution taking place all around him.

Then, ultimately, at the age of thirty-six he died of leukemia, so he actually was very young. Prior to his death, he wrote another classic work, *The Wretched of the Earth*. It is a work that many people have sort of subtitled themselves "the handbook of the black revolution." That's a work that also is very controversial, especially with respect to the chapter on violence. It is just a hugely important work.

In addition, he wrote a book called *A Dying Colonialism*, or at least that's the English title for it. Then there was a collection of his writings that came out after his death that was edited after his death. The title of that work in English is *Toward the African Revolution*.

MYISHA: What was it about Fanon that got you interested?

DOUGLAS: I've always considered myself a rather fierce humanist. And perhaps more than anything else, Fanon's fierce, unapologetic humanism is what I think really drew me to him and still today draws me to him, not only as an inspiration philosophically or intellectually, but also as an inspiration for how I should live my life and how I should approach my social and political commitments and so on.

Fanon was someone who lived his ideas, and that's quite rare. He, I think, in many ways embodied the idea of praxis, where you have theory on one hand and action on the other. Some people do only one of those, which is perhaps never really good. Fanon had his ideas, but he put them into practice and he risked his life doing so; absolutely, he did. That was something that I found remarkable about him, not only biographically, but also ideologically and philosophically.

MYISHA: You say that Fanon was a psychiatrist. He wasn't a philosopher by training. However, you were able to write a philosophy dissertation on him. You also said that philosopher Lewis Gordon does work on Fanon. And I see this pattern from philosophers who work in Africana philosophy, a pattern of gaining philosophical insight from those outside of professional philosophy. How is this possible?

DOUGLAS: I think that's a great question. I would say, first of all, that even if Fanon was a psychiatrist, he can also be a philosopher in addition to that. It doesn't have to be necessarily an either/or situation. But it is true that his training was primarily in medicine, though he did study philosophy as a student in France with Merleau-Ponty and many other thinkers, many of whom are associated with existentialism.

MYISHA: What is existentialism?

DOUGLAS: I would say that Existentialism, with a capital "E" refers to a particular philosophical and literary movement that is generally associated with sort of mid-twentieth-century continental European thought. And there are certain figures who are associated with that: Simone de Beauvoir, Jean Paul Sartre, Maurice Merleau-Ponty, and many, many others. But I think it's also important to realize that many of the questions that animate Existentialism with a capital "E" have been around for a very long time.

I tend to think of existentialism not exclusively in terms of that specific moment in the mid-twentieth century. I tend to think of existentialism as a much broader category. And in terms of the kinds of themes that are important within existentialism, perhaps more than any theme, it would be the theme of freedom. Existentialists are deeply committed to the idea of human beings as free beings, as dynamic beings, and also as beings who need to take responsibility not only for their lives but also for the social conditions and the political conditions around them.

So there is at least for me a kind of humanism in existentialism. And of course, Sartre actually wrote a work called *Existentialism Is a Humanism*, but that is how I've always thought of it. There's something deeply humanistic about existentialism. Because I've always had these normative concerns about social injustice, for me, existentialism provided a certain amount of theoretical resources to think about issues of alienation and exclusion, exploitation, oppression, and dehumanization.

MYISHA: Would you say that Fanon captures these particular themes and you were able to gain philosophical insight as a result?

DOUGLAS: Most definitely. Another thing that is worth pointing out is that one of the big questions in philosophy is the question of humanity: What does it mean to be a human being, how should we understand who we are as human beings in the world? And there has been a tendency to think about those sorts of questions in terms of what some people refer to as "ideal theory." When people do work in ideal theory, they are often doing work that is incredibly abstract, incredibly theoretical, and often kind of divorced from reality.

As a result, there is sometimes a tendency to forget, for example, that we are embodied beings. We aren't just these floating concepts or floating consciousnesses going around. We have bodies and our bodies are different. People are embodied differently. Many philosophers don't really consider that as very important. In existentialism—and not exclusively existentialism, but within existentialism—there is a recognition of the importance of our embodiment of the concrete world in which we are embedded and how we understand that.

What I would argue—and I'm not the first person to argue this by any means—is that while that kind of ideal theorizing can be a very good thing, it can provide us with certain normative principles that we should strive for and so on. I think it's also important that if we really want to understand the human being, if we want to understand the human condition, it's incredibly important to consider the experiences and the articulations of people in the world whose humanity has been denied.

If you're only thinking about the anthropological question, ideally, there's going to be a whole lot you're going to miss. That was one of the reasons early on, to be honest, that I was very attracted to some of these debates taking place within Africana philosophy and the philosophy of race. It was because there was a concreteness to it, there was this recognition of embodiment, there was a recognition that the world is, unfortunately, a profoundly unjust place in many, many ways. And then the question is: Okay, where do we go from here and how do we think about that? So I think that existentialism has a lot to offer there. I think that Fanon as a thinker himself has a tremendous amount to offer there.

MYISHA: You mentioned that Fanon's *The Wretched of the Earth* is sometimes referred to as the handbook for the black revolution. What insights, having to do with social protest, does Fanon give us?

DOUGLAS: A few things, I think, are worth pointing out. Fanon, in the very first chapter of *The Wretched of the Earth*, which is titled "Concerning Violence"—and it's a very lengthy chapter and it's a controversial chapter—makes the argument that colonialism (and we might also extend that to say white supremacy, institutionalized anti-black racism) are things that are very real in the world. And to challenge them may, and probably will, require very real conflict.

Fanon recognized—and he's not the first person to recognize this either—that often positive social and political change can only take place if there is struggle. This is an argument that Frederick Douglas famously made as well. But Fanon talks about this in terms of a necessity in some historical cases of more than just nonviolent, pacifist means. This is one of the things that a lot of people find both very compelling about Fanon but also troubling because in the United States when we think about protesting and so on, we tend to have this ideal of nonviolence.

One of the things that Fanon warns us about—and this appears in *Black Skin, White Masks, A Dying Colonialism*, and in *The Wretched of the Earth*—is to not allow the oppressors, the people who are doing the exploiting, oppressing, and the dehumanizing to define the appropriate terms under in which people who are being exploited, oppressed, and dehumanized can and should protest.

There is a tendency, for example, if we're talking about maybe Occupy Wall Street or the Movement for Black Lives, for a lot of people in the media, a lot of fairly well-known talking heads, to criticize what the protesters are doing. They like to say, "Well, we're kind of sympathetic, but why do they have to do this and why do they have to do that?" There's this sort of backseat driving or whatever that's sort of taking place. But the problem is that the people who are privileged and quite likely directly part of the problem should not be setting the terms for what a protest in the search for justice should be.

MYISHA: I feel the same way concerning anger. The way people try to police the way in which groups protest, the same policing happens when individuals express their emotions (which is a form of moral protest, some may argue). They say, "Your social protest is not appropriate" and they also say, "Your anger is not appropriate."

DOUGLAS: I was at a march to protest the nonindictment of the officers in the Eric Garner case. I made a sign, and if I remember correctly it said something like "Don't lecture us about peace if you're not struggling for justice" or something along those lines. And it's not about getting up on my high horse, but there is this tendency for people on the side to be very judgmental and to nitpick what people are doing in the street. I just don't think that's appropriate. That doesn't move me.

MYISHA: I was at home in New York when I heard about the nonindictment of the officers who killed Eric Garner. I took part in the march throughout the streets of New York and also went to a die-in at Grand Central Terminal. There's a variety of ways today in which people can socially protest. Marches and die-ins are examples.

There have been comparisons made between present-day activism and the activism of the civil rights movement. Some have implicitly suggested that activists today are not risking their lives like activists of the past. This judgment is often used as a way to minimize contemporary activists and their work as well. Tell me a little bit about the virtues, diverse ways, and the impacts of contemporary activism that you are witnessing on the ground.

DOUGLAS: You mentioned one of the virtues, and I think that just right off the bat, one of the virtues that I think we have to recognize is the virtue of people who are willing to take strong, normative positions

having to do with justice and do this in a time when a lot of people regard any kind of normative beliefs whatsoever as passé.

There is a kind of postmodern malaise that a lot of people are in
that keeps them from really having any strong beliefs, because having
strong beliefs is seen as somehow outdated or inappropriate; people
don't want to present some grand narrative or people don't want to
engage in binary thinking. But I think it takes a lot to go out and to get
in the street and protest.

In terms of the different approaches that some people might take,
whether we're talking about die-ins, or for example, getting in the
middle of traffic and basically blocking off major streets and major
highways, I'm all for it. A lot of people, again, on the sidelines say
things like "Well, wait a minute. This isn't very effective protesting because you're just inconveniencing people and that's not a good way to
bring them to your side."

I think that the people who say things like that are appealing to
a kind of politics of respectability. For example, I saw in the Occupy
movement and I see in the Black Lives Matter movement, activists
are interested in speaking truth to power and I don't think they're interested in necessarily being seen as respectable as they're doing so.
I think what a lot of people recognize is that the politics of respectability
doesn't get you very far, because essentially, you are constantly lim-
iting what you are doing as a protester or an activist by the rules of the
person that you're actually trying to change.

MYISHA: What do you think about those who say that it's not radical
enough?

DOUGLAS: I agree that many of those things may not be revolutionary, but I also would say that they are not nothing. The Occupy
movement was in a very obvious way not successful. I think a lot of
people agree on that. I spent a lot of time down at Zuccotti Park. I was
there a lot. And I can say, yeah, it wasn't very successful if you want
to point to some concrete policy change. In terms of reform, it wasn't
particularly successful. In terms of transformation, it definitely wasn't
successful. But it did introduce a new vocabulary. It did introduce certain questions regarding economic justice that no one was really talking
about. That may not be enough. It definitely isn't enough, but I think
it's still something.

In terms of the Black Lives Matter movement, I think it's going
to be very interesting to see how it develops in the coming years because many people are recognizing that there are still some very serious problems. They are recognizing that people need to stand up, get

in the streets, and actually try to do something about it even if it just means being with a community of other human beings who are similarly disgusted by the injustice.

MYISHA: I remember when I was marching in the streets of New York, there were chants going around and we were saying, "Black Lives Matter, Black Lives Matter." It was a mixture of people from different backgrounds, from different races. Then we got to Times Square and there was an argument that was going on between a black male bystander with some protesters. The black bystander was suggesting that the protesting was dividing us. And even while we were marching, there were some people that were saying, "All lives matter, all lives matter."

As a white man who was protesting through the streets, what is your reaction to that kind of vocabulary, where some are saying, "Black Lives Matter" and others are feeling the need to be inclusive and add "all lives matter"? What do you think is the importance of the distinction, or do you think the distinction even needs to be there?

DOUGLAS: My reaction to white people who respond so negatively and with such a degree of insecurity to a sentence like "Black Lives Matter," my reaction to that is there's something silly about it. There's a complete lack of understanding. The idea is this: When people say, "Black Lives Matter," that is not an exclusive statement. You can imagine maybe at the end of that sentence, there should be a "too" and then a period, but why add that?

People who say, "Oh, come on, Black Lives Matter. All lives matter." Well, of course, all lives matter. Of course, that's true. The problem is that within a racist society, certain lives, namely white male lives, have generally mattered much, much more. So to affirm that black lives matter is not to take away from white people in any way. I think to interpret it that way is very insincere. If it is sincere, it's incredibly insecure. And quite likely, that is an insecurity that comes from a sort of hidden guilt about the reality that there is white privilege, that there are people who do know that their lives matter more.

Myisha, you've written a piece for salon.com that is very good in talking about privilege. And there's another piece I've read, where the author says something like "To understand privilege, think about video games." That was the beginning of this piece. And I was like "Video games? This is strange." But the idea was today when you start a video game, one of your first choices in the game is, "What is the difficulty setting?" You want to choose easy, medium, or high difficulty. Sometimes they'll have clever names for the different settings.

But that's not a bad way of thinking about privilege, which is to say that if you are white in a racist, anti-black society, you are essentially playing the game of life on the easy setting. It doesn't mean that you're not going to have struggles, it doesn't mean that there aren't going to be setbacks. But things are going to be comparatively much, much easier. I thought that was a very interesting way of thinking about that question of privilege. That was an interesting analogy to use as a kind of teaching tool.

15

Rachel McKinnon on Allies
and Ally Culture

MYISHA: Social movements in America are as old as America itself. What we notice about many historical social movements is that they were not just made up of those directly affected by injustice but also included nonaffected or less affected people like Jews and Protestant whites in the case of the civil rights movement. We tend to call "outside" individuals supporting other people's causes "allies." What is an ally for you? Do you see any positive roles that allies can play in social movements?

RACHEL: That's a tough question actually. Maybe readers should imagine me always putting scare quotes around the word "ally" because I don't think that they really exist.

Typically, when we think of allies, we think of people who have some sort of dominant group identity or social location that serves to help someone with a disadvantaged identity or social location. We tend to think of allies like straight people helping out queer people, men helping out women, white people helping people of color, and so on. I think that's our typical conception of an ally. I think that that gets things a little bit wrong because immediately a queer person can't be an ally to another queer person. That just seems wrong to me. I think that ingroup members can be supportive of other ingroup members. I think what allies do is use some amount of social power to help out someone with maybe equal or lesser social power, in whatever context.

Now, what positive role can they have? That's the tough question. I think the positive they can do is recognize that they have more social power and then use that social power. For example: I'm a white woman and I teach a lot of issues of critical race theory and race and racism in the classroom. Part of the reason I can do so much of that is, unlike professors of color, I won't receive the same amount of punishment or pushback from students or administrators. In a sense, I can use my white privilege to affect good. I think that that's the good thing that allies can do. They can recognize that they have more power and then use it.

MYISHA: You say in your work that allies can engage in what you call *gaslighting*. What is gaslighting? What are some examples in which allies engage in this kind of behavior?

RACHEL: Gaslighting traces back to a 1938 play and then a 1944 movie called *gaslight*, where the central plot is one of a man engaging in what we might call psychological warfare on his wife. He is basically trying to convince her that she is not perceiving the world properly. His aim is to drive her crazy and he succeeds. Now, that form of psychological warfare isn't typically what we're using for gaslighting these days. More typically, we mean something as a form of epistemic injustice where a few things are happening: (1) The gaslighter downplays the seriousness of an injustice that someone claims to have suffered and (2) The gaslighter tends to directly attack the reliability of the affected person's perceptions of the events or their memory of the events.

For example, if someone comes up to you and says, "Dave just sexually harassed me, he groped me at the bar." Well, someone might gaslight the speaker by saying, "Maybe you came on to him or you are just overreacting. It's not that serious. He just had a couple of drinks. Besides he is married, he wouldn't do that sort of thing." These are all sorts of ways we might gaslight someone's claim that something bad has happened to them.

MYISHA: Are there any other "sins"—if we can call them that—that allies can commit?

RACHEL: Some of my work lately in feminist epistemology has to do with standpoint theory. Standpoint theory is the idea that having a certain social identity or location produces certain epistemic effects. One of them, I think, is that if you have a certain identity and you are sort of struggling against systems of oppression based on that identity, you are better epistemically situated to understand how that oppression works and, I suspect, know how to react to it. One of the sins that allies commit is not recognizing that lacking this social locatedness means that they are at an epistemic disadvantage.

What I see allies do a lot is if someone claims that some injustice happened to them, they will use their own background information as equal epistemic weight to the claim of an injustice. They will say things like "well, maybe he's done this to you before but I've never seen him do it." Somehow they are putting their own experiences on equal epistemic footing to the person who is claiming an injustice. I think that that's not right. We need to be putting more trust in the testimony and assertions of the disadvantaged person.

Another thing that allies do (this is what irks me the most and prompted me to write a whole paper on it) is that they use their allyship as an identity and they use that identity as a protection from criticism. So, if an ally screws up and they inevitably will, and you try to criticize them by saying, "Look, you are screwing up." They'll say, "Yea, but I am an ally, like cut me some slack" or "You're just going to push me away, why should I even bother if I can't get it right."

Often what I find is that allies want positive recognition for not doing bad or not doing worse than others. They say, "Well, give me some credit. At least I didn't do this worst thing to you, right?" I see a lot of bad behavior from allies.

MYISHA: There is a scene from Spike Lee's *Malcolm X* where a white woman walks up to Malcolm X (played by Denzel Washington) as he is on his way to give a university lecture. She comes to him and says something like "I'm dedicated, I understand your struggle. What can I, a white woman, do?" His reply was, "Nothing!" He walks away and you can see the disappointment on her face. Some readers may think that your criticism of ally culture means that they cannot join in the struggle with disadvantaged folks. But I don't think this is what you are saying. So Rachel, is there something we can do to move from this ally culture you are describing?

RACHEL: I think it's so messy. I don't have a sound bite for what can be done. I think part of how we have to approach this is by recognizing the epistemic disadvantage of not having a particular identity, of not living it every day. With this recognition we then have to trust more the people who do have the identity, who are telling us stuff. The worry I have though is that allies think it should be easy to do it well. I find that they want to read a couple of books and feel like they know what's going on when they don't.

Coming to understand how to properly engage in an anti-racist project or an anti-transphobic project or whatever is understanding that it is going to be a lifelong project. It's going to be a lot of work. I think it's more work when you don't have the identity. It's a lot of work even if you do have the identity. It's even more if you don't. I continually find people just thinking it should be easy. So when you try to show them "No, you need to work harder" they react negatively. They say, "Well, give me some credit." It's like cookie seeking (the act of seeking praise or reward for not being bad) pops right up.

I think they can also engage in the work of trusting more the claims of the disaffected people by not telling people to "get over it, you are overreacting." They can also begin doing a lot more of their own research and struggling with things on their own time, not expecting the disadvantaged person to always educate them, and respecting that maybe the disadvantaged gets burnt out sometimes from always fighting these battles.

One of the really sticky situations is I find that allies are often afraid of making a mistake and that leads to complete inaction. They know they probably should do something, but they don't want to make a mistake because if they do they are probably going to get crap from the disadvantaged person too. What I tell people is: just do something, be prepared for criticism but just do something. Something is generally better than nothing.

At least in my own case, I know that lots of people have refrained from saying something even to just be minimally supportive because they think I can fight my own battles, which is for the most part true. But what that results in is no one ever fights my battles for me. I never see people stepping up for the most part because they are like "Well, she is capable of it, I don't need to do anything." Whereas I'm sitting there like "No, I'm only fighting my own battle because no one will fight for me." I find that this fear of doing something wrong is getting in the way of actually doing anything.

MYISHA: Is this what you describe as an "active bystander"? An active bystander would do these things?

RACHEL: Yeah! Part of my work is saying that we have to get rid of allies and ally culture and a replacement is active bystanders. One of the benefits of moving to an active bystander model is I think it removes some of the identity claims, where you can't claim to be an active bystander if you are not actively doing anything. Whereas I found a lot of people claim an ally identity without ever having done anything to earn it. So an active bystander just does stuff. You can't claim, "Well I'm an active bystander, you should give me some credit" if you didn't do anything in the context.

Active bystanders are people who actually engage, who actually participate in helping in some way. Whether it makes it worse or makes it better, active bystanders are at least doing something. They are stepping in, they are saying: "That's not cool." If someone is already fighting their own battle, the active bystander is chiming in, in support. That's something I see lacking almost in its entirety. People stepping in and being like: I agree with this person. What I see instead is a lot of back-channel people sending an email or a message saying, "Yeah, I totally agree with you," but they are not doing it publicly. An active bystander has to do it publicly; otherwise, it's not being an active bystander.

MYISHA: Let's put this into a specific real-life context. When Caitlyn Jenner's 2015 historic *Vanity Fair* cover was first released, how did you witness allies behaving badly? What can we learn from that, particularly as it relates to being an active bystander for the trans community?

RACHEL: What I see, in general, from a lot of allies is that they want to do token display support. Something like cheering on a *Vanity Fair* cover for a white, wealthy, Republican woman fit the bill for most allies. They wanted to do something that was fairly safe for them. Allies don't want to take on personal or cultural risks. So often, "allies"—again scare quotes—don't want to alienate their current set of friends, whereas people in disadvantaged groups are often having to distance themselves from friendships all the time because of stuff going bad. Allies, however, do not want to take that risk. They tend to make very, very safe displays of token support. I felt like a lot of support of Caitlyn's cover was of that sort.

There were also these critiques of beauty in saying that Jenner was perpetuating gender beauty norms and that we shouldn't be praising her but instead critiquing her for this. Well, that's well and good. But why is it that this critique only happens when a trans person gets attention? When cis women are on the cover of *Vanity Fair* every month doing the exact same thing, the critiques never happen. There was a lack of awareness of "why are they doing it now, why are they picking a trans person as somehow having more responsibility for not perpetuating gender norms than the person voicing the concern themselves."

When it came to critiquing the cover, I think cis folks just needed to sit down and shut up because we'll (the trans community) do the critiquing ourselves. There were tons of critiques of what was going on by trans people. Cis folks didn't need to do it. They needed to recognize that they're doing it had a different set of social weight than trans people ourselves doing it.

There were also signs of support based on the comparison between the gender transition and the possibility of transitioning race. I've argued a bit that this just isn't there. Allies said, "I'm supporting Caitlyn because at least she's out in the open and she's honest, whereas I don't support Rachel Dolezal[1] because of the deception and dishonesty." However, I thought that what they were really saying is that trans people should be out and if they are not out, then they are deceiving. This is one of the biggest problematic tropes of trans people.

Moreover, the statistics on being out and trans are that you are far more likely to be assaulted, to be murdered, to be fired, to be denied work, to be denied housing, all sorts of horrible things. So the cis "allies" were essentially saying, "I'm only low key with you if you do these sorts of things that create harm for you" with complete unawareness of what they were saying.

MYISHA: Your claim is that allies can stop committing these sins by leaving ally culture behind and becoming an active bystander? And if they are an active bystander, they will not commit the sins that you are describing?

RACHEL: Exactly! I think part of the problem with ally culture is that it incentivizes these token displays. There is this feeling that you need to put on such a display to prove that you are an ally. The way that people think that you do that is by these shows of support which—because they are coming from such disadvantaged epistemic positions—tend to cause more harm. I honestly think a good case could be made that allies and ally culture create, on balance, more harm than good.

[1]Rachel Dolezal is an activist, lecturer, and former president of the National Association for the Advancement of Colored People (NAACP) chapter in Spokane, Washington. She was forced to step down after it was revealed that she lied about her race. Her parents accused her of being a "white woman passing as black." In 2016 she changed her name to Nkechi Amare Diallo. She chronicles her life story in her memoir, *In Full Color*.

16

Kyle Whyte on Indigenous Climate Justice

MYISHA: What is the difference between climate change and "anthropogenic environmental change"? Why do you think we are not united on this issue?

KYLE: "Anthropogenic" is a term that refers to anything that's caused by humans. In environmental fields, it really got used heavily with respect to anthropogenic environmental change or anthropogenic climate change. What it is used to point out is that whereas, historically, it seemed like a lot of changes in the climate were things that humans can't really control—it seems like more recently in the last two centuries, humans are doing things that bring about those changes. If we know that humans are bringing about changes, then it brings up this issue of: Are some of the humans that brought about those changes actually responsible for any harms that might befall people who experience those types of changes?

Climate change or anthropogenic climate change is a good example of this because, according to the science, we know pretty well that it's industrial and capitalist activities that have triggered some of the environmental systems that are creating warming, and changing rainfall and rain patterns. Those changes are actually harming a lot of people. They're harming people that live along the coasts. They're harming people that live in areas that are prone to drought. Those droughts become worse. They're harming people that depend on certain types of agriculture where you need to be able to predict rainfall patterns. There's also this whole issue of: Should the people whose economic activities benefitted from activities that are now harming other people be held accountable?

MYISHA: It's hard to gauge or measure someone's sincerity, but how do you make sense of what's behind a person's denial of anthropogenic climate change?

KYLE: The way that I look at it in my work, where I focus a lot on indigenous issues, is that that raises a larger ignorance that we experience in the US, Canada, but many other countries in the world. When we think of climate change today, oftentimes we think, "Oh, this is the first time ever that humans have, say, gotten powerful enough through their industrial, capitalist, and other polluting activities to actually change the climate system. This is a question that we now have to consider for the first time ever." What I think is actually funny about that is that for indigenous people, but also many other groups, including many people of color in the United States, it's actually not the first time that another human society has imposed environmental change, even climate change, on us as part of the way that they dominate us.

For example, in the United States in the nineteenth century and the end of the eighteenth century, one of the key things that many US settlers did was they completely deforested indigenous people's lands; they changed the hydrology, that is, the water system of those lands; they forced indigenous people onto tiny reservation areas; and in some cases like with my tribe, the Citizen Potawatomi Nation, they made us march from the Great Lakes region, which had been our homeland for many hundreds of years, to Oklahoma. This meant that we were literally changing from one climate region to the next in a very short period of time. Oftentimes, I think a lot of people forget that it's oftentimes part of oppression to impose environmental change on another group or another society for the sake of the dominant society benefiting economically, culturally, and socially.

MYISHA: Give us some examples of anthropogenic environmental change impacts that may surprise some people.

KYLE: In the world of indigenous climate change, we've seen some stories of indigenous people featured in the media. And I've been trying, with a number of other people, to point out that there are perhaps some better ways to interpret these situations, these stories that

I think would surprise people. One of those stories is people that are having to permanently relocate their communities due to sea-level rise. So in the Arctic, for example, a lot of Alaskan-native villages are having to consider whether they should literally pack up and create a new permanent residence because of sea-level rise.

In the media but also in other sources, including in philosophy, people say, "Oh, well, it's just bad luck that these are folks that were already suffering tough times having gone through several hundred years of US or Canadian colonialism. And now they happen to be living in areas where they are more susceptible to these climate-change impacts that are products of industrialization and capitalism." Myself and others have been trying to point out: Wait a minute. There's a pretty big irony here that, historically, for a lot of these peoples, sea-level rise wouldn't have been a big issue because they lived in a massive region where they moved throughout the year to different locations to harvest, to subsist, and to engage in economic and cultural activities. They were highly mobile people. And the reason why they're now vulnerable to sea-level rise is because the US forced them onto a tiny jurisdictional area so that the US could develop the rest of their lands to benefit US settler populations.

The fact that they're confined to this small area and they can't move is what makes them susceptible to sea-level rise. That means that the solutions for the best way for indigenous people to weigh the options of how they should relocate need to address this larger failure of the US to support the types of land bases and conditions for self-determination that they need.

MYISHA: You talk about the sea rising. You also talk about the fact that there are indigenous people suffering from this because they've been forced to leave a land that they were familiar with to go to another land. You're suggesting that this is one of the reasons why indigenous peoples face heightened climate risk. Give us some more examples.

KYLE: We've been really trying to bring out a lot of different dimensions of how people face climate change. So, for example, in the Great Lakes region, you have a lot of different tribes that have reservations, which are a fraction of the size of their historic territories, but they also have treaty rights to hunt, fish, worship, and engage in other activities off-reservation. These were rights that their ancestors guaranteed in treaties that they endorsed in the nineteenth century.

What has happened in these situations is that since the signing of those treaties, a lot of those areas that are off the reservation, they've filled in with private-property owners, businesses, and other US settler activities. That's actually shrunk the area of land that tribal members can now go out and use, enjoy, and relate to and be part of. If you take a particular relationship, such as to medicinal plant or to a key plant for food but also for ceremonies like wild rice or even an animal like moose, over time the area of land where you can relate to those plants or animals has shrunk. When climate change, such as through warming or changes in precipitation, reduces those places even more, then it might mean that significant numbers of the tribal population will no longer be able to relate to those plants or animals.

It's not just an economic impact in the sense that, say, if you were consuming or even selling the products of those plants or animals, the consumption or sales would be affected. It's a deep psychological impact because your community may have been relating to that plant or animal since time immemorial. Your culture, your family relations, your stories—are all tied to particular plants and animals. To lose that relationship and to not be able to take any action to stop that is deeply disturbing. It contributes to what in indigenous studies a lot of people refer to as "historic or intergenerational trauma," which is the idea that as indigenous people—but obviously this is for many other people of color, and other groups too—that our experience today is a compounding of just years of trauma imposed on us by the US settler society.

MYISHA: What is climate injustice, and why is it "more like an experience of déjà vu"?

KYLE: The philosophical question of climate justice is a really diverse one because it's really quite different depending on what group you're talking about. Climate justice in a general sense refers to this idea that it turns out that the people who benefitted the most from the activities that have made climate change occur at a pace so fast that it's hard for people to adapt to are the least likely to be harmed by those changes. The people who are harmed are actually oftentimes the people who are the least responsible for the activities that caused the spike in warming.

There are groups of people in the world that are experiencing some of the issues that we're talking about right now, like, say, sea-level rise or drought. But the reason they're going through it is because of industrial actions that occurred in the nineteenth century. The responsible parties are no longer alive, and you could even claim that at the time, they didn't know what they were doing. This has created a range of theories and ideas to try to figure out: How do you hold people responsible who either didn't know what they were doing or they're no longer with us? I've tried to show that for indigenous people, broadly, that's not actually the best way to look at the issue of climate justice, because actually, there is no unbroken chain of responsibility.

If you look historically in the nineteenth century, indigenous people were forced by the United States to get off their land. We were dispossessed of our land to make way for these industries that have brought us the current spike in global average temperature. The US designed a number of policies, such as the reservation system, but also other things like the boarding-school system which divested us of our knowledge, that made it possible for these industries to move into our lands.

What we find is that if you fast-forward today, and this is relating back to the example I was sharing before about relocation in the Arctic, the reason why indigenous people suffered the most from climate change or climate-change risk is because of those very same policies. That means when we talk about "Oh, what do we do about the fact that we're facing greater risks than other populations from climate change," we still have to actually go back and address those policies that were the original ones that made way for the industries that caused anthropogenic climate change. So it's déjà vu.

MYISHA: I've noticed that one of the things you haven't evoked in our conversation is the issue of sacredness. What role does the sacred play for you when thinking about these issues?

KYLE: It makes a huge difference. In another paper I have, I am looking at a lot of what indigenous people have said about spirituality and sacredness and how we oftentimes use that term in our environmental activism and in our environmental-justice work. What oftentimes you find is that, different from maybe how those terms are used in other religions, when we use "sacred" or "spiritual" often in English, we're referring to respecting and honoring the fact that we're all highly interdependent on one another. And our interdependence connects us to the environment, to plants, animals, to nonhuman entities like water, to other people, and to other cultures.

A lot of my friends, for example, who are from Standing Rock, if you ask them, "Well, what is the idea that water is life or water is sacred mean?", it's not only the idea of a kind of reverence for water as a nonhuman entity or in a sense having faith in water. It's actually recognizing just how complex the interdependence between humans and nonhumans as water is, which is why it was actually quite ridiculous that the Dakota Access pipeline builders keep saying, "Oh, the pipeline doesn't technically go through the reservation." If you look historically, and this is again bringing back this déjà vu, the Standing

Rock tribe had not only secured a reservation but a larger treaty area where they could continue to participate in those relationships of interdependence. For them, that's what matters. It goes way beyond the reservation. For someone to suggest that it's acceptable to put a pipeline through that land that's part of that sacred world, that spiritual world, is an injustice and it's forgetting what those Dakota and Lakota fought for.

It really goes back to the question you were asking earlier about climate justice; that when somebody tells me, "Oh, it's really bad luck that indigenous people seem to be impacted more severely than others by climate change," it's like "Wait a minute. The reason why we're more impacted is because the US still maintains this very rigid policy about reservations and about blocking off our opportunities to adapt and to live in those worlds of interdependence that our ancestors enjoyed." And so it's an erasure and forgetfulness that as peoples, we're not just confined to these small areas of land.

MYISHA: There have been solutions to climate change proposed. Lowering emissions is an example. Why do you think tackling solutions like this without addressing colonialism is problematic?

KYLE: In a lot of my educational work, especially with nonnative people and nonnative environmentalists, this is a tough question that we have to really talk about. Because for a lot of indigenous people, and I think for a lot of nonnative folks, this might sound strange, the environmental-conservation movement has actually been just as harmful to us as the extractive industries.

When national parks were created and ecological restoration processes or projects were designed, oftentimes they displaced indigenous people or they used terms like "wilderness" or "historic landscape" that didn't include any humans. That actually erases that indigenous history. What we see, again, is that many environmental projects, even solutions to climate change, while at one level you can see how they're trying to solve the problem, are always at the expense of indigenous people. Recent efforts to, say, conserve forests and create programs for carbon credits from conserving forests oftentimes still require displacing indigenous people. In the US when there's been polices to create better conditions for people to use renewable energy, they're often very silent on providing resources or capacities for leadership or voice for tribes. We're seeing this all over again: solutions to climate change come at the sacrifice of indigenous people. And so for us, are those actually any better?

MYISHA: I used to work for an environmental organization in Brooklyn. I remember one of my friends saying, "We need to take care of our environment so that our children can have somewhere to live in the future." Rhetoric, like this, often points to this futuristic thing. Plus, it was always about "our" children. But rhetoric like this fails to recognize that there are people presently suffering and they may not be "our" children. And it doesn't make it less morally pressing. Here we see that even those who are on the front lines of environmental justice are thinking in a self-centered futuristic way that I think is problematic.

I also think that living on the East Coast is very different from living in the Upper Midwest. On the East Coast many do not have interactions with indigenous peoples and thus may be unaware about on-the-ground struggles and issues that you are discussing. One of the things I hope that this conversation will do for readers is enlighten and challenge them.

Here's a final question and a big one. If colonialism is the problem, then what are some solutions to colonialism?

KYLE: That is the question that guides a lot of my philosophical work. When we think about what does it mean to engage in decolonizing praxis or what does it mean to affect and transform this kind of colonial situation that we live in, what I've argued is that there's a key idea which I think makes sense to me from my experience and many of the tribes that I've worked with. For Anishinaabe people, Potawatomi people, our major philosophies are actually about the importance of being able to adapt to change. Because a lot of changes that get thrown at us, they're not things that we control. But it takes a society around us to be able to support our capacity to adapt to those changes.

If you look at what colonialism actually is and what it uniquely does that's bad, in connection with capitalism and other forms of oppression and domination, it cuts off our capacity to have a society that will support us in our capacity to adapt to change. A further step is we see that what colonialism actually does is attack the moral fabric of our society, and teach us that we can't trust each other and that we can no longer live in societies where consent means anything. If we're going to engage in decolonialization, we actually have to create and support the strengthening of the moral fabric of our society so that we can actually be able to, like a lot of our ancestors did, withstand and be resilient to the different types of risks and changes that we are encountering.

For climate change, for example, say for a tribe that is losing its capacity to relate to a particular plant or animal, the reason why it's losing that capacity is because the US says, "Oh, all you have is a right to this particular territory, which I can draw it in a little box" instead of thinking, "What does that tribe need to be as adaptive as possible for the well-being of the people?" And so instead, they should actually go back to what many of our ancestors thought they were getting into in the treaty era, which was that there would be ongoing relationships of renewal with the United States where we would check in and actually think about "Well, what does each group need to do to adjust so that each can pursue its well-being in a way that's best for its own people?" This is kind of the basic idea of what decolonialization needs to go for. And this idea is both about institution building and about motivating direct action like we saw at Standing Rock—the water protectors, the ceremonies.

Decolonialization has to include both a willingness and motivation to stand up and to stop domination but also to engage in that institution building that will restore, strengthen, and maintain those moral fabrics that colonialism has damaged so greatly.

17

Andrea Pitts on Resistance to Neoliberalism

MYISHA: I think the word "neoliberalism" has been loosely thrown around these days in a way that makes me uncertain about what a person means when they use the term. What is neoliberalism?

ANDREA: I think that's a great question and an important question. There are a few things that get generally referred to when people use the term "neoliberalism." One would be a set of economic policies and the other might be a kind of broader political view that people consider neoliberal in character. I think meanings between the two are related, but it also depends on the context and who's saying it and when.

Generally, I think neoliberalism is a term that's been used by political theorists and economists a lot to refer to economic policies stemming from around the 1970s and onward that tend to share the view that nation-states should try to prevent interfering with or impeding market relations. For example, the International Monetary Fund and the World Bank offered a series of guidelines for loans for a lot of Latin American countries in the 1980s that sought things like deregulating trade, promoting foreign direct investment, privatizing natural resources, and removing these other kinds of impediments that might impact market relations.

A specific example would be something like in Bolivia in the 1980s, a party called the Revolutionary Nationalist movement implemented some policies that privatized the tin mines in Bolivia. That effectively led to the loss of employment for thousands of miners who were working these mines. The government also sought around to deregulate labor laws, which effectively weakened the unions there. There's a general set of policies in that sense that were enacted. There's also stuff like what's called the "Washington Consensus" from 1989, which is a kind of shorthand for the economic policies recommended by these major lenders like the IMF and the World Bank. They're usually about monetary flows from the Global North to nation-states in the Global South that were deemed "developing nations" that needed these kinds of loans.

In the context of the US, these kinds of policies are also associated with fiscal and social reforms of someone like Ronald Reagan. So including, for example, the firing of 11,000-plus air-traffic controllers during the early 1980s when they were on strike. That was a pretty big blow to trade unions at the time. I think it's also associated with someone like Margaret Thatcher as well.

That's the economic sense, and then there's also a kind of political sense that people tend to use, which is referring more generally to individualizing, privatizing, and as Isabel Altamirano-Jimenez states in her recent book *Indigenous Encounters with Neoliberalism*, a kind of "commodification of nature."

Neoliberal policies might operate to dissuade or prevent employees from joining or forming unions, or they might support the privatization of previously state-run social goods like education, health care, water sources and gas. For example, the privatization of gas means that gas is something that you'll pay for individually from a private company and not something that your community or your state collectively owns and endeavors to protect, sustain, or distribute.

There's also maybe this other broader sense, which is related to the first two for sure. It's a sense in which the wealth and power of a nation-state benefits from these types of policies. So these could include the use of military force or economic sanctions to preserve the financial interests or the corporate interests of a given nation-state. The military force at Standing Rock, the military deaths of Lenca activists that were done in Honduras, and the military deaths that were caused in response to the Agua Zarca dam are cases in which people tend to refer to the military's implications in the preservation of private corporate interests. There's another sense in which we could talk about private industries and contracts that support state surveillance and national security measures, which can also be a way to talk about the nation-state's role in preserving individualized and privatized investments.

That's kind of the general take. I think maybe what's neo or new about these policies is that they apply some basic liberal tenets of freedom, individualism, and state power with policies and trends that focus on private, often corporate, global, capitalist, and economic relations. That tends to be, at least from what I've gathered from the folks that I'm reading and working on, where some people put the emphasis.

MYISHA: It seems that the term "neoliberalism" is not just descriptive, but it's also value-laden. Do you think that employing the word itself always has this negative valence to it?

ANDREA: I'm committed to this broader epistemological or philosophy-of-language view about meaning itself. Even our best objectivist efforts are going to be value-laden. Neoliberalism is value-laden, but so too is everything else. "Is it a pejorative term?" Has it been used to critique and that kind of thing?" Yeah. I think it's use is probably similar to how the term "capitalism" in a Marxist context has been used in a critical sense. You don't often see industries describing themselves as capitalist. Neoliberalism has operated along those terms as well.

As a political idea, I think there's a pretty fairly robust set of debates about the relationship between, say, the classic neoliberalism of John Locke or Adam Smith and what these neoliberal economists like Friedrich Hayek or Milton Friedman have done. I think, again, maybe some common threads would be something like an emphasis on the relationship between the individual, the state, and freedom. If neoliberalism and liberalism are connected, how are they connected and that is something that people are debating. David Harvey's *A Brief History of Neoliberalism* has a really great overview of some of these same concepts and ideas.

MYISHA: How are indigenous peoples uniquely affected by neoliberalism?

ANDREA: I think a number of indigenous scholars and activists have long pointed out that the effects of economic policies and specifically neoliberal economic policies are often particularly violent against indigenous peoples. The impact of neoliberalism policies on indigenous peoples follows what a lot of folks refer to as a kind of "settler-colonial logic." This is in the case in which a colonizing nation-state considers itself more capable than indigenous communities to determine maybe the importance or value and use of, say, traditional territories, waterways, forests, or other natural resources.

When I use the phrase "settler colonialism," it's important to note that, as Patrick Wolfe has argued, it is a structure and not an event. The expropriation of native land through these kinds of economic policies is an ongoing organizing principle of the structure of settler colonialism. It's not just something that happens; rather it's an ongoing, organizing structure. In this sense, Eve Tuck and Wayne Yang have a great piece called "Decolonization Is Not a Metaphor." They basically say that according to settler colonial logic, land is the most valuable commodity to preserve. Because indigenous land is their new home and a source of capital, this requires the disruption of indigenous life ways and cosmologies in relationship to place.

I mentioned Isabel Altamirano-Jimenez's work, and she has some really thorough and great work on what she calls "green neoliberalism." She says that her work is tracing an environmental stance that holds the view that various animals, plant species, and ecosystems would actually be better protected by treating them as commodities. That's the kind of neoliberalism approach to saying that now it is better to commodify things like fisheries and have corporations use them and work over them than the indigenous communities to whom they're in these relations of place. In a piece called "The Sea Is Our Bread" she outlines some of the ways in which Zapotec and Waveh peoples have been basically treated as "entrepreneurial, petty producers," who are unable to protect the lands in which they're fishing. And she discusses the ways in which there's these private interests that come in to gain control of those lands and use them.

Another example would be by Rebecca Tsosie, who has a really great piece in the *Routledge Handbook of Epistemic Injustice*. She uses *Lyng v. Northwest Indian Cemetery Protective Association* as an example of hermeneutical injustice. The case was an injustice against the intelligibility of indigenous lifeways in the court systems in the US. The federal government was allowed to extend a logging road through a sacred site that's impacted indigenous groups in northern California. They were able to do this because these indigenous peoples couldn't show that their belief, something that was sacred, was prefaced upon it not having a logging road in it. These private interests in the timber industry were weighed as more valuable and, certainly, more intelligible than the cosmology and sacred beliefs that these indigenous groups had. I think the Bears Ears monument in Utah, Dakota Access, and Keystone pipelines are also an example of the US and Canadian settler-colonial states using and implementing neoliberal policies. Kyle Whyte (Chapter 16) has some really excellent work on a lot of these issues as well.

MYISHA: You note in your work that indigenous peoples are not passive to neoliberalism. They've taken up projects to resist it, and you specifically note indigenous communities in Bolivia and Mexico that have done so. Tell us more about their work, their strategies, and also their successes.

ANDREA: I should say that as a nonindigenous person and as someone who's a descendant of both white settler and Central American mestizo migrants, I take it to be important for me to focus specifically on the work of indigenous-identified scholars for the kind of work that I'm doing. Particularly in this project, I was really drawing from the work of Chickasaw scholar Shannon Speed and the Aymaran scholar Silvia Rivera Cusicanqui.

What I take from this literature are the differences between the political relationships between indigenous peoples and the nation-states in each context. So, for example, the current Bolivian president since 2016, Evo Morales, is an Aymaran labor union organizer who developed his political base and platform from fighting for the rights of coca-leaf farmers. Many of those farmers who became part of this coca-leaf industry had actually lost their jobs when this mining industry went privatized. There's also this interesting kind of movement from the mining industry into coca-leaf farming. Coca leaves are also known to be a sacred plant used by indigenous communities across the Andes, and cocaine is made from it. It's also part of the US's crackdown on the War on Drugs, which has also had a pretty big impact on a lot of Andean communities who rely on the coca leaf.

I mentioned the shrinking of unions as part of the impact of neoliberalism, and Morales and Movimiento al Socialismo (the Movement to Socialism), which was a political party that he joined and now leads, directly contested those kinds of neoliberalism trends within Bolivia. The Bolivian government is currently directed by an indigenous and socialist leadership, and their stated aims are to work against colonialism, neoliberalism, and interventionism. That's that national context.

So while the outcome of indigenous organizing efforts led to this renewed political life in Bolivia during the 2000s, indigenous communities in Mexico continue to struggle under a set of policies enacted under the North American Free Trade Act (NAFTA) and other reforms of the 1990s and 2000s. For example, in 1991 the then-president Carlos Salinas de Gortari effectively ended all forms of land redistribution to indigenous communities. That was a huge blow for the indigenous communities who held significant claims against the state. Part of this meant that there was this detrimental impact from NAFTA. There was this decision to no longer respect nor respond to land redistribution claims. That led to some organizing efforts. But the 2000 president Vicente Fox also refused to honor the self-governance rights that were agreed to during a series of accords in the mid-1990s. This was also a huge failure by the Mexican government to affirm the policies that they had agreed to that would impact indigenous and peasant peoples in Mexico.

Part of the formation of the group, the Zapatistas, was in response to this. This indigenous rights movement moved to the region of Chiapas, Mexico, and this led to the declaration of the region as an autonomous region. Against the state's wishes, Zapatistas began to develop their own health care, educational, and agricultural systems. In terms of state presence, those are very different kinds of outcomes in the 1990s and 2000s.

With respect to women in those two movements, given those two different contexts, you have these different negotiations for indigenous women with respect to these different structures. In the context of Bolivia, the group Mujeres Creando call themselves anarcha-feminists. They're responding despite the work of the Movimiento al Socialismo and Morales. They effectively argue that a lot of work remains to be done for indigenous women in the country.

I think one really poignant piece that I used when writing about this work was an essay written by María Galindo that's called "If Evo Morales Had Been Born a Woman." Galindo responds to this seemingly heroic narrative about Morales in the coca-leaf industry. She claims that things would have been quite different if he had been Eva Morales, an indigenous peasant woman. Galindo's point here is that her opportunities would still remain quite limited under the current state policies in Bolivia. She writes that Eva wouldn't have been able to marry outside of her community; or if she did decide to migrate, she would be viewed as having turned her back on her community; or if she left domestic life to go work in the city, she most likely would have been confronted with a traumatic experience of rape or sexual harassment. Galindo traces the story of Evo Morales and reframes it through this narrative of Eva Morales and what the conditions would have been like for her to make those similar moves.

She does say too that had she been able to become president, there is no doubt for a minute that she would decriminalize abortion, condemn rape within the party, and require that each and every member of the Movimiento al Socialismo provide financial compensation to the families caring for their children that they've abandoned along the way. Then she says, "Eva would understand each and every one of the dreams of Bolivian women." I feel like this is a call for Mujeres Creando and for Galindo in the essay. It's a call for what people call a "de-patriarchalization" as part of decolonialization. So despite the state's pointed efforts to decolonize and to resist neoliberalism, there's also these other really important facets of the ways in which the state has framed the possibilities for indigenous women.

Regarding Zapatistas, I think there's an interesting shift in recent Mexican politics. For some time, the Zapatistas were choosing not to participate in state politics and they had severed ties and fought against the state government. But more recently, the Zapatistas announced that they will have an indigenous woman candidate running in the 2018 presidential election. María de Jesús Patricio Martínez is a Nahua medicine healer who was designated by the National Indigenous Congress to serve as their candidate.

One thing too that the Zapatistas, I think, have really done is foreground indigenous women in their organizing through representational politics of indigenous women. There was this really key moment in March 2001 where they had a woman named Comandanta Esther take the central platform in the Mexican Congress. She has this speech where she notes that her presence as an indigenous woman in front of the Mexican Congress will have this interesting effect of not making anyone feel attacked or humiliated or degraded. She knows that some people might choose not to listen to her or they might refuse to speak to her because it will be her that's the one that they're now having to address. But she says that the Zapatistas are aware that she is placed there as an indigenous woman, representative, and speaker and an authority on indigenous politics and demands made to the state. I think that's a really interesting moment in which the Zapatistas used a political platform to highlight indigenous women as the voice for self-governance rights within their organizing. It's another interesting difference between the ways in which we see these political situations differing and also the tactics that these different groups are using to highlight indigenous women.

MYISHA: Thank you for providing clear examples of indigenous forms of resistance. You claim that there's a possibility to exoticize or romanticize these forms of resistance. What might that look like, how is it problematic, and how can we resist it?

ANDREA: One thing I try to highlight is that both Comandanta Esther and María Galindo of Mujeres Creando are pretty clear and adamant that one thing that they don't support is the idea of indigenous cultures as static, inherently sexist, or any notion like that.

Pitting gender and sexual liberation against non-Anglo or European cultures would be a false dichotomy. I think Shannon Speed writes about this as a kind of multiculturalism that makes people have to choose between a cultural identity or a gender identity. I think in some ways to "romanticize indigenous resistance" might also require overlooking the claims that women within those communities are making in response to their communities. I think that we wouldn't want to have that very dichotomous read.

What are ways to resist exoticizing or romanticizing indigenous resistance? As many of us are settlers, immigrants, or descendants of people forcefully brought to this land, it's not just learning and listening that we need to do. I also think we need what Mariana Ortega calls in her paper, "On Being Lovingly, Knowingly Ignorant," a kind of prescription to check and question whether the things that we're analyzing actually respond to the communities that we're engaged with.

I did email Mujeres Creando and was corresponding with them in the construction of my paper on this work. That was part of me thinking about how I can be responsive to these communities. My engagement with the Caribbean Philosophical Association has been really great because as a conference it puts you in conversation with folks from a lot of different philosophical and geopolitical sides to move some of this work. I had a really great opportunity at an early presentation of this paper to talk with a scholar, Catherine Walsh, who works with Afro-Ecuadorian communities, and get her take on how this resonated with her and that kind of thing. That was a really fruitful dialogue.

In thinking more generally about romanticization, there's some really interesting insights in the Tuck and Yang piece, "Decolonization Is Not a Metaphor." There they highlight this phrase by Janet Mawhinney about settler-colonial efforts to move to innocence, to try to purify or cleanse one's own complicitness with settler-colonial violence. For example, they state things like when people claim some kind of small percentage of native identity to take some authenticity. Or when someone uses the phrase "We're all colonized as oppressed or marginalized people." I think this erases the specific responsibilities to, say, issues like land redistribution or other complicities with settler-colonial logic.

Tuck and Yang have a really great set of ways in which they try to talk through what folks call a "native-settler-slave triad," which actually upholds settler colonialism and then relies on both the elimination of native peoples and the exploitation of black and brown labor. They challenge us to remain attentive to how one's concrete practices are maintaining or upsetting settler-colonialism.

MYISHA: What are some lessons to learn from understanding the struggle of indigenous communities in the Global South?

ANDREA: To frame some of the discussion, I want to emphasize that a lot of these things are not particularly original to my reading or my contrition on this part. On a general level, I think it's important to note that the struggle of indigenous communities can't be reduced to their effectiveness for the ends of academics. I think often we seek to extend our influence in representational capacities, and sometimes those extended networks might still remain insufficient for challenging, and may be complicit with, the policies and economic trajectories of neoliberalism.

I think the goals of decolonial practices through scholarship should also seek nonacademic forms of engagement and dialogue. So some questions for scholars and readers thinking about resisting settler-colonial logic are: What, beyond academic work, are you doing to support the self-determination or views? Anishinaabe scholar Gerald Vizenor's term "collective survivance" of indigenous people is relevant here. Where do you spend your money, where and for whom have you put your body on the line, with whom do you seek to learn from, or with whom do you seek critical engagement, guidance, or comfort? I think these are all important ways of thinking about what our academic writing isn't necessarily doing on its own.

Another important way to frame some of the issues that we've been discussing is through ways to resist, replace, or dismantle what some folks call the "modern colonial nation-state." Folks like Kwame Nimako or Sylvia Winter have called this a kind of "Westphalian model" for the nation-state. The model stems from the 1648 Treaty of Westphalia, which is a mutual recognition for the territorial sovereignty among European states. So basically, all other peoples are left outside of those agreements. Against this, Chickasaw scholar Jodi Byrd has offered a model of Chickasaw sovereignty, which she says isn't founded on territorial claims over property, but rather in diplomacy, disagreement, relationships, intimacy, and kinship. The association here is about building models for solidarity and coalition that work across the imposed boundaries of settler-colonial nation-states. An example of this comes from Evo Morales. He cites the Idle No More movement, the First Nation's Native American movement of 2012, as a kind of transnational movement. We could also think about how the Zapatistas have had a worldwide movement as well.

Section 4

RACE AND ECONOMICS

18

David Livingstone Smith
on Dehumanization

MYISHA: What is dehumanization?

DAVID: This is a word that's used in all kinds of different ways. Some people think of dehumanization as the use of animalistic slurs. They see it as sort of a linguistic phenomenon. Some people see it as disrespectful or degrading treatment of others.

There are about ten different logically independent notions of what dehumanization is in the scholarly literature alone. Then when you go to common uses, it's even more all over the map. So dehumanization can mean a lot of different things. I'll tell you what I mean by "dehumanization," which is just really fine grain. We dehumanize others when we think of those others as subhuman creatures.

So dehumanization is something that happens in your head. For example, you might think of me as appearing to be human, but not really being human on the inside where it matters. If you were to engage in that kind of thought process, you would be dehumanizing me.

MYISHA: Can you give me some more examples of dehumanization?

DAVID: In the book I'm writing now and in the talks I give now, I use as a sort of Exhibit A the examples of spectacle lynchings in the United

States. A lot of people don't know what spectacle lynchings were, so maybe I should explain that a little bit.

The stereotypical view of what happened during lynchings in the United States was that five or six guys would ride up with their Halloween costumes on (their hoods and shit like that), and they'd grab some African American person and string him up to a tree, and that was a lynching. I mean, things like that did happen and did happen frequently, although that's a very cleaned-up version of what happened. Because of course, what generally happened even in these small-scale lynchings were torture and bodily mutilation of the most gruesome sort.

Spectacle lynchings were these lynchings that were widely advertised, were attended by thousands of people. There were professional photographs taken, and there were cases where even the screams of the victim were recorded on primitive gramophone rolls. And what's regarded as the first one of these attracted a crowd of between 10,000 and 20,000 people to observe an unbelievably horrible sequence of tortures before this man was burned to death.

Now, what interests me about these was the way that the victims are described mostly in the media at the time. These events were covered very widely, so there are lots and lots of information. Henry Smith, a man lynched in 1893 in Paris, Texas, is described as a beast, an animal, a monster, a subhuman creature very, very consistently in the press; not only in the press but also in the reminiscences of people who actually attended the lynching.

You might think, "Well, weren't these people just speaking figuratively?" And my response to that is, "Well, some of them might have been." But very, very often the case, when black people in the United States were described in those terms, particularly acutely from the late nineteenth century to the early twentieth century, this was meant quite literally. And we can see this from the racist literature of the period.

So dehumanization in that sense is very closely related to the commission of atrocity, atrocities which would be very, very difficult for many of us—not all of us—but many of us to commit unless we thought of the victims as less than human. Spectacle lynchings are an interesting set of examples of thinking of others as subhuman creatures, but you can go to virtually any genocide, any episode of mass atrocity, and find this way of thinking playing a role.

MYISHA: Do you think that this thinking, this dehumanization, is a true belief? Is it a justification for the treatment that they're engaging in? Is it both? What comes first here, the chicken or the egg?

DAVID: Well, I guess it could be either. But I think it's primarily an actual belief. It's not just a post-op thing after the fact. "Oh, it was okay to do that because he's really a monster, a bloodthirsty beast." Rather what we see, if we look at dehumanization, is that we find it in the buildup to mass violence.

I don't think it's just a way of people exculpating themselves as they're getting ready to do violence. Here's why I don't think so. Actually, unless you're a very special sort of person, performing such acts is actually difficult. It's very, very difficult to look at another human being in the eye and kill them or torture them. For some people it doesn't bother, but they are deviations from the norm.

And the reason for that is something about the way human beings are. We are highly, highly, social animals. There's no other mammal that comes anywhere near to us in sociality. In fact, I think it's going to be our undoing because we care more about Hollywood gossip than we do about anthropogenic climate change. So our interests are so socially skewed that we often don't pay attention to things that really, really matter.

Any social mammal has to have inhibitions against violence, against violence directed against members of the kind. This is just a truism in biology. Strangers, say, in nonhuman animals—these would be individuals outside the breeding group—often have terrible violence unleashed on them. But within the breeding group, within the community, there have to be very, very strong inhibitions against violence or else they couldn't exist as social animals.

Now, we hypersocial animals have to have extremely powerful inhibitions against doing violence to one another. And we've got these great, big brains that allow us to very easily recognize that all human beings are part of a single extended human community as it were. Now, this creates a problem. What's the problem? Well, the problem is, not to put too fine a point on it, that it's often advantageous to kill, harm, and enslave others. We steal their stuff, we can exploit their labor without compensation, we can do all sorts of awful things. So that recognition, that cognitive recognition, bumps up against the emotional inhibition.

Over the millennia, human beings have found various ways around that. One way is religious ideologies, another way is the use of drugs to dull one's senses so that one can kill, and that goes way, way, way back; certain kinds of mind-altering rituals to put us in altered states of consciousness that allow us to do these things. And dehumanization is one more way, I think, of disabling these inhibitions against doing harm. It's kind of a solution to a problem.

MYISHA: It's interesting that you say that dehumanization is a way to do these things that we as humans wouldn't naturally do. Before our conversation I was wondering if dehumanization was part of human nature. It seems that your view is "It's not human nature to do certain acts to individuals. But through dehumanization, we're able to do those particular things."

DAVID: I think you've got it right there. We're, unfortunately, endowed with psychological capacities that make it possible for us to dehumanize people. And that's a very important and very particular set of psychological capacities. People who have an interest in us doing harm to others can very easily manipulate these capacities. So we're suckers for a certain kind of propaganda or a certain kind of entrenched ideology just because we tend to think in this sort of way.

What I'm talking about is what psychologists call "psychological essentialism." There's a robust literature on this that got going in the late 1980s. This idea is: Human beings just have a tendency—philosophers would say "an intuition." I call intuitions "cognitive biases." We have a set of biases that lead us to do two things. One is to divide the world up into what philosophers call "natural kinds"—real divisions out there in the world like biological species, for instance. That comes very naturally and easy to us.

The second is the really important bit. We tend to think of those natural kinds as having essences. And what I mean by that is there's some deep fact about them that all and only members of the kind share. "What makes something a dog?" is an example of that way of thinking. It's not its appearance. It's something somehow inside the dog, in the dog's blood, or nowadays people who know nothing about genetics say, "in the genes" and that's the essence. And that essence is supposed to be causally responsible for the typical doggie features like wagging tail and four legs and stuff like that.

Now, what's really interesting about that, if you think about it, is that the essence can come apart from the appearance. So you might have a dog that's born with three legs. Well, it's still a dog. Why is it a dog in ordinary folk thinking? Because it's got that inner "dogginess." You might have a dog, because of some genetic peculiarity, that looks more like a cat; but it is still a dog. What makes it a dog? Something "inside."

Now, we tend to apply this way of thinking to other human beings as well. The whole idea of race in my opinion is rooted in this way of thinking.

MYISHA: So let's talk about that a little bit. Given the history of dehumanization in the West, how does this history intersect with racial-formation processes or racialization practices?

DAVID: Very, very importantly. I think dehumanized groups are not always, but they're almost always, racialized before being dehumanized.

Let's go into what's involved in racialization. I think the precondition for racialization is conflict. There has to be something in it for the racializing group to subordinate the racialized group. So, what is it to racialize? What I think it is to racialize is to treat a population of people as belonging to a different and inferior human natural kind.

So you and I would be classified as different races. Depending on the historical epic, we would be classified differently, right?

MYISHA: Yes.

DAVID: The idea of that classification is that you and I are members of different human natural kinds. That means there's some deep difference, something in our blood (in folk thinking) or in our genes (in pseudoscientific thinking), that sets us very fundamentally apart from one another and determines our different appearances. But the appearance isn't constitutive of being a member of a race. It's a symptom.

Let's look at the story so far. A group of people is kind of situated as a distinct and inferior human natural kind, and that justifies exploiting them in some sort of way or doing harm to them in some sort of way. So they've been made fundamentally other.

Dehumanization is just taking that a step further. When we racialize people, we don't exclude them from the category of the human. We just say, "Well, they're kind of an inferior sort of human being." Dehumanization crosses that categorical boundary. "They're not really human. They just look human. Really on the inside they are subhuman creatures." And of course, then this frees the dehumanizing population up to harm them in ways, which would be difficult to hand out to those whom we regard as fellow human beings.

MYISHA: Does extermination necessarily follow from dehumanization?

DAVID: No, I think that's relatively uncommon. We dehumanize a lot more than we exterminate. One of my very favorite examples is the description written by a man named Morgan Godwin, who was an Anglican clergyman in Virginia and Barbados in the late seventeenth century. He was very, very explicit when he's writing particularly about what was going down in Barbados, that the planters regarded their African slaves as nonhuman, as subhuman creatures, and that they treated them accordingly. These guys weren't interested in exterminating these people.

They were interested often in working them to death, but death was merely a consequence of working them, of exploiting them. So it's not just extermination. In fact, there are certain very distinctive exterminationist patterns of dehumanization such that if you notice this kind of pattern, you have reason to be justified that extermination is in the offing. But it can be any kind of brutality or atrocity handed out to others that goes with dehumanization.

MYISHA: It's one thing to conceive of someone as not human. How then do you go about conceiving of someone as a monster?

DAVID: This is really important and this is stuff that my new book is going to be about, which is going to be titled *Making Monsters*.

Here's the idea. I'm looking at a picture of you right now and I can't help but respond to you as a human being. I'm looking right on my screen at your face, and that just says "human" to me. And that's not something I'm in control of. Now, suppose I was a member of one of these white nationalist organizations, like Stormfront, who were marching in Charlottesville, Virginia, in 2017. Some of these Stormfront people would consider you as a subhuman creature.

Imagine I'm one of them. I'm looking at you. I'm looking at your face. I can't help responding to you as a human being, but I've got this kind of theoretical classification of you as a subhuman creature. Now, this has a very interesting implication, I think. And the implication of this actually goes back to a literature that began in 1906 and is very well developed now but has not been brought into relation to dehumanization theory at all.

Back in 1906 there was a German psychiatrist who wrote a paper called "On the Psychology of the Uncanny." This word translated as "uncanny" from the German. I don't think it's the best translation of it, at least in these contexts. The word is *unheimlich*, and I prefer to translate this as "creepy." The English "uncanny" can be used in a very neutral or even a laudatory way. "She has an uncanny ability to throw the basketball through the hoop" or something like that. "Uncanny" in German in most contexts is a more negatively toned word.

What was interesting for Jentsch is what is going on when we get creeped out by something. And the conclusion he came to was super interesting. This is my rendition, my philosophically cleaned-up version.

MYISHA: Okay.

DAVID: We experience something as creepy when we can't decide what kind of thing it is. We treat it as belonging to two different, contrary, natural kinds at the same time. If we go back to Jentsch's paper, he gives the example of figures in a wax museum. So they're these real, realistic human figures. You go to Madame Tussauds or something, and say you see a figure of the Forty-Fifth President of the United States, God forbid, but you might have that experience, and it looks just like the guy. But then you look a little closer and it's not moving, it's not breathing, the eyes look kind of dead, the skin just doesn't seem like real skin.

On one hand, you're reacting to it like a human being, that sort of human recognition system is turned on; while, on the other hand, you're thinking, "No, this is just a chunk of inert matter." As long as your mind can't really decisively settle on one or the other and is pulled both ways at once, it elicits a thought, this creepiness feeling, feeling of *unheimlich*.

Now, this kind of links up with a whole other literature and I'll skip the whole story. I'll go right to a philosopher named Noël Carroll, who wrote a wonderful book on the philosophy of horror. And one of the things he asks in this book is, "Well, what's a monster? What's a monster in horror fiction?" And what he suggests is a monster in horror fiction is a being with two properties. One is it's physically dangerous, it's out to get you, it's out to hurt you.

The other property is what he calls "cognitively dangerous," I call "metaphysically dangerous." By that we mean it crosses these boundaries. It transgresses boundaries between natural kinds. So think of a vampire, which is alive and dead at the same time; or a werewolf, which is a wolf and a human being at the same time. This is the very essence of unnaturalness. It doesn't fit into a natural kind. It transgresses.

What happens when we dehumanize people—I'll circle back to where I started—is, on one hand, we can't help responding to them as human beings. On the other hand, we classify them as subhuman. And these two things are going on at the same time. Now, what happens first is that we experience them as highly disturbing and highly threatening, both physically threatening. This is what motivates us to dehumanize in the first place. We see them as bad, dangerous, nasty. But now we consider them as metaphysically threatening, and that metaphysical threat, that crossing the boundaries, kind of amps up the danger that we attribute.

This is why very often we see dehumanized populations as having these sort of superhuman characteristics. If we can go back to my initial example of the dehumanization of African Americans in the late nineteenth century, early twentieth century, particularly African American males, by the way, by whites, they're seen as having various super-human capacities: insensitivity to pain, prodigious sexual appetites, and so on.

This idea of superhumanization, what psychologists call the "superhumanization bias," is a function of the dehumanization process itself. And it's not just that case. If we look at the Nazis' characteristics of Jews—interestingly, both cases illustrate what I described to you earlier, the racialization preceding the dehumanization—Jews were seen as being extremely formidable enemies of everything that was good and right and decent in the world. They had superhuman intellectual powers and it was a life-and-death struggle. This was a tiny percentage of the population, but my God, how dangerous they were seen.

So that's the monster bit. When we dehumanize others, the intention isn't to turn them into monsters. The intention is to just relegate them to a subhuman status. But because we can't shake a recognition of their humanity, we end up turning them into monsters. Then they become much, much more threatening and dangerous than we had ever imagined—dangerous and threatening, of course, in our own imaginations.

MYISHA: I've been thinking about this superhuman aspect and how I believe it's a form of dehumanization. You talk about the superhuman aspect as being threatening. As you were talking, I was thinking about the Officer's report of his encounter with Mike Brown, a black teen who the officer shot and killed in Ferguson, Missouri, in 2014. The officer likened Mike Brown to the Incredible Hulk. On the officer's account, Brown then had this physical ability to not feel pain and to be strong and therefore dangerous.

You also mention Jewish intellectual ability as being perceived as dangerous. But I wonder if we can flip it just a little bit. You have this notion of superhuman as it refers to danger, but I wonder if we can think about superhuman abilities, those that are perceived as virtuous, as a form of dehumanization as well.

I'm thinking of black women being seen as supervirtuous: for they are able to forgive no matter what pain they encounter, no matter what oppression they encounter. They just love everybody and they're going to offer up forgiveness. That's at least the thought. In some way we are celebrated for being able to achieve some type of miracle, to be stronger than what we are. We celebrate that virtue. But in some ways, I'm beginning to look at that celebration as a billboard of superhumanization, which is connected to dehumanization.

Tell me how off I am, how right I am. What do you think about that?

DAVID: My view is you are right on some accounts of dehumanization but not on my account of dehumanization. So it depends on how we use the term. I think what's going on there is a profound failure of empathy. A person who indulges in this sort of attitude that you describe is kind of denying ordinary human sensitivities to the person that they're regarding as—what is it called—"black girl magic" or something like that.

Certainly, my impression is that when white people indulge in this sort of thinking, it's not seen as particularly virtuous. It's basically a way of minimizing the harm that's been done to a person. So you should be able to just forgive and forget, and that's that. And I think actually that sort of attitude is much more widespread. It's much more widespread when people say, "Black people should get over the past," or the most ridiculous one, "Get over slavery" as though the oppression of African Americans ended in 1865. But that's to a great extent a combination of ignorance and wishful thinking. I think that is a really destructive attitude, but I wouldn't include it in the category of dehumanization.

MYISHA: Is it because the person is not seen as dangerous?

DAVID: Well, I don't think that a person who's thought of in that way is thought of as a subhuman creature. Remember, for me that's definitional of dehumanization.

MYISHA: If we have dehumanization, if it's been part of history, if it's taking place now, how do we combat it?

DAVID: Well, that's the question I wish I could answer very definitively. Let's look at it on two fronts. Remember, we've got something to build on here. We have a basic tendency to recognize one another as human beings. That's really hard to turn off. In fact, that produces a lot of the problems because that's what results, like I explained, in us seeing people that we try to dehumanize as monsters.

So how can we dehumanize people? Well, I think there are two sources of that. One is entrenched ideology and the other is propaganda. There are always people who are keen to make one group of people harm another group of people and to portray that other group of people in such a way as to make it easy to harm them.

Let's take that first. We need to be really, really vigilant about the sort of language that's used to characterize vulnerable groups of people. The vulnerability element, by the way, if I can come back to something said earlier—it's one of the paradoxes of when we turn people into monsters, these very formidable, very dangerous beings. That's characteristically the most vulnerable members of a population that are seen as the most outrageously vicious and dangerous members of the population. It's ironic and tragic.

We keep track of that and we take a strong line. Now, the line that you take depends on your views, the politics of speech. It might be counterspeech, it might be suppression of that sort of speech as so-called hate speech. I say "so-called" because I think calling it "hate speech" is actually a misrepresentation of the moral psychology of what's going on, but that would be for another day.

MYISHA: No, no, no. What should you call it?

DAVID: I'm not sure what to call it. I think a little label is probably always going to be misleading. But we can hate good things and love bad things. Think again of the Stormfront people. They love the idea of a superior white race. They love it. You can kind of call it love speech. So love isn't always a good thing, right? Hate isn't always a bad thing. Often it's contempt rather than hate. We need a much more nuanced vocabulary to describe these sorts of things if we're going to understand them.

We need to really be vigilant about the sorts of language that we use, because that kind of language plays on these psychological sensibilities, which allows us to very easily slide into dehumanization. It's not just ignorant people or bad people. It's very, very easy to dehumanize.

That's one side. The other side is ideology. There are long-standing systems of beliefs and practices which set the stage for dehumanization, if not actually uphold dehumanization. We need to pay attention to dismantling this ideology. The two things work in tandem because an ideology can be latent, and then you get some propagandistic rhetoric that just sort of sets it on fire, enflames it.

Those are two political fronts. There's also education. It's education on two fronts, actually, and I'm thinking of the course I teach that you did me the great favor of visiting on Skype, "Race, Racism, and Beyond." One thing you discover teaching this to American students is they don't have a clue about the history of black Americans, who are still horribly dehumanized in this country.

That helps because I think the only way you can understand ideology—you can't do it by engaging in some kind of Cartesian meditation on your own beliefs. The only way you can understand that you're in the grip of an ideology is looking at the history of the beliefs. So that's kind of therapeutic and that's really, really important and it's a kind of education which Americans do not receive. Frankly, most white Americans—and I can't speak for African Americans but most white Americans—do not have a clue, unlike Germans.

My spouse and I were in Berlin earlier in the year and we visited the Sachsenhausen concentration camp, and there are groups of schoolchildren visiting and it was being explained to them. I would like to see American students visiting the sites of these spectacle lynchings I spoke about and have museums set up on these sites to explain to them what was going on in its full horror.

That's one side of education. The other side of education is making it clear to people what their vulnerabilities are. If we're all vulnerable just in virtue of being human beings and have a certain kind of psychology, then we need to know that, because if we don't know that, we can't be vigilant. If you go back with respect to the propaganda, there are always going to be people who are trying to get us to commit violence on others. I mean, that's what elites wishing for power do, and we can't effectively resist that unless we understand something about our vulnerability to it.

19

Linda Martín Alcoff on the Future of Whiteness

MYISHA: You say that whiteness is a historical and social construct rather than a singular idea. What do you mean by this?

LINDA: There's been some really good historical work now on tracing how whiteness emerged in the United States in particular but also in European colonialism. You can trace it to certain legal judgments that had been made to privilege European Americans, for example, settlers, in certain societies to give them economic advantages and political privileges over others.

You can really kind of find the origin of this idea of whiteness in legal judgments and in these histories. But I think sometimes people are making a mistake in concluding from that that those events constituted white identity and are sort of the originary moment and sufficient cause of everything that white identity has ever meant or can ever mean into the unending future.

I think that's a mistake. It's sort of like taking an essentialist position or a certain kind of realist position to whiteness. I think whiteness emerged. It had multiple causes, it was constituted in multiple experiences from people at the top to people who were pretty far down the scale of labor and power, yet there was a unified experience of being settlers, of being immigrants sometimes fleeing persecution, sometimes looking for new opportunities, and also being told that being European was an advantage, a privilege, being part of the vanguard of the human race.

So there's multiple experiences that involve racism and colonial ideologies, about the human race, differences, and who's the vanguard and who's behind. But there's multiple experiences, so I think we have to understated whiteness as a plural rather than a singular, as something that has changed, as something that will continue to change, and as something that is not something we just find but something that we make. And its future will be dependent on what we make of its history and its present configurations.

MYISHA: As a black woman in America, I grew up in a time in which we embraced our blackness. I was taught that it is something that I should be proud of, it's something that I should embrace. I am in no way encouraged to distance myself from blackness. If I did, that would be morally problematic for many in the community that I am a part of. Why do you think whites try to distance themselves from whiteness?

LINDA: Well, it's a whole different ballgame, isn't it? Because the more history you know, the more you find out about unfair privileges, atrocities, genocides, colonial annexation of land, holocausts over and over that were justified on the grounds of white superiority and in which whites, even poor whites, participated in and sometimes gained some economic advantage out of those atrocities.

It's painful and there's a question of responsibility about that. I think it has a lot to do with why in the United States we say, "History doesn't matter, we can just escape our history," because if we look at our history, it raises a number of moral and political questions about the particular distributions of land and goods and resources in existence today—the particular distributions we've got today are based on that old history.

It's obvious people find this uncomfortable, don't know what to do with it, and don't know how to emotionally relate to these histories. Then there's also the sort of worry that whiteness is associated with white bread, mayonnaise, blandness, culturallessness, an amalgamation of rich and thick ethnic identities that just got flattened out through intermarrying in this hemisphere in such a way that it doesn't really mean anything interesting or substantive anymore.

I think the main reason really has to do with the difficult history of whiteness. It has to do with people's desire to escape the implications of being tied or being who they are today and having the benefits that they have today in relation to that history.

MYISHA: So some people may be thinking, "Hey, you guys are talking about blackness, whiteness; all these identities are just problematic whether they're racial, whether they're ethnic, or whether they're gendered. They disunite us as America and we just need to be one."

LINDA: That's such a bizarre view, but I know it's a common view. Difference was not created by philosophers of race. Difference is something we try to understand. Difference has always existed. It was given a certain ranking analysis by colonialism that decided to put people in ranks and value-laden hierarchies. And yes, we should rethink those value-laden hierarchies and ranks by which we organize human difference.

But difference is real. Consider our relationship to, for example, slavery in the United States. It makes quite a difference if you can imagine your ancestors being enslaved or if you worry that your ancestors perhaps were slave owners or slave masters, or if you were a family that were bystanders or came later. That's a different emotional reaction to those histories that will probably generate a different set of actions on your part. Those differences are not something that are theoretical constructs. They are real as a feature of the way in which we interact with our worlds and our histories and with each other and the way in which we live our lives.

I take what I call a "realistic realism" about racial identities, ethnic identities, and gender identities. It's realistic because it understands all identities as historical products that are changeable and changing, and who knows what the future will bring. But it's a realism in the sense of acknowledging that these are not things that we can wish out of existence. These are part of our social realities and our psychological individual realities as well.

MYISHA: Even if someone concedes to the point that our identities do not disunite us, is there a case that identity politics does?

LINDA: I think the truth of the matter is that what has disunited us is a refusal to acknowledge the truth of history and the fact that history still has an impact today. That's what creates disunity between people who just talk past each other and can't understand one another.

I think one of the first ways in which identity politics was first thought about was in the Combahee River Collective, a collective of mostly African American lesbians writing in the 1970s. What they were arguing was that identity has a political relevance. They weren't arguing that identity entails one particular kind of politics or that identity is not complicated, because they were women who had been involved in the anti-racist civil rights movements but had been frustrated by the gender politics and sexual politics; they had been involved in feminist movements but were frustrated by the race politics and the sexual politics. They were fully aware that any identity like race or gender or sexuality or class is complicated and there's multiplicities, contradictions, conflicts, and differences within each of our identities. And yet it's still the case that there are different ways that we react to history and political questions today. People can more readily believe the idea that somebody can be walking down the street doing absolutely nothing and get thrown to the ground by the police for no reason, beat up, and possibly terribly harmed. Some people find that kind of a story incredibly plausible because that's their experience and that's the experience that people they know have had their whole lives. Other people find that really implausible and they need a videotape. They need three videotapes before they believe that actually happens in the United States of America. And that can make a big difference on juries, prosecutor offices, and political campaigns.

Your initial starting knowledge and your assessment of what story is credible or plausible has to do in part with your identity. That's just a fact that I think everybody sort of knows. It's commonsense, but there's a real worry that if you start talking like that and if you start acknowledging that identity can make a difference in what we know and what we can know, that it will lead to some kind of stalemate or rationality where we can no longer talk to each other or hear each other or come to a united agenda.

That's just not true. We can come to a united agenda. The way to do that is precisely by understanding that we are differentially situated vis-à-vis these kinds of social experiences. And those of us who don't have that kind of experience need to listen carefully and learn from those who do. It goes in every direction, but identity often has epistemological implications that have political implications, and that's just a real fact of social life.

MYISHA: You talk about two forms of what you call "white exceptionalism" in your book. What are they and why are they problematic?

LINDA: You were talking about black pride earlier. Think about the movement that emerged in the '70s of black power. When you try to apply that to whiteness, it doesn't quite work. When we try to think about a future multiracial, multiethnic society in which we can have a rainbow and everybody is acknowledged and has their place without ranking and rating, whiteness really stands out as difficult to be included. I mean, when you think about the category of white pride, it's a little worrisome sounding.

It is very different from black pride. So white exceptionalism has been a tradition. There's both a racist form of white exceptionalism and an anti-racist form. The racist form of white exceptionalism is just the racist idea that whites are better than others and they can't mix with others—this was the reason for the laws against miscegenation. If whites mix with others, they would be degraded and go down. There was the idea that whiteness had to remain pure. Other groups could mix; didn't matter. But whites couldn't mix. So a lot of the laws in the United States were around protecting the borders around whiteness.

But there's also a kind of anti-racist exceptionalism about whiteness that also sees whiteness as unable to change, unable to mix, constituted by racism forever. And I think that anti-racist form of white exceptionalism is actually also mistaken both empirically and metaphysically. It's mistaken empirically because there are a lot of things that went into the development of white identity. Racism was an incredibly important central feature of it, but there were others. There was the experience of European immigration, experience of ethnic amalgamation, and so forth.

I think it's also wrong metaphysically to think that one originary moment like the US Constitution could constitute a form of social identity forever into the future. So I think white exceptionalism is based on some mistaken claims. Even though I would agree that whiteness is different from other identities, it poses more challenges to creating a multiracial, pluralist future in which we can live without rankings and live without racial vanguardism. But I don't think whiteness is forever constituted by some originary racist moment and can never change.

MYISHA: The argument that you're criticizing, I've heard so many times. The idea in some ways is something that I've never really been conscious of. But thinking that just because someone is white, their fate is to have this exceptionalism, is to have the kinds of beliefs that you are referring to.

But I wonder, and maybe we can address this a little later, what do you think needs to change that will get rid of this white exceptionalism? Because I think the doubt or the lack of optimism seems to be that it's so entrenched. And I know if anything is a social construction, it can come in and it can leave as well. But I wonder since white exceptionalism is so entrenched in our society, historically and presently, that it is considered naïve to ever think that white exceptionalism will ever go away?

LINDA: I think we have to avoid naiveté, but we also have to avoid fatalism. That's what I was trying to do in *The Future of Whiteness*. I am trying to construct an account that would be neither naïve nor fatalistic. I mean, some people are naïve and think that as the United States becomes majority minority and whites become a minority after 2042, that racism will wither away. As Marx once said, "The state would wither away on its own without any kind of social activism or movement."

I think that's totally naïve. There are plenty of countries that are white-minority in Latin America, where I'm from; also today in South Africa in which there is retained an inordinate amount of white or light-skinned political and economic power. So minority status is not going to be a guarantee of a reduction of racism.

But I don't think fatalism is warranted either. I mean, history always surprises us. There's no way that we can predict exactly how things are going to play out in the future. And the truth is there are multiple causes of whiteness and multiple things going on. There's a lot less belief among younger whites today—it's not gone, but it's less than it used to be according to any opinion survey you consult—a lot less belief in the old ideas of white vanguardism. The United States and Europe are not less violent than any other parts of the world, they're not less unjust, they're not more rational than other parts of the world. They're causing the possibility of a global devastation. It's not just a possibility, it's already happening, of course. So the idea that white people are the vanguard of the human race I think is no longer plausible to a lot of people.

I think the question is how to move from that to a better political society which will redress the injustice of the past and formulate the possibility of new kinds of social relations across group differences.

MYISHA: W. E. B. Du Bois is famous for coining the phrase "double consciousness" in relationship to blacks. You introduce the notion of "white double consciousness." What is that?

LINDA: It was definitely inspired by Du Bois, but I think white double consciousness is in some ways very different from the kind of black double consciousness he was talking about. I mean, on one level double consciousness is just seeing oneself through two different perspectives: as he talked about African Americans seeing themselves, always knowing how white racists would see and interpret their actions or their dress, and so forth on the one hand, but also knowing—having access to another perspective, their own community perspective that provided some positive alternative and some way to deflect the white racist interpretations. You had a kind of internal perspective that was more reliable and an external perspective that you always had to negotiate and deal with.

For whites it's kind of the reverse, because the internal perspective is the one that's not very reliable, and it's the external perspective that has actually helped to change and improve people's understanding of how they are in the world and who they are in the world. So today our public sphere is way more variegated than it was when I was growing up in the south in the '60s. You have to do a lot of work today to engage in any kind of media and not come across nonwhite perspectives on drone warfare or gun violence or the crisis in public schools or racism in the prisons. Something happens and there's going to be voices and perspectives in the public domain that are going to give different points of view about whatever the current event is.

Whites have access today to nonwhite points of view much greater than they have in the past. And this gives them, I think, a kind of double consciousness, realizing that the white point of view is not the only game in town, maybe not the most plausible analysis on some topics. And I think whites are more hesitant to make certain kinds of jokes and certain kinds of comments. They're a little self-conscious now about saying certain kinds of things, at least in some scenarios depending on who they are talking to, because they're aware that what they're saying might be construed differently.

That awareness is actually, I think, a potential for development and movement in a positive way. Unlike for African Americans, it's coming externally to whites from outside. But it can be a source of reflection and thoughtfulness and give people a motivation to try to understand why is this seen in this way and why my point of view is not the only one. I don't think it's a panacea. I don't think that we should be naïve that this will always lead to enlightenment, but it is leading to reflection and enlightenment in many cases.

MYISHA: I'm going to ask for you to put on your prophet hat here. What do you think will happen when whites become a minority in the United States? How do you think this will affect the future of whiteness?

LINDA: I think some will adjust. I mean, most of our cities today—the city you're in, the city I'm in right at this moment—are majority minority. They're minority white cities—Los Angeles, Chicago, Philadelphia, Washington, D.C., Miami, Atlanta, New York—I mean, on and on. Four states are minority white, and of course, this is a growing number.

So you can already see some of the ways in which people are responding. Some people adjust and embrace the new pluralism and find it an interesting place to live and one that connects you to the rest of the world outside of the United States, and some people will adjust. But there are others, of course, who will try to circle the wagons and create a white space, a gated community or a gated apartment building in effect. People are moving. They're actually from Florida but move to North Carolina, Kansas, Idaho, or to Wyoming to try to seek out a place in which they can rely on the schools their children go to, their workplaces, neighborhoods, and town council meetings being white dominant or white only even. But that's getting harder to do.

I think the strategy of trying to maintain a white-only workplace, neighborhood, and school system is going to shrink, but some people will continue to try to do that. There's always been a class difference. Poor whites don't have the option of opting out of public school and sending their kids to some private school that's white majority, whereas the upper class does have that option.

If people opt for trying to live in the spaces in which they find themselves and live as members of groups that cannot claim the right to culturally and politically dominate the space anymore, then I think people will have to develop some new skills of communication, coalition and alliance, understand the role of identity and difference in our political and social cultures.

20

Chike Jeffers on Black Thought

MYISHA: What is Africana philosophy? Is it all about race?

CHIKE: I would say that Africana philosophy is philosophy as it arises within the black world. So here we're thinking Africa, particularly Sub-Saharan Africa and the diaspora. Even as I say "Sub-Saharan" I shouldn't even limit it that way because one of the things that I have worked on is ancient Egyptian thought.

So in a way, I think that Africana philosophy is maybe among the oldest philosophical traditions, not under that name; for the term "Africana philosophy" only really comes into common usage in the 1990s. Lucius Outlaw was a major figure promoting the use of that term. Lewis Gordon took it up and started promoting the use of it. I take it to be that which is philosophy that emerges from the black world and which is distinctively related to it.

As far as the question of whether it's all about race, I would say that a lot of Africana philosophy, especially that which emerges from the diaspora, is centrally about race. But I don't think it is all about race. The fact that I, for example, would include ancient Egyptian thought (which some would argue can't be about race given the fact that many believe that race is something of the modern world rather than something of the ancient world) is evidence that I do not think it's all about race.

When I say that it's distinctively related to Africa and the African diaspora, what I mean is that I could choose to contribute to contemporary debates in "epistemology" or "philosophy of mind" as they tend to go in the Western world. If I'm doing that, I don't think the mere fact that I am of African descent makes it Africana philosophy. I think it makes more sense or is certainly more informative to say that, yeah, it's Western philosophy.

It seems to me, then, that Africana philosophy is philosophy produced by people of African descent that is somehow distinctively related to their experiences, cultures, situations, et cetera. In the modern world that does mean that race becomes a very central topic. But if you have a situation where people of African descent are working on a topic even today and it's not a topic that is specifically about race, but for whatever reason maybe they all went to this particular grad school in Africa and so there's a kind of like trend in, let's say, philosophy of mind or epistemology but that's kind of distinctively coming out of the African world somehow, at that point I'm willing to call it Africana philosophy.

MYISHA: Let's talk about Africa for a little bit. You edited a volume entitled *Listening to Ourselves*. Can you explain that work to us, and why did you decide to put the collection together?

CHIKE: It was something that I worked on actually throughout my time in grad school. And the subtitle to *Listening to Ourselves* is *A Multilingual Anthology of African Philosophy*. It's a collection of essays, new essays by African philosophers written in indigenous African languages. The book is then in a dual-language format where there are English translations of the essays on the facing pages of the book.

I was responding to debates, themes that have been talked about a lot in African philosophy and then within African thought more generally. So Ngugi Wa Thiong'o, for example, is a Kenyan writer who's very famous for having promoted the use of indigenous African languages for writing. He has especially used his own language, Gikuyu, for his creative writing.

African philosophers have been talking about whether African philosophy, to be truly African, needed to incorporate more usage of indigenous African languages. Without trying to suggest that, I wanted to get that started as one among the things that it was normal for African philosophers to do.

There's a variety of topics addressed in the book: truth, time, gender, morality, proverbs and their relationship to language and naming practices, and the relationship between language and thought.

I'm pretty proud of it. I think if you happen to come across it in a bookstore, even just flipping through it, I think, it is kind of an interesting visual experience, seeing these African languages being used for philosophy by professional philosophers.

MYISHA: To get more specific about African philosophical work, tell me about the "Tale of the Peasant." Why do you think it's important to political philosophy?

CHIKE: The tale of "The Eloquent Peasant" is an ancient Egyptian work. That title would be given to it by modern scholars and wouldn't have borne that necessarily by the author.

It's an interesting story to begin with. It's a story involving a peasant who is going to the capital to do some trading and he ends up being robbed by the greedy nobleman of all his belongings. So the peasant goes to a steward of the king to complain. When the steward reports the speech of the peasant to the king, the king says to the steward, "Well, don't give him an answer, keep him talking, surreptitiously send food to his family so his family doesn't starve and make sure he doesn't starve."

But they keep him talking basically because he was so eloquent. He makes a total of nine speeches over the course of the work, and then he's ready to give up at the end and potentially commit suicide. It's then revealed that they actually had been writing down his speeches the whole time. The steward has them read to the king. The king is pleased and tells the steward to go ahead and make a judgment. All of the greedy nobleman's belongings are actually awarded to the peasant.

It's interesting, first of all, in terms of the structure of the story because there's this weird way in which you empathize with the peasant's frustration, as he is continuously seeking justice but not getting it. There's the irony that you know that it is his very eloquence in pleading for justice that is the reason why this is a prolonged experience. It's why he's not being given justice. So there's an interesting structure.

The bulk of the work is the nine petitions or speeches of the peasant. I think of it as a really important work of political philosophy because through what the peasant says in the petition, we are given a certain picture of the role, function, and value of political authority.

That's the basic reason why I think it's a fascinating work. I'm happy to have published on it and that piece has gotten a nice amount of attention. I think that that's pretty important because of the fact that ancient Egyptian thought has been generally ignored by philosophers. I think that it's time for that to change, and I was glad to use this really, really fascinating work to help change that.

MYISHA: Prior to having this discussion with you, I've been thinking a lot about the Western canon: what we include in it and what we exclude. I wonder if the Western canon excludes work like this because philosophers in the West are obsessed with rigor. And I wonder if we have neglected a lot of work not only from the African world but also the Eastern world because of this perception. Why do you think certain kinds of work from other parts of the world have not been included in the Western philosophical canon?

CHIKE: I think that, historically, it does have to do with white supremacy; that is, with a belief in the superiority of Europe such that whatever can be learned about other parts of the world does not rise to the level of philosophical superiority of Europe. I think that's an important part of the story of how it came to be that in the Western world. There are so many who learn so little about philosophy that comes from elsewhere. Very few languages have as much translated into them as, say, English does. And I think that racism has to be part of that story as to why so many learn so little.

In terms of the idea of rigor, I think that it's important how bias ends up shaping notions of rigor such that people will take the time to read, say, the Pre-Socratics but not read works from ancient Indian and ancient Chinese philosophy. You may be attracted to Plato's dialogues as a model of philosophy, but there's a lot that's considered philosophy in the ancient world that is not written in that style. There's this diversity of style in ancient Western philosophy even between Plato and Aristotle. So there's not really a good reason why someone wouldn't be able to engage with other stuff.

In both ancient and in subsequent periods of Western philosophy you, of course, also have the entwining of philosophy and religion. Yet sometimes people mistake texts from other traditions as just purely religious without seeing them as philosophical in the ways that they might read an Aquinas. I think it's more bias than the fact that the texts are not measuring up.

MYISHA: Du Bois seems to be a main figure in Africana philosophy. Tell me more about him. Why do some claim him as a philosopher? What other contributions has Du Bois made to Africana thought?

CHIKE: The sociologists claim him with great justification. He is a pioneer in sociology and he was also an accomplished historian, journalist, and groundbreaking social activist. He was many things. When we claim him as a philosopher, what we're doing is pointing to the fact that he was also a philosophical thinker; that is, someone who raised and sought to answer fundamental questions about justice, about ethics, about culture. I think it's hard to read significant amounts of Du Bois and not recognize him as someone who thought philosophically and gave interesting answers to philosophical questions.

The contributions he made to Africana thought are many. Some of what he's most known for today would be the notion of double consciousness, the idea of the Talented Tenth, and his dispute with Booker T. Washington. All of these, I think, he talks about in *The Souls of Black Folk*, his most famous book. But there's a lot more to learn and know about him.

MYISHA: Explain Du Bois's notion of double consciousness.

CHIKE: First of all, I would say that double consciousness is an interestingly evocative phrase and that its popularity has a lot to do with that. I don't want to suggest that I don't think that Du Bois made an interesting philosophical move when he kind of developed this idea, but he developed it under that name really only in one work. And so I do think that part of its great power in terms of the fact that lots of people cite and talk about it has to do with the fact that it ends up being flexible in various ways, and you can see this if you look at different interpretations. Even the language that he's using when he's explaining it is flexible to the point that a lot of people are able to read into it what they would like to read into it.

My own particular reading would be that double consciousness is a matter of being black in a majority-white society and being, as a result of that, very conscious of how black people look from the outside. When explaining it with students, I often give the example that watching the news sometimes, if there's reports of, say, a violent crime, a shooting or a stabbing or a robbery or something of that sort, it is often the case that a black person watching the news will begin to hope that it wasn't a black person who did it.

This is something that is extremely common and it's, of course, interesting to talk about this with students, because we talk about the fact that this is not very common for white people. They don't hear about violent crimes or crimes of any particular kind and start wishing and praying that's not a white guy despite the fact that they clearly perpetrate the majority of crimes, as they are the majority of the people in society.

The reason for that has to do with a kind of sense that people are getting more reason through watching the news, to view black people as violent, as criminals, et cetera. And this has an impact on your life. More people buying into that stereotype may affect your life chances in particular ways. That's the reason that you are extra conscious of that outside view: that nonblack view upon black people. I think that's what is central to double consciousness.

But in the passage where he talks about double consciousness, he also uses this term "twoness." Twoness is beyond just the kind of thinking about how you look from the outside part of the situation. He's also talking there about what we tend to call today "hybridity." I often then talk about the term "African American," which wasn't in common usage at the time that Du Bois wrote *Souls*. Nevertheless, it is very useful for looking at what he's saying about how there's a divide, a twoness that the American Negro is trying to reconcile. What he goes on to say is that he wouldn't want to give up the "American" part, he wouldn't want to try and bleach away the "African" part. He wants this to somehow fit into a whole.

So it's the idea that: How can you be both—African and American? How can you both be an American and a Negro? This shouldn't actually be something that is hard to fit together because African Americans are among the oldest portions of the American population, but he's talking about the fact that it can feel that way, it can feel as if somehow these don't go together.

Those are the two dimensions that it would probably be most important to highlight when thinking about double consciousness: the sense of looking at oneself from the outside; and the sense in which one's identity is made tense by the fact that one can't ignore being different, but on the other hand one can't ignore being American as well. He's trying to push towards the idea that this could one day fit together as a comfortable whole.

MYISHA: Explain Du Bois's dispute with Booker T. Washington. Who do you side with? What do you think we can learn from it today?

CHIKE: I guess it's maybe not a surprise given that I write and think about Du Bois a lot that I side with him. But I think what's most important in terms of understanding Washington is gaining historical perspective.

Washington was what is called an "accommodationist." Washington was active at a time in the US right after Reconstruction, a period where there was much black political participation. But it had been squashed through various means by the southern state. At this time there was also other aspects of segregation such as separate facilities and things of that sort.

Washington was called an accommodationist because his reaction to that is to say, "Well, don't push for political power at this time, don't push for full civil rights in terms of being able to use the facilities you want. Concentrate on learning practical skills—stuff like agriculture, trades like carpentry and so on. Learn this practical stuff and build up your economic base. And if you build your economic base, you will eventually get to a point at which this capitalist country, that is America, will simply have to recognize your power as an economic force. The other stuff will come; the equal rights in the political sphere, in the social sphere so to speak—that will come later." I think that it's useful to help people understand the ways in which Washington was saying things that made sense in important ways in that context. Given the fall in terms of power from the end of Reconstruction, there's a lot of practicality to his view that is worth understanding.

Now, Du Bois, representing the alternative view, believes that you cannot wait for your rights to come later. You have to press now for full political and civil rights and he also pushed back against the emphasis on so-called practical or industrial education and championed a higher education. He does not say that everybody would be suited for higher education but that there should be black colleges that provide that.

Chapter 3 of *Souls* where Du Bois makes this argument is a fascinating piece of political philosophy. It's one of those moments where it's hard to see how someone could deny that Du Bois is a philosopher. Because part of what he does is make what we call internal critiques of Washington's view, where you kind of accept certain basic premises of your opponent and show how on the basis of those very premises, their conclusion fails. For example, Du Bois argued that Washington is misunderstanding how politics and economics work because the idea of building up your economic base while lacking political rights means that you lack the ability to protect your economic power from political attack. If you don't have a say in the political system, then it's possible for laws to be passed, for example, that will make it hard for you to build up your economic power.

He also made the point that what Washington was encouraging was this sense of self-reliance, confidence in black people's ability to do for themselves. Du Bois argues that the various ways in which segregation made clear that black people were inferior and the kind of acceptance of inferiority that goes along with just accepting, for example, that you have to use this different water fountain, undermines the self-confidence needed for the kind of self-reliance that Washington was arguing for.

He also makes an internal criticism of Washington on the issue of higher education by basically saying that even a place like Tuskegee, the institution that Washington was the head of, runs on the fact that you have people who've gone to higher education and thus teach there. So at each turn, he's arguing that Washington's own premises show the failure of his conclusions.

MYISHA: We've spent some time now talking about *Souls of Black Folks*, which I think is Du Bois's most popular work. Let's talk about some work that is not so popular. Tell me about *The Conservation of Races*.

CHIKE: *The Conservation of Races* is, you might say, less popular in the sense that many people in many disciplines who know a lot about Du Bois may not think of that as particularly important. Interestingly, in philosophy it is the most important work by Du Bois. It is arguably, significantly more important even than *Souls* because philosophy of race itself as a kind of subfield is greatly shaped by the work of Kwame Anthony Appiah. And Appiah in the 1980s wrote about *The Conservation of Races* and inspired many people to also write about it. I myself have joined that tradition and published something in the journal *Ethics* in 2013 that was focused on *The Conservation of Races*.

It's interesting that in a way it's kind of the most popular work from a philosophical point of view despite not being his most popular work overall. Why it's so important to philosophers is because of the fact that it's partly about the question of: What are races in the first place? It's asking that big metaphysical question: What is a race? And then the other thing that ends up making it interesting is that Du Bois is clearly trying to go against the grain of the kind of biological essentialism common in the nineteenth century. He's arguing that races are, first and foremost, social and historical groups.

Now, Appiah in his first work on *Conservation* critically examines the extent to which Du Bois has successfully managed to develop a sociohistorical concept of race. Appiah argues that Du Bois fails, that he ends up falling back upon biological essentialism. Others have disagreed and argued that he does develop a useful sociohistorical concept of race in that piece. These are the kinds of debates that *The Conservation of Races* has produced.

MYISHA: Let's talk about some obscure work of Du Bois. Why is *Whither* significant for you?

CHIKE: *Whither Now and Why* is a piece that he wrote very late in life. One of the impressive things about Du Bois is that he lived to be ninety-five and was productive for most of his life.

MYISHA: I want to be just like him.

CHIKE: There's a good seventy-five years or so during which he was like a fascinating thinker. *Whither Now and Why* comes from 1960. He was giving a lecture to, I want to say, social studies teachers, black social studies teachers at a conference at a black college.

I take *Whither Now and Why* to be a kind of interesting sixty-three-year sequel to *The Conservation of Races*. What's interesting about the way that *Whither* starts out is Du Bois acknowledging how legal equality is coming even faster than he expected. This is after *Brown vs. Board of Education*. King has been very active at this point and Du Bois is foreseeing what would come within a few years. By 1964 you have the Civil Rights Act. By 1965 you have the Voting Rights Act. He's foreseeing the coming of legal equality. He's arguing that this does not somehow put to rest the questions of what it means to be African American and it doesn't mean that now everything is going to be okay.

Part of what he is arguing for is to preserve the cultural distinctiveness of African Americans and preserve their sense of being tied to the rest of the black world. There's a cultural nationalism and a Pan-Africanism that he's arguing for there, which he had already been arguing in *The Conservation of Races*.

In both pieces he's suggesting that we need to press for full political, economic, social equality. But part of what black people also need to be doing is understanding that they do not just bring to the table another set of humans. They bring a distinctive experience and a distinctive cultural background to the table. There is tragedy if that is lost.

That's an interesting, you might say, tension but a productive tension that I see as kind of a major thing running through Du Bois's work: the idea that we need to be integrated basically on a political and economic plane; in certain important ways on the cultural plane as well. But it's important to him that gaining equality, which is to say making race less of a dividing thing from the sense of who has which opportunities, need not mean losing diversity. He thinks that race, when understood as cultural diversity, is actually a really important and productive thing, a positive thing, a thing to value rather than something that we should be seeking to transcend.

21

Lawrence Blum on Teaching Race

MYISHA: You've written a lot about race and you've taught college students for decades. But you did something very interesting that a lot of college professors have not done. You have taught race to high schoolers. That is the experience that sparked the book *High Schools, Race, and America's Future*. How did you end up teaching a high school course on race?

LAWRENCE: I have three kids and they went to the public schools in Cambridge, Massachusetts, which especially at that time, though still true, is a very racially diverse city. The public high school population is more diverse than the city is in a sense, and especially it's more diverse than the Harvard community, you might say. I got involved as a parent activist on racial issues at the elementary school. I teamed up with two other black parents, and we ran a little group. We called it the "race and class committee." We would have people come and talk about concerns they had, either teachers or parents, and we talked about racial or culturally related issues at the school.

That just kind of drew me into a concern with race. It started bleeding into my professional thinking. And I just drifted into work on race, and now that's the main thing I do. But at the same time, I also started teaching in the education program at UMass, Boston. I taught a course on anti-racist education. I was teaching preservice teachers, people who weren't yet teachers. And I was feeling a sense of dissonance that I had never experienced a classroom below the college level, and yet I'm teaching these people to go into those kinds of classrooms.

I wasn't sure what to do about it. But one day just by chance I was talking to one of the history teachers at the high school. This teacher had been a teacher of one of my kids, and I asked her about the extremely diverse high school that's minority white and has every multiracial group there. At the time there were seventy different home languages. Cambridge is also an immigrant-receiving city, so that's part of the ethnic diversity as well.

I asked the teacher whether she thought that the diversity among the students was being made use of in a good way by the school and by the different courses in the school. And she thought about it for a minute and she thought, "Well, we could be doing a better job." So I said, "Well, I would be interested in running an after-school program in which kids from different racial groups talked about race." I have no idea why I thought I was qualified to do something like that. I just was moved in the moment. And she said, "Well, let me talk to the head of social studies and get back to you about that." So the next day the head of social studies calls me and she says, "Your idea is good, except we can't have an after-school program like that because students have too many different things to do after school. What you'd have to do is give a whole course at the high school."

MYISHA: How long was the course?

LAWRENCE: At the particular time—the school has changed the way it's organized—but at the time they were semester-long courses. I had no training as a high school teacher. I had no idea why I agreed to do it. She almost left me no option. She kind of said, "Well, you wanted to do this after-school thing, but the only way to do it is to give this whole course, so you're going to give the whole course." That's sort of the way I remember it.

After teaching it that one time, I also taught it with a black graduate student of mine who was in my education class at the time. The school wanted me to pair up with a teaching assistant of color, I wanted to do it and they wanted me to do it, so that worked very well.

I didn't know what I was doing the first time out, but then they asked me back three more times in three successive years to do the course. So I taught it four different times. And of course, over the years I got better at it. I felt like the last time I did it was the first time I really knew what I was doing. But it was a really, really fascinating experience to teach it. I was very happy each time they reinvited me to come back. I never experienced anything like dealing with high school students. They're really different from college students in a lot of ways.

The students were from a lot of different racial groups. The school and the guidance counselors helped me shape the class so that it had a certain demographic that basically mirrored the demographic of the larger school. So, for example, Cambridge has a lot of Haitian students. The Boston area is kind of a Haitian-receiving area. And there were a fair number of Haitian students as well as other Afro-Caribbean Anglophone students as well as the Haitian students. And the Latino students were also always from very different national backgrounds. So there were a lot of both ethnic and racial diversity as well as the economic diversity that the public school system in Cambridge serves. It's less true now fifteen years later because the city has gotten much more gentrified than it was then, but as I say, it was extremely diverse and that was part of what was fascinating about teaching.

MYISHA: In the book you lay out some of the lessons that you went through with the students, and you also lay out some things that you learned from the students. On the first day of class, you had students introduce themselves and also tell a racial or ethnic stereotype that they object to. Why do this on the first day?

LAWRENCE: It was a little bit artificial, I have to admit. But the idea was I wanted something that every student would be able to contribute to. From the first day, I wanted to establish the idea that this is a class that everybody is expected to participate in because it's such a charged terrain talking about race. I thought it was really important to establish the idea that nobody was going to be able to sit back and let the other kids kind of take the lead, that everybody was going to have to do it. And everyone has a stereotype of their group that they object to. So I just thought it would be something that would be a way of getting that kind of buy-in from the students.

I wasn't sure about this, but I thought that the stereotypes that they came up with would then be useful later as reference points to come back to. I wasn't going to critique each stereotype when it came up the first day because that would inhibit a little bit. It was also just really an icebreaker in a certain way. I just wanted them to hear each other out. I wanted everybody to speak.

MYISHA: Was it a stereotype of their own group?

LAWRENCE: It had to be a stereotype of their group, but they could think of their group in any way they wanted to. I had one girl who had a black parent and a white parent, and then she had an anti-white stereotype that she picked and I didn't say, "Oh, well, why did you do that?" I just let her pick that. The fact that she presented a white stereotype, I just filed that away if that would come in handy later. It was kind of an indirect way of that girl's coming out as mixed in the class.

MYISHA: You have a lesson on moral symmetry and race where you talk about whether it's equally wrong, for example, for black students to exclude a white student because of his race. What is your view and did it differ from your students? If so, how?

LAWRENCE: Well, I think of it more as sort of a framework issue that there are both symmetries and asymmetries in thinking about race. The stereotype exercise is an example. Every kid had some stereotype that was objectionable about his or her group. So you could say that's a symmetry; it's something that everybody shares.

On the other hand, each of those stereotypes carried very different social meanings. There was one girl who was African and she said, "Africans are seen as spearchuckers" or something like that. It was a very degrading stereotype, whereas a white student said, "Yes, white kids are all thought of as preppy." Well, okay, that's something that there's reason to object to, but clearly, it doesn't carry the stigma that the African girl's stereotype carries. That's an asymmetry.

I sort of feel like the whole issue of symmetry and asymmetry comes up in a lot of different settings, and it came up in different settings in the class. One of the places that I discuss in the book where it came in was around a reading that we had done from the black abolitionist writer David Walker. He wrote a really important and quite fascinating book in 1830 and we read some portions of that book. Walker is criticizing Thomas Jefferson, who had died just a few years before, for Jefferson, as many people know anyway, had written these very demeaning things about black people in a book that he wrote in 1787. Walker has this kind of outraged response to Jefferson, but it's also very argumentatively structured. So it's just a fascinating text.

Walker takes Jefferson saying that black people's skin color is unfortunate, and then he just tears that to shreds. I had the students read that aspect and then I asked them what they thought about Walker when he says, "Every person has the skin color that God wanted them to have." So that's a very complicated idea; not all students believe in God or not all of them would agree with that view exactly, but I wanted them to engage with Walker and kind of say, "He's saying that black people should be able to have pride in their skin color rather than shame in their skin color as Jefferson was implying." But then I asked them, "Do you think he's also implying that white people should be able to take pride in their skin color? Because after all, God gave it to them also."

That just prompted this fascinating conversation where the students implicitly recognized the asymmetry in the sense that they recognized that expressing pride in a white skin color has a completely different social meaning than 'expressing pride in being black. They were struggling to figure out how to articulate that difference. Some of them would say, "Well, it should be the same, but if a white kid said, 'I'm proud of being white,' I would be upset about that, I would object to it." But they weren't quite sure why.

It was a fascinating conversation that I sort of recount in the book in which, ultimately, they got to a sense that there are these different meanings attached to skin color and pride in skin color depending on your group and that those differences are a product of history.

MYISHA: What are the different ways that you discussed slavery in the course, and how did students respond to that?

LAWRENCE: The slavery aspect of the course was a very important and central issue in the course. I connected slavery to the course's framework, which was understanding the historical development of the idea of race itself. So I was trying to get them to understand what's now the consensus view that the idea of race, as we understand it in the West, is not something that was always there. It was a product of slavery and colonialism as well as certain scientific ideas that interacted with slavery and colonialism and rationalizations from those oppressive systems. I was very eager for them to recognize race as this historically constructed idea. A very small number of them had been exposed to this before, but none of them had studied it in the depth we did.

Changes in the character of slavery were also connected to changes in the development of the idea of race. The history of slavery was being looked at in part because it was important in its own right and in part because it connected to the understanding of the idea of race. In the class, the study of slavery was quite serious. We read some slave narratives that were very painful and difficult and sometimes hard to discuss, but many of them, while they had often been exposed to slavery in other courses that they had taken, basically had a kind of frozen image of slavery as the plantation system.

They hadn't understood the changes in how slavery wasn't always like that. Sometimes slavery had more of a kind of personal servant dimension and there were differences in different parts of the south, and then of course, there was slavery in the north for a long period, and then that had a different character than the plantation form. So even understanding the differences, the regional and historical differences, was something students hadn't been exposed to before.

Now, of course, studying slavery on the one hand is this thing in the past. The fact that it had happened a long time ago, I think, sometimes made it easier for them to engage with it without having to bring it into the present. But on the other hand, I wanted them to bring it into the present and they were sometimes inclined to do that. It's sort of like "Think about, well, what does slavery mean for us now?"

I had an exercise in which I asked them to write down what the experience of studying slavery had meant to them and they came up with different kinds of things. Some of the black students said, "Well, when I read about slavery, I realize that my own problems are not as serious as I sometimes think they are as a teenager." Sometimes they would say, "I feel pride in my ancestors because they struggled against this terrible system." And some of the black students would say, "I'm really glad that I live now and not then."

There was a real range of different views. One of the things that some people worry about in teaching slavery in mixed groups is that the black students will come down on the white students and be resentful and the white students will just go into either guilt or resentment. I can't say that never happens, but it didn't happen very much in my class. I think it's partly because I worked very hard to create a space in that class where it was like a joint project that all of them were engaged in to learn this history of slavery. And it was intellectually challenging. It was difficult. It was college-level material. So the intellectual challenge, I think, in a way helped to mute a pure sort of way of teaching slavery in which you emphasize that white people oppressed black people.

Some students did sometimes say that it made them feel resentful of white people, but it was usually of white people who put down the study of slavery. It wasn't really white people as the people who are the current instantiations of the group of people back in the 1830s so much as it was people who now had a view of slavery that was objectionable. I think this is a perfectly reasonable and healthy response.

MYISHA: You mention in the book that you were discouraged from having a class on the n-word. Why was a parent worried about this, and what did you learn about your students after an unplanned discussion of the topic came up?

LAWRENCE: I talked to an African American parent at a meeting that the school held to have parents have more input into the curriculum. So I thought it was a really good thing that the school did.

In a previous year, I had taught a unit on the n-word and I had a kind of pro and con setup for that particular unit, and I was planning to do it again. This meeting with the parents was right before the next year's class. The African American parent said, "It's fine for you to teach that at the college level where students are mature enough to see this as an issue that they can discuss kind of dispassionately and look at both sides." But she felt at the high school level, it should be a disciplinary issue. That is, "We should just say, 'You cannot use this word in high school' and the teachers should have a disciplinary way of dealing with it."

I was very caught up short by this parent, but she was an extremely thoughtful person and so I really took seriously what she said. I just decided to play it safe and take that unit out. I thought, "Maybe this parent is right. She probably knows more than I do about this, so I'm going to do what she says." I always felt ambivalent about going down that path, but that's where I went.

But the thing is, you can't control a high school class like that. And one time the issue came up in class. I can't remember exactly how, but I talk about it in the book. When it came up I thought, "Oh yes, someone said that I should just crack down on this and say that you can't use that word," but I couldn't figure out how to do it. I just couldn't do it. I just sort of thought, "Okay, I'm just not up to this challenge. I didn't think through how I would do the thing she said. I just thought in my mind, 'I'll do it.'" But then when it came to it, I couldn't do it. So I guided the conversation. I actually think it was quite productive.

Students have a sense that it matters who's using the word, and there are symmetries about who gets to use it and who doesn't. But they haven't generally been in contexts where they've been invited to think through why. They don't talk about that in their courses. This is actually one of the reasons that I thought it was good for them to have this conversation.

There was a wide range of views among the black students. No one thought that it was a perfectly fine word, but they differed as to whether they actually thought it was wrong if a black student used it. Some black students did think it was wrong and thought that basically it's just a word that nobody should ever use. But some of them thought, "Well, I'm not that comfortable with it, but my friends use it and it's okay for them to use it. But it's not okay, especially for a white person, to use it."

I made them articulate why it mattered whether—what group you're in affects your permission to use a racial slur. That's a general moral point about asymmetrical uses of racial slurs. But it applies especially to the use of the n-word, which is more charged than almost any other racial slur.

It was very interesting and the dynamics of the classroom were very interesting, because in the beginning only black students spoke, which is very unusual. And I think it's because all the nonblack students thought, "I'm not getting into this, I'm sitting this one out." But then over time, though, the conversation developed in such a way that there seemed to be an opening for nonblack students. So one of them would venture in and their venturing in made it easier for some other student to venture in. And at some point, basically, every student felt like they could chime in on that conversation.

22

Tommie Shelby on Dark Ghettos

MYISHA: What is the ghetto and what makes "dark ghettos" different from other sites of poverty?

TOMMIE: People define ghettos in different ways. For me, dark ghettos are predominantly black metropolitan neighborhoods with a high concentration of seriously disadvantaged people. I say "metropolitan" here rather than "inner city" since not all ghettos are in the inner city. Some are on a suburban ring of a broader commuting region, and that's been going on for some time.

The word "ghetto" is used to refer to disadvantaged, black, urban neighborhoods. It's been used that way for a long time. It kind of came into use among black intellectuals and scholars around the 1940s. I think the idea was to suggest that the treatment of urban blacks who had recently migrated from the South to various urban centers was very similar to the treatment that Jews received from the Nazis. So the ghetto is a site where race and socioeconomic disadvantage and metropolitan space come together to form a distinctive form of black subjugation. Horace Cayton and St. Clair Drake in their famous book, *Black Metropolis*—published in 1945—have a chapter called "The Black Ghetto." They were trying to draw those connections and thinking about, "Here are these blacks moving to Chicago, and look how race and space, and class kind of constrict them in ways, almost like there are invisible walls holding them in various forms of subjugation."

A number of intellectuals have tried to take this up. Kenneth Clark wrote a book in 1965 called *Dark Ghetto*. And a lot of the things I'm trying to do in my book is pick up on themes and ideas I thought he was expressing in that book that haven't been taken up. That's part of the reason why I call it *Dark Ghettos:* to properly pay tribute to him and to emphasize that I'm drawing on things that he's doing there. I think that ghettos are still with us. I want to emphasize that continuity in terms of a subject of investigation for those of us interested in black life.

MYISHA: You consider several explanatory factors of dark ghettos. Let's discuss four of them. Tell me first: How does mass incarceration and crime explain the presence of dark ghettos?

TOMMIE: I'm drawing on lot of social science in the book and I'm trying to offer a philosophical interpretation of some of their findings. I'm not exactly trying to offer empirical explanations of ghettos, but I try to take seriously some explanations people have given, some factors people point to when they do it. Then I try to ask various questions that a moral and political philosopher might ask about those things.

Crime, and in particular violent crime, negatively affects poor black communities in lots of different ways. One of the ways it does is it tends to deter people who have more financial means from living in those communities since they have the means to leave them. And thereby as people with more means are able to leave communities where they perceive crime to be a problem, that is going to concentrate the number of disadvantaged people, people who have fewer means and are less able to leave those environments. That concentration of disadvantage is partly what people are talking about when they're talking about ghettos.

That concentration of highly disadvantaged people is also going to affect neighborhood schools, because you're going to have a higher proportion of very disadvantaged people in those schools. That's going to make it more difficult to instruct them, given the limited means that the school typically can use to educate them. It's also, of course, going to deter businesses from setting up shop there or remaining. So you end up with businesses that are primarily there to prey on the poor rather than businesses that might be better for the people in those communities. Clearly, it's sort of stressful, I think, for residents, particularly I think for women and girls who are exposed to street crime and various forms of sexual harassment. Some people are clearly attracted to street crime, especially adolescents. And that's going to have an effect on or can interfere with their education. Sometimes it can send them to prison.

In the case of mass incarceration, it obviously affects these communities in lots of ways, too. One of the ways it does is it takes away people who could have otherwise provided various forms of financial help and childcare assistance. Even once people leave prison, when the formerly incarcerated return to their communities, they're often much worse off as a result because now they have this felony conviction and that's going to make it very difficult for them to find work and housing. It's going to make them ineligible for various forms of public assistance. And it probably is going to end up leading them back into the illicit economy, which could put them back in jail.

There are other ways, but those are some of the ways in which I think people have pointed to how crime and incarceration can help to perpetuate these communities.

MYISHA: There are two controversial factors that people have offered up to explain ghettos: culture and single-mother families. Can you elaborate on these explanatory factors?

TOMMIE: Those are more complicated in that—I think you're right—they are certainly more controversial. The social scientists tend to emphasize the cultural factors. The factors they emphasize vary depending on where they are on the political spectrum. But I think that they tend to think of cultural factors as shared attitudes, beliefs, values, and social identities. They think that some of these things have been forged under ghetto conditions and at least some of these patterns, cultural patterns, inhibit poor people in these neighborhoods from seizing available opportunities or making the best use of the opportunities that are available to them, even if those opportunities are insufficient, as I think a lot of social scientists, especially sociologists, believe. Some of those cultural characteristics have to do with street crime, but not all of them. I think a lot of times people are pointing to things like attitudes toward work, school, family life, consumption patterns, or things like that. They think that some of these patterns make it harder for the poor to escape poverty.

I do not view some of these transgressions against mainstream norms as pathological or anything. I tend to think of them often as a kind of healthy defiance in the face of various forms of injustice that the people in these communities face. I wouldn't want to deny that it can sometimes make the practitioners worse off when they engage in some of these things, but I don't think that that then licenses the state to, say, engage in various forms of cultural reform or behavior modification.

It certainly doesn't justify the withdrawal of public support in an attempt at a kind of tough love and what not. I think sometimes some of what's being seen as suboptimal cultural practices that kind of make people worse off are probably better seen as, at least among some people, people's refusal to just go along with expectations that they regard as unreasonable.

In the case of the family, social scientists that tend to emphasize family structure have a long history, obviously. Their primary concern is that they think that single women who have limited education and limited job-related skills are going to have a lot of difficulty earning enough income to maintain a household and also finding enough time and energy to properly look after their children. They're also going to find it pretty challenging to escape ghetto poverty. Therefore, they're going to end up exposing their children to some of the hazards of life in these communities.

I don't, myself, think there's anything wrong with single-parent families, provided they get the public support that they're due, which they typically don't. I tend to think that much of the difficulty people point to for the family structure is better understood by looking at the way the labor market is structured. Its best understood by looking at the way we tend to devalue the parenting work that women do and not see women's role in rearing the next generation as playing a very important part of maintaining the social life that we all share together. So I don't regard family structure as the right thing to focus on, but I can see why some people have done so.

MYISHA: If dark ghettos exist, and according to sociologists, they may exist for these particular reasons, then I'm interested in what we are doing and should do about them. You are critical of the ways in which the US Government has tried to address the problems of the ghetto. And one of the ways has been what you call the "medical model." What is the medical model? What are some examples of it? What serious limitations does it have?

TOMMIE: Most of the public debate that's been going on for some time, certainly since the mid-60s around issues of ghetto poverty, is disagreement between people who focus on so-called structural factors (e.g., lack of jobs, race discrimination, substandard schools, and so on) and the people who think that "No, there are these behavioral factors" (e.g., reproductive decisions, subpar parenting, avoidance of work in the licit economy, criminal conduct, so on). Then of course, there are some people, like former President Barack Obama, who insisted that it's both. That's a standard position a lot of people take about these issues. That debate tends to move from talking about "Well, how much of it is structure, how much of it is behavior?" to a debate over "Okay, once we identify the factor, how can the government intervene into the lives of the ghetto poor?" It is almost like the government is a kind of doctor. Now you got the diagnosis. "Let me see if I can intervene in a way that's going to be most cost-effective, get the biggest bang for your buck as it were." "Should that be a jobs program, should we integrate neighborhoods, should we increase crime control measures?"

I think that way of framing things in this kind of social-scientific policymaking way tends to marginalize crucial questions of political morality—both the ideals of social justice that we should be striving to realize in practice, but it also tends to marginalize questions about morality of activism and resistance. And so in the book, I identify what I regard as three main pitfalls of framing things in this way: status-quo bias, downgraded agency, and unjust advantage blind spot. Let me see if I can quickly gloss those.

Status-quo bias is what it sounds like. When you go to see the doctor, they are going to assume basic anatomy and physiology in that they're not going to try to change the structure of your body. But they are going to try to figure out how to intervene in a way that leaves that body in place. Similarly, you can have the same kind of way of thinking about ghettos. You can say, "Look, here's this problem. How can we figure out how to get them to fit in with the rest of the structure but leaving the structure in the background and not giving it the kind of critical scrutiny they might have? Because obviously, a social structure can be changed in a way in which the body's anatomy cannot." So I do think there's a tendency to do that, and I think you want to bring that structure into the light so that you can give it proper scrutiny.

I think there's also a problem of downgraded agency. Again, a lot of the social scientists, especially sociologists, tend to be pretty liberal, sometimes pretty left-wing. But they also have a tendency to think of the ghetto poor as people in need of other people's help. They try to think about "How can we get people to help them, either wealthy people, private foundations, or the government?" And not "Let's frame things in terms of how can we, now, as fellow citizens, as residents of this country, work together to try to make it into a society we can all feel good about and want to support to make into a more just society?"

Maybe that's an occupational hazard; I don't know. But there is a tendency not to see the people who are being studied (the disadvantaged in these neighborhoods)—there are exceptions, obviously—as active moral and political agents in their own right. I think there's a tendency to not see all the ways in which the advantaged are benefitting from an unjust social structure. I mean, they're taking advantage of opportunities that are not afforded to others but that should be made available to those others. They have a lot of ill-gotten gains. And so it's very easy to lose sight of those ill-gotten gains and just think, "Well, how can we use our privilege, as it were, to help them" as opposed to thinking that maybe that privilege and advantages are themselves a sign that the society is unjust. So I wanted to reframe things away from that way of thinking in order to avoid those pitfalls.

MYISHA: Let's get to some specific solutions that are often offered in these models. You mention integration in the book. When we hear of integration, for lots of us, it sounds like a good idea. But according to your criticism of the medical model, you have a problem with integration. What is it?

TOMMIE: Well, I think it depends on what people mean by "integration" and how you want to justify it. I think a lot of people when they've thought about this point to segregation as a problem, which you cannot deny. But people mean different things by that.

If desegregation means let's prevent people from discriminating in housing, say, in renting and lending generally in the real estate market—if it means preventing that from occurring and if it means making sure that people have their fair share of economic resources so that they can live where they can afford, be given what they are due economically, then who can deny that? And I think it's appropriate for people to have the liberty to choose their neighborhood communities free from that kind of discrimination, exclusion, and be equipped with the resources that they are due.

But I think some people, when they talk about integration, are focused on so-called social capital deficits. They think there are disadvantaged black people who could do better if they were in neighborhoods with people who were more advantaged, because the disadvantaged could then find their way into the advantaged's social networks. And that would help get them greater access to opportunities.

Now, I find that troubling for a number of reasons. Some of the reasons just have to do with the unjust -advantage blind spot problem. Because what you're basically asking of the ghetto poor is that they work their way into the lives of the privileged, and the privileged can then dole out these privileges on them so that they could do better—which I think is not a tenable position from the standpoint of many people. People might be forced into doing that, because maybe the best they could do is try to get an affluent person—and I don't just mean white people; it could be an affluent black person—to see them with favor and help them. But I think that's a degrading way of dealing with the problem.

But also I think people should have the liberty to choose their communities. There is nothing wrong with wanting to live in a black community. We have a long history of living in such communities, and some people really enjoy them, they're very attached to them as a place that feels like home to them. I don't see any reason why they should be dispersed in that way in order to try to get them to work their way into the lives of more affluent people. But what should happen is they should be protected from unjust forms of exclusion and properly equipped economically so that they can choose the neighborhoods they want to live in.

MYISHA: How about welfare reform as a solution?

TOMMIE: Big topic! There's so many dimensions to it. One dimension of it that I try to spend a lot of time on has to do with work requirements. Welfare as an entitlement to poor people was abolished. So now for the last twenty years, if you want to get access to basic necessities beyond, say, basic food stamps, if you want anything more substantial in terms of support from the public, then you're going to have to go through a pretty onerous and austere welfare system. This welfare system has various requirements, including work requirement with time limits on how long you can receive such support. But you're not entitled to a job. You have to find one in the economy as it currently exists. And the economy as it currently exists is not terribly hospitable to people who don't have highly developed skills and a fair bit of education. It's often inaccessible to people living in these neighborhoods.

So you're then just pushed into part-time marginal and service jobs if you can get them. It seems to me that that's not an appropriate way to respond to the plight of the people who are confined to these neighborhoods. I don't think it's a good response to any poor person. But I think in particular it's not a good response to people in these neighborhoods.

MYISHA: The subtitle of your book doesn't just have the terms "injustice and reform" in it but it also has the word "dissent." Given that the ghetto poor live in unjust conditions, you claim, "Some of the conduct poor, urban blacks engage in is harmful to others, self-destructive. On the other hand, some of their actions are best seen as a moral response to injustice that is a form of resistance or dissent."

You list several forms of dissent. Let's focus on refusing to work and participation in crime. How can they be "expressions of justified rebellion"?

TOMMIE: You're trying to get me in trouble. But okay, I did say it. If we were under just conditions, then I'd say, "Look, everybody who's able should make some kind of contribution to the maintenance of their society, do some kind of valuable work. I don't necessarily mean that work has to be something that the market will reward. There's work that's important to be done that the market won't reward, but we should make some kind of contribution of that sort. People benefit from the work of others, and so you should do your part. Share the reciprocity to help make these benefits possible."

But in an unjust society, and particularly at the site of the economy, I think sometimes refusing to work can be an appropriate form of protest. So suppose you thought, as I go back to the example we were just talking about, it's unjust to make access to basic necessities conditional on your willingness to work in a low-wage, menial service job. You might say, "I think such a system is demeaning to the poor" and not go along if you can. (Not everybody can, some people, just by economic circumstances are forced to have to submit.) But if you could refuse and you're willing to absorb the cost of doing so, that might be one way of conveying your dissatisfaction with the way that welfare is structured.

You might similarly feel that way about the work that's available, the way it should be rewarded. You might say, "Look, I mean, you're not getting a living wage. You're working a lot but you're not able to live with any degree of comfort or economic security." Rather than, again, just submit to that and say, "Well, I'll just go along and just accept the jobs that are available," you might say, "Well, I won't go along, I refuse" as kind of a way of withdrawing your support for certain features of your society that you regard as deeply unfair. I think that kind of action can be justified.

I don't want to make it sound like I think everybody who refuses to work is doing it for that reason. I think that's probably implausible. But I think some are and I think if more did so and they did so in a way that was open—that is, they made it very clear that's the reason they're doing it—others might be willing to join in in support. You can maybe galvanize people around getting some change. You can also galvanize people around the way the labor market is structured and the way work is rewarded.

Crime is harder. Take Martin Luther King Jr.'s discussions of ghetto riots. He would emphasize that unlawful actions that are directed towards symbols of wealth and objects of need can be an expression of dissatisfaction with the economic order; that is, distribution of income, distribution of wealth, distribution of work itself. I think that's right. And I also agree with King that the violent crime, whether that's ordinary, say, robbery or something like that of a full-scale riot for that matter, is not permissible nor do I think it's really a productive form of dissent.

But there might be some nonviolent economic crimes that are not only a means to acquire needed income but can be a way of refusing to go along with a set of unjust property relations and unfair tax schemes. I don't advocate it because I think we're living in a very punitive moment in US history, and the penal system will come down really hard. As a practical matter, I think it's probably not a terribly effective way to express your dissent. But that's different from saying it's impermissible. I think it can be permissible to refuse to obey certain laws when you believe that your society is seriously unjust, especially seriously unjust at the site of the economy.

And I do think people do that sometimes. I think they feel like, rather than just submit to the expectation that one will just work these jobs and become a part of the insecure workforce of people living without a living wage, mostly engaged in doing the work of being a kind of professional servant class to the affluent—many of whom's wealth is unjust, some people say, "Well, no, I'll just participate in an illicit economy to try to earn money and I'll thumb my nose at those who expect me to accommodate myself to my place in such an unfair economic order."

MYISHA: It seems that the issue is a problem of justice, it's a problem of structure. Some people may be skeptical that politicians and institutions can really help solve the problem of dark ghettos, particularly if those same politicians and institutions show a lack of concern about justice-related issues. What can normal folk do, in the current moment, to help eradicate dark ghettos?

TOMMIE: I think if you can overcome the various collective action problems and build some solidarity and do things jointly—that is, you can get a lot of people to engage in refusing to go along with injustice, which is a tall order—I think that will be helpful. There does seem to be a lot of sentiment around cutting across various lines of difference. There are ways in which people are more willing to find forms of solidarity that they might not have been able to forge in a previous time. I think maybe they can forge them now. We should be on the lookout for those links; ways that we could collectively support one another and refuse oppression.

It's hard to know what to do when there is a kind of withdrawal of public support in the case of, say, the US Department of Housing and Urban Development HUD, which does a lot more than just try to support integration. It also provides a lot of income support for housing, housing support for people who don't have housing. If that gets stripped of a lot of its funding, it is going to make a lot of people quite insecure. But again, I think probably we'll have to support each other in that way too; that is, try to find ways to support those who are insecure when it comes to housing. We could raise a lot of money online to help people to be able to afford housing. You could allow people to live with you like family members or friends in order to protect them from being on the street.

That's a kind of a save-as-many-as-you-can kind of approach, but at the same time it's about looking forward to try to make some progress in the future. This means doing the work on the ground locally, at the state level, and trying to strengthen organizations fighting for change. That's more of a long-term view, but I think we have to be engaged in that kind of activity as well.

23

David McClean on Money
and Materialism

MYISHA: Why does what happens on Wall Street matter? Particularly, why should the working class and the poor be concerned about what happens on Wall Street?

DAVID: I think I can answer that question with another question: Why would anyone be interested in the space program? I mean, all of these things are connected. When one thinks Wall Street is irrelevant, it's important to realize that by "Wall Street," we're talking about the financial services industry, which is a collection of industries from commercial banking to investment banking to money management. They all are relevant to everybody's life. Most people can't get a car without financing it, so the financial services industry is part of your life when you buy a car. If you have a pension, 401k, you may not be interested in what's in it, it may be like metaphysics to you, but in fact, Wall Street firms are investing your retirement money.

Given what happened in 2007–2008 with the financial crisis, we know that Wall Street can actually wreak havoc on the lives of very wealthy people and extremely poor people. After the crisis in 2008, there were people that committed suicide, there were people that lost their homes, there were people that became destitute. Obviously, attendant to all those things are mental health problems, so it's all interconnected.

One of the mistakes I think people make, especially people who are focused in one area, whether it's the academy or business, is that they don't see these interconnections. In some sense it is the job of the public intellectual to make those interconnections plain.

MYISHA: When the crash happened, there was this rhetoric of "They need to be held accountable." There were corruption and greed. There were predatory lending practices. Do you think Wall Street can be fixed from the inside or through regulation? Can the public have a hand in fixing Wall Street?

DAVID: Wall Street lends itself to bad acting for a variety of reasons. I think that you're always going to need regulation. There's always been regulation of Wall Street. Although back in the days of the crash of 1929, the regulation was scant. There were tremendous "nods" essentially, by the courts, and government in general, to the robber-baron classes. Since then, especially since 1933, there has been a lot of regulatory reform on Wall Street that has snowballed ever since. What Wall Street really needs is reform, and that's cultural reform. I don't think that passing regulations like Dodd-Frank will do the job. What needs to happen on Wall Street is a mindset change; a paradigm change in how people think about what they're doing there. It needs to move from a model of self-indulgence to a model of service, or what I call a "ministerial model."

There's no reason that that shouldn't happen. There are doctors in Europe, all throughout Europe, that don't look at what they do as something that should lead to tremendous amounts of personal wealth. They look at what they do as a public service. So, anything can be changed, any culture or any industry can be changed. It just depends on whether or not there's a tipping point where there are enough people talking about the need for the change, and enough people grasping the need for the change to affect change. Some of that is top-down; some of that is bottom-up. My job—I just wrote a book on Wall Street reform—is to make that as plain as I possibly can.

In the dominant discussion right now is a coercion model; it says that we are going to beat these people (Wall Street) into submission. I think some of that is necessary. Believe me, I've seen bad things. But I think that if you really want to reform anything, you have to go back to Aristotle to some degree, and change habits, including habits of mind. There are many good people on Wall Street; they just happen to work there, like some people happen to work in universities and other people happen to work in agriculture. They would love to see a change because Wall Street has been smeared so badly that many people who are accountants, lawyers, and back-office clerks are almost embarrassed to be associated with it. It's also a necessary industry. The world has always had banks; it always will.

MYISHA: To someone who is focused on living a philosophical life, a self-examined life, and/or a virtuous life, how should they view money? What should their relationship with money be?

DAVID: I think that money is extremely important. There's the old adage that says, "Money is the root of all evil." That's what people think, but that's not what it says. It says, "The love of money is the root of all evil." It isn't even just the love of money that's the root of all evil. It is the sort of teleopathic interest in money, to borrow a term from a business ethicist named Goodpastor, where the pursuit of money makes almost everything else fall to the periphery. That's the root of all evil.

There's a problem in believing that money is problematic. It is not. Money is fluid for life and everybody knows it, from the most ardent leftist to the most reactionary conservative. If money is something that one needs—if it's almost axiomatic, it should go without saying that it is true—then one needs to be disciplined in how one handles it, one should understand that there is an ethics of money and moneymaking, saving, and investing that one owes to oneself to explore.

So much wealth in African American communities went up in smoke partly because of predatory lending, unaffordable subprime mortgages, unemployment, bankruptcies, and the destruction of credit that took place at the same time that people were losing their homes and their jobs. Prior to the crisis, the ratio of white wealth to black wealth, household to household, was 12:1. That is, whites had 12 times as much wealth on average as the average black household. Now it's 20 or more to 1, post crisis.

I believe that one needs to have a tremendous amount of respect for the dollars they earn. One of the principal things that needs to be done is saving. You want to know how to get wealthy? It's very simple: Save your money. What difference do the returns you're getting on your mutual fund make if you're buying a pair of Ferragamo loafers every Friday? It doesn't make any difference what your return is. You have to look at money holistically and understand that saving is the beginning of investing. If you don't have any money, you can't invest it. It's a critical thing. It allows for one to take advantage of opportunities. The people losing money in the market are people who are panicking, because they were never told how to manage money or what to do with it. So, they panic, the little investor panics, and they sell. They sell low because they fear that the market won't come back again. This is just one example of how people who are not used to money need to learn how to save it, and then learn what to do with it once they have it.

What I do with my money—not to brag because I could do much more—is when someone in need asks for money I give it to them, whether or not it's a loan, or whether it's just a gift. It could be someone that's trying to get an apartment, or someone who is just down and out. I give money to various charities and I like to be able to do that. It gives you flexibility to be of assistance to people, to family members, to friends, to people that are in jeopardy. It doesn't mean that you live your life so that you can continue to make lots and lots of money, because then you can become unbalanced.

But I can't emphasize enough how in the African American community we need a culture of saving and investment, and we need it really, really fast. Because right now we are in dire straits when it comes to how we treat money, how we deal with money.

MYISHA: I was talking with a friend of mine from the Continent, and we were having the kind of typical African and African American conversation where I get their perspective about what they think of us, they hear my perspective of what we think of them, and then we try to answer all these questions together. But I remember talking with her and she was telling me about a perception that Africans have of a lot of Americans: that, first of all, they're rich.

She doesn't speak for all Africans, but another thing that she shared with me was, "African Americans are very materialistic." She told me that the way they know this is through the media, and the media—particularly rap videos and hip-hop culture TV shows—depict black Americans as being very materialistic. You think about the songs, you think about the jewelry, you think about the cars; everything that's in the media, and music videos, et cetera, gives away this materialistic perception.

I responded to her, but I'm interested in what you have to say. Are African Americans materialistic? Do you think materialism is a side effect of living in a capitalist society in general? Or do you find something else interesting that's going on?

DAVID: One has to be charitable with respect to the state of African Americans. While one could be critical of a number of the conditions that we find ourselves in, one also has to understand the history. Part of that is a history of depravation, doing without—being *forced* to do without—in a culture that is a consumerist culture, that has bought into the ideology of consumerism, not just capitalism. The word "capitalism" gets overused, but I think a better word is "consumerist."

In this consumerist culture, the mandate is to go out and increase the GDP by constant consumption. You're watching everyone around you being enticed into this frenzied consumption activity, and you're unable to participate in a big part of the culture, the sort of meme of the culture, this notion of being a consumer. We're judged because we can't participate; we're judged as being unable to participate. So, it's not a big surprise that when we can participate, we go crazy. We become hyperconsumerist. A lot of that is quite understandable. I have a great deal of sympathy.

These are broad generalizations. You and I both know people who are not caught up in this, and I'm not trying to paint everybody with the same brush. Having said that, it's destructive on a number of levels. One, you define success simply on the basis of one's ability to consume. So, one of the things you see in hip-hop culture is that the ability to purchase high price-tag goods and services is somehow the pinnacle of a life. Well, it certainly isn't. There's great idolization of symbols of wealth without understanding what wealth really is or, for that matter, what power really is. A lot of the false bravado used in hip-hop culture, especially in hip-hop music and videos, is a kind of false machismo, a false bravado, that I think shows an ignorance of what power and wealth really is. That's a tragedy. It's got to be addressed, but it can't be addressed through simply being hostile and critical. It's got to be addressed with an understanding of how it is that this came about; otherwise we're not going to fix it.

24

Vanessa Wills on Marxism Today

MYISHA: Who was Karl Marx, and what is Marxism?

VANESSA: I knew you were going to ask me this question, and it's actually a much harder question than it sounds. I'm going to say some things that I take to be true. Karl Marx, of course, was a German theorist, economist, political scientist, philosopher, and activist. He was very much influenced by the work of Hegel and the traditions of German idealism. He is most important, intellectually, for his formulation of historical materialist method, or sometimes called dialectical materialism.

That dovetails into the second question of Marxism. There's different answers I could give, but focusing methodologically, I would say that Marxism as applied to the study of humans, of social development, is a method that proceeds by looking at the way in which human beings produce their own conditions of existence. It examines the way that the economy functions, the ways that people literally produce the food they need or acquire the goods they need, and so on.

Specifically, if we're talking about class societies, they are organized in such a way that the society produces the things it needs by organizing relations of production and relations of ownership that distribute this work across different economic classes. If you can understand the relations of power among these classes, and the conflicts of interest between these different classes, then you will have a basis for understanding all sorts of things about the society, like the ideas of the society, the reason it has developed in such a way; ideally, how to change the society in order to better meet the needs of human beings.

MYISHA: What are some of the misconceptions about Marxist thought?

VANESSA: People often think that because Marxism applied to class societies, it's only a class-based analysis. It's as though Marxism has no resources to describe other forms of identity, or axes of oppression because "Wow, don't those folks just care about class?" I think that's a fundamental confusion about what Marxism aims to do.

Another misconception about Marxism has to do with the role of determinism and the nature of the materialism at the base of Marxist theory. I mentioned earlier this concept of dialectical materialism. It's dialectical because it is seeking to understand the interaction between matter and ideas. There's a tendency to conflate Marxism with what I and others call "simple or vulgar economism," which is the idea that the relation of causation or influence only goes upwards from an economic base to a superstructure of ideology. That just would not be a Marxist analysis. We have to understand how the superstructure of ideology, of politics, reacts back onto that base and, in turn, influences the economic conditions.

Both of these are tendencies to oversimplify Marxism. I often find that critiques of Marxism are actually directed against these oversimplified versions, and therefore miss the mark.

MYISHA: Why has Marxism—and you alluded to this in your previous response—been so attractive to a variety of oppressed people?

VANESSA: I think there are a number of reasons. One is that Marxism holds out a vision of a different type of society. That sounds simple and maybe sort of obvious. But Marxism says a different world is possible, and if you're oppressed, then maybe that sounds like a really comforting message. It also sounds like a call to action; it is an inspiring message. I think that Marxism has been appealing because people can see in their own lives how oppressions based on race, gender, or nationality are often organized and produced by bosses, by those who are in power in capitalist societies, the capitalist ruling class. There's an appeal to seeing the ways in which the explanations of forms of oppression actually correlate pretty directly to who's passing the laws and who's controlling employment.

I think that Marxism has also been appealing because it suggests that the struggle of different groups has a common basis. That different oppressed people around the world can work together and have something in common to struggle for. It provides a theoretical and practical framework for a more universal struggle to achieve things, like genuine freedom or genuine control over our lives.

MYISHA: I want to talk about capitalism for a little bit. I know you said that you don't want to minimize Marxism to capitalism, but when people think about Marxist thought, they think about capitalism. What is so bad about capitalism?

VANESSA: When I teach a course sometimes called "Philosophy of Karl Marx," the first thing that we do is very carefully read the *Communist Manifesto*. Near the beginning of it, there are lots of really nice things about capitalism. Marx describes all of the ways in which capitalism has been revolutionary, the ways in which capitalism has allowed for an explosion in humanity's ability to satisfy its current needs, develop new ones, and develop new modes of interacting with the world. He talks about the way that it connects people all around the world with one another, creates common interests, and has overthrown feudalism; that's a biggie, that's a victory for humanity. This could also be another misconception about Marxism: the idea that Marxism or Marx just hasn't noticed the incredible positive role that capitalism has played in the development of humanity.

The way that Marx formulates his critique of capitalism is not that capitalism is all bad, which is a historical way of thinking about capitalism. Marx argues that capitalism, at a certain point in history, was exactly what was necessary, was this good force, but perhaps it's outlived its usefulness. At one point, it was the best way to organize production and now it no longer is. Certain contradictions are produced by capitalism, like the fact that there's this incredible wealth produced and yet an increasing proportion of humanity falls deeper and deeper into poverty. We have these incredible inequalities of income and wealth. There are housing booms and there's rampant homelessness. So the idea is that that doesn't have to be the case. There's a way to resolve some of these contradictions. The way to do that is to abolish class society. We have a system where the decisions are made, by and large, by a narrow band of folks at the top. The thought is that that is no longer necessary, and no longer the best way to organize things. We can democratize, or socialize, control over production and decisions about what gets made and where it goes.

MYISHA: In a capitalistic society people are able to create goods and services, and sell them. Competition in the market also creates innovation. This is all I've seen as a member of such a society. I'm trying to imagine life without capitalism. Help me to imagine an alternative to this economic system.

VANESSA: In one sense, the simple thing to say is, the alternative is a classless society. A society where everyone participates in setting the direction, everyone has a role in making decisions, and people are able to exert more influence over their own lives.

Is the question what would we do if we couldn't sell? There's a kind of fear, that by socialism or by communism, Marx is describing a limitation on freedom, or a limitation on the expression of individuality. To put it sharply, I think that fear doesn't survive even a cursory reading of Marx. It just doesn't. Marx talks often about individuality, about the development of individuals, and is very concerned with promoting freedom. One way of thinking about Marx's project is it seeks to promote an expansion of human activity, an expansion of ways of intervening into our natural and social worlds. So the ideal, "I can create anything I want," well, good. I don't see that as something that would be lost.

This brings me to an interesting point. In liberal political philosophy, we're accustomed to thinking of other people as limitations on our freedom. If I have this sphere within which I could act, no one could tell me what to do because I'm a private citizen. Here's my private property to prove it; I can do whatever I want with it. We see one another as limitations on our ability to act outside of ourselves or to act on the world. Marx rejects this picture of what freedom is. He proposes instead that we think of others as the ground of our freedom; the people around us are what make our freedom more possible. They allow us to develop greater freedom. We can see that if we think about the fact that many of the things we do depend on a huge amount of social labor. Whatever it is that you make and sell on the street requires a street and all sorts of things. We tend to think about those things in a very private, individual way; "Well, don't get in my way!" We forget that, actually, it is through our interconnection with one another that we have this freedom to explore and to develop ourselves. It's not in spite of it.

I think that's an important piece of thinking about what socialism is for Marx. It's this idea that we don't lose freedom. We actually gain it by interacting with each other in a way that more fully honors the fact that we require one another in order to develop as individuals. That requires that we live in a society where we all have the ability to exert this type of influence.

The contrast is our current society, the United States, where most people are highly excluded from important decision making about our lives. Whether it is decision making about who will receive economic relief and who won't. Apparently, the banks will get it and hurricane victims not so much. In Pennsylvania, they've had huge cuts to public spending on education, and at the very same time they constructed a new state prison at a cost roughly equivalent to what was cut out of the school budgets. We live in this society where the focus is, "Well, yeah, I don't have this decision making at a social level, but I'm here watching in my house and no one can bother me in my private sphere, so that means I'm free." That is an illusion. I offer that to add more concrete detail to why thinking of ways we can transform our society so people have more ability to exert influence in the fields that really matter to all of us would obviously create more freedom, rather than less.

MYISHA: If I was to start or join a freedom-fighting or social-justice organization today, name at least two things that I can learn from Marx that will help me in my struggle for freedom.

VANESSA: Oh, that is interesting. I think one thing that would be really important is to think about the ways in which fighting for liberation is not a zero-sum game. Think about the ways in which the struggles of various people of color and people of various gender identities depend upon and require one another. I would hope it would be some kind of Marxist organization. (Laughter.) That would be great. But even if it's not, I would argue that thinking these things are connected, by the fact they're questions of whether people will be able to have meaningful control and influence over their lives, or the parts of themselves that they're able to develop or express, means a critique of the class relations of the society is happening. So one would just be to think about how looking at economics points us towards the interconnectedness of various struggles against oppression.

The second one would be to understand the importance of history, of knowing the history of struggles around the world, and drawing lessons from them. I think lots of people think like this; you don't have to be a Marxist. Sometimes we think that what we're going through is new. There's this tendency to always think that the struggles we're dealing with are new and therefore we need new ideas. I would encourage everyone to look at some of the old ideas, Marxism and older.

Sometimes there's a kind of been-there, done-that attitude towards Marxism and other ideas. I think this underestimates the continuity between the struggle for black liberation now and 100 years ago, between workers' struggles today and at the beginning of the twentieth century. History is important. I think we should really dig in and find out what people thought about their conditions, what organizations they built, what was successful and what wasn't. That's hopefully something anyone can take on, but I think we forget it often, too often.

Section 5

GENDER, SEX, AND LOVE

25

Nancy Bauer on Pornography

MYISHA: What is pornography?

NANCY: That's a question I never answer. I don't think it's quite the right question. I think it's kind of like asking what is anything and expecting a philosophically precise definition—not that you are, but usually when philosophers talk about this—that's what they mean.

When I think about pornography, very casually speaking, I think about it the way everybody else does. It's stuff that's produced in order to sexually excite people and help them have an orgasm. A long time ago most philosophers and feminists gave up on drawing a line between erotica and pornography, although there are people that are reviving that project. I'm not very interested in that line. To me the very simple, sort of intuitive notion of what pornography is, is perfectly serviceable.

MYISHA: In your book *Doing Things with Pornography*, you consider the issue of: Is pornography an expression, is it actual speech, or is it just performance? Do you want to take the everyday idea of what pornography is, or do these distinctions also matter?

NANCY: Those distinctions would matter if we were asking a question in which they became salient. It depends on what we want to know about pornography, or what we want to do in our work in thinking about pornography. It's not as though I think those things would never be interesting or that we shouldn't make any fine distinctions, but it really depends on what it is we're trying to do. For me, there are lots of things to say about pornography, but they don't necessarily depend on making those distinctions a priori.

MYISHA: Let's talk about some views on pornography. There must be some people dying to at least try to figure out: Is pornography good or is it bad? Can you summarize some arguments from either side?

NANCY: As always, I'll approach these questions by indirection, so I apologize to readers. I think it's really not surprising that to be human is to find things arousing in sexual advances from someone with whom we're in a committed relationship, or a reciprocally open one. To me it's just the case that sexuality involves potentially all of our senses and that any number of things can turn us on. For people who are visual, visual images of people and things can be very sexually arousing. For some people, reading a story that describes sex in very explicit ways, or listening to someone tell a story, can cause arousal. In a way I sound like an idiot because this is absolutely obvious, I know.

Pornography has been around forever. In the drawings on cave walls, we see pornographic sketches. The first two things that came off the printing press when it was invented were the Gutenberg Bible and pornography. The Gutenberg press was invented by a man and what came off the presses was controlled by men. I certainly don't want to say that this is just a ho-hum natural phenomenon among human beings, that they get turned on by these sorts of things. I do think it matters that control of the media has been for most of human history in the hands of men, and that we live in a really, really sexist world. That skews things to me.

MYISHA: You mentioned that the objectification argument is probably one of the most popular anti-porn arguments. What is the objectification argument? Why do you find it or the use of it problematic?

NANCY: Let's just talk about pornography that involves objectification of women, just to make it simpler. The idea is that what's wrong with pornography is it objectifies women; it makes them into things that are just there to be used and potentially abused, or even likely abused by men. There are other people who make a more quasi-moral political argument. They make a moral claim that objectification is just a really bad thing; we should never objectify another person, and we should never use another person as an object for our purposes.

I've not participated so much in that argument because I don't think that objectification is the right place to focus our philosophical attention. Martha Nussbaum's 1995 "Objectification" is the locus classicus of this conversation. She makes the argument that there are many, many different features of objectification. I think she lists seven or so of them. She wants to point out that not all instances of human behavior that involve these kinds of features count as objectification. A good example she gives is that I can take a nap with my head on my lover's belly. I can do this even though I would be using my lover's belly as a pillow, and therefore as an object. But it doesn't count as an objectification because it's in the context of a loving relationship. To me that's all screamingly obvious. We don't really need a philosopher to tell us that that's not necessarily a bad thing.

Here I follow Simone de Beauvoir, and think it is inevitable that we will not be able to have relationships in every moment with other people, in which we are fully acknowledging their subjectivity without it being a moral calamity. For example, I'm walking into a concert and there's a person there who is taking tickets and is very busy. He just sort of grabs mine and gives it back; there's not even time for me to say "thank you" or "hello." Is the treatment of that person an example of objectification? No. Is it objectionable? No. I just think there are tons and tons of cases like that. I also think that in sexual contexts, people sometimes enjoy the relief of having somebody focus on their body, as opposed to the exhaustion of having to be a subject for someone all the time. I don't think this is a disaster.

However, I do think that in the culture at large, in many contexts and for centuries, women were endlessly encouraged to self-objectify and do it in two ways. Firstly, they're encouraged to present themselves as sexually attractive in a kind of generic way that is dictated by the media. Secondly, there's absolutely no emphasis on women's pleasure. Sometimes self-objectification can be pleasurable if you draw the kind of attention that you want. But there are lots of ways in which women have been and now are supposed to objectify themselves, and it is just not pleasurable. It's disappointing. It involves a disciplining of one's body and of one's appearance that is strenuous and doesn't always reap the rewards that one thinks it will.

If you're a feminist, you just see objectification in the world. It's there. It's something you experience. We don't need a philosopher to rush in and justify it. I'm really opposed to that way of proceeding philosophically. We're not doing what we owe to the public for supporting us via institutions if we're doing that kind of work.

MYISHA: What made you think of J. L. Austin when doing work on pornography, and how does your reading of his work inform your view?

NANCY: From the very beginning I was interested in Austin. Austin is really interested in what, unfortunately, to my mind philosophers call the "pragmatics of our speech." That is to say, as Austin discusses, many philosophers who work in language divide the various ways to approach it into three categories—syntax, semantics, and pragmatics. The syntax stuff, which is in the purview of linguistics and by philosophers interested in linguistics, has to get worked out. Semantics gets worked on by those in philosophy of language. Semantics is the idea that we have to figure out how words mean what they mean. This is where the action has been for a long time. Then after that, of course, we'll have to do pragmatics to determine how words actually work, and we'll do that later. The key thing is semantics.

What Austin is saying is that you can't separate the three things. You have to look at what he calls the "total speech act" and the "total situation." What he thinks is driving speech acts is that they do things. Right now, for example, I am performing the act of elaborating—that's the doing. But I'm also explaining why I find Austin important, and lots of other verbs could be used to describe the action I'm doing. One of the things I argue is that Austin thinks that as we are talking, we are often positioning ourselves in the world in relation to other people. We are trying to make clear where we stand with respect to our own words.

In the early 2000s, MIT philosopher Sally Haslanger was doing a workshop. She called me and said, "Oh, will you comment on Rae Langton's *Speech Acts and Unspeakable Acts*?" I said, "Who's Rae Langton and what's *Speech Acts and Unspeakable Acts*" because I wasn't in the middle of the road of analytic philosophy. I'm kind of neither fish nor fowl. So I said, "Oh, well, I'll read that. That's interesting to me." I read it, and I immediately admired its virtuosity as a piece of argumentation and as a piece of philosophical writing. At the same time I thought it was just much ado about nothing.

The argument was that pornography is speech, at the same time, it is a kind of action. Pornography does things, it doesn't just say things. Given where I was coming from, I thought, "Well, duh. I mean, all speech say things." I just thought that was a really bizarre argument. And in order to make the point that she was making, Rae really focused on the standard reading of Austin. She argued that pornographic speech, including obviously films and photographs, has the power to subordinate women and to silence them in the sense that it makes it impossible for women to refuse sex. This is because the "no" that they say when they're refusing sex, because of pornography, doesn't come off as a refusal but as a kind of coy move in a language game. I thought this was totally wrong.

This snowballed into me thinking a lot about articulating my views of Austin, trying to shift the conversation about pornography so that it was actually about pornography in its complexities, not just a nice and neat argument about pornography's elocutionary power, as Rae Langton thinks Austin would put it. And then Rae moved happily and wonderfully to MIT shortly thereafter, so I had many, many occasions on which to discuss these matters with her. That was enormously helpful.

MYISHA: Nancy, can I be a feminist and enjoy nonfeminist porn?

NANCY: It depends on what the "can" means. I think people are often turned on by stuff they wouldn't necessarily morally approve of, and this is true even outside the realm of pornography. For example, somebody who decides for principled reasons to be a vegetarian could be tempted to eat some meat. Even if they were able to resist the temptation, they could still be in effect, as it were, turned on by the prospect of eating meat. So yes, in that simple sense you could.

What is nonfeminist porn? Let's say that nonfeminist porn is porn in which a woman is shown being demeaned or having no agency. Let's say it's porn where the sexual pleasure that she takes from whatever's going on in the pornography doesn't seem in the cold light of day to be what you would expect from what's happening to her. It's porn in which women are shown endlessly, over and over again, enjoying things that women very well may not actually enjoy in real life (e.g., being penetrated with no buildup of any kind). Let's call that nonfeminist porn.

Then again, it depends, I think, on the context. I don't think it's a moral sin to find oneself turned on by that kind of porn. On the other hand, what's a problem from my point of view is that there's so much porn like that and it's very, very easy for people to get conditioned to watching that kind of porn. Anne Eaton has written about how people get conditioned to look at various kinds of porn. I also think though that some people—to be very technical about this—have these pervy things about them. Freud was right about this. Everybody is pervy in various ways. Who knows why some things turn us on and some things don't. They may be hardwired; there may be simple reasons.

The issue would be if someone routinely finds that only really misogynistic porn can get them going. That would be concerning for obvious reasons. But I think it's complicated. I really do. I say this having four children between the ages of nineteen and twenty-five. The major problem with porn in our era is that kids are learning about sex from porn at a very young age. By the time they're ten, if they live within a world in which the Internet is everywhere and it's accessible to them, they have seen porn, and in many cases, lots of porn.

One major problem that I am particularly interested in is that in porn, almost always there are no horrendous consequences of whatever it is that happens. Mostly everybody has an orgasm or at least they're okay. And in lots of porn, even in fetish porn, everybody looks the way that you want them to look. So for example, in fat porn, everybody looks the way they want to look and everybody has an orgasm. Everything is okay. In his famous book, *Civilization and Its Discontents*, Freud talks about civilization as a byproduct of our sublimation of erotic desires. You're a little baby; what do you desire? You want to eat, you want to sleep, you want to pee and poop, and you just do those things whenever you want. You don't do them when you don't want to. And we learn later on that you can't just pee and poop whenever you want; you're constantly socialized so that you're controlling yourself.

That kind of control produces architects, philosophers, and taxi drivers—people who are doing productive things. We are channeling our erotic energy, not necessarily sexualized, into the rest of the world. But what Freud thought was that unbound erotic energy is incompatible with civilization. In porn, there's never that tension. The housewife cleaning her middle-class home answers the door. There's the mailman and in five seconds they're just humping all over the room. And then the mailman leaves, but the mail still gets delivered; the house is immaculate and everything gets done. It's like you can have it all.

The fact of the matter, though, is that kids learn from pornography that sex is great, you always have an orgasm, and everybody ends up being okay even if they're hurt or bruised, or whatever they are. We don't give them any other counternarrative. What we do is we go into schools and we say, "Here, kids, have some condoms. Make sure you get consent (we never really explain what that looks like)." We say, "Make sure the person really wants to do it with you. And then have a condom and good luck." But the kids have this whole other powerful eroticized narrative in front of them. And to me this is a major problem with porn.

MYISHA: Some US states have attempted to pass anti-LGBT laws in the last few years. North Carolina and Mississippi are examples. What we find is that Mississippi was ranked sixth overall in the number of gay scenes screened on a popular pornsite. The top three porn video searches in North Carolina one year were searches involving trans porn stars. How do you explain this?

NANCY: I don't know if I'm in a better position than anybody else to explain this. But I do think that what is taboo is sexy for many people. One of the things that's interesting is that it's hard to know how to talk to kids, even if you wanted to, in frank terms about what sex actually is really like.

Sometimes you have sex with someone that you're fond of, in love with, or care about. You marry them because you really care about them. And even though you don't feel like it, you just have sex with them anyway in the same way that you would do anything with them that you didn't feel like doing. And it's okay. Other times you really want to do it, but it's not going well. It is consensual and rather than stop in the middle of it, because you love the person or whatever, you instead make a grocery list in your head. Or another time you say, "Note to self, don't have sex with this person again." It's very complicated and I think we should talk to people about that.

All of that said, I think for many people, a lot of what's sexy, what turns them on are things that are taboo. Obviously, I am not an experimental psychologist. I don't have any data to support this, but I don't think it's surprising that if you live in a state like, for example, Mississippi or North Carolina, in which there's a very heavy, fundamentalist Christian presence, with a very strong set of taboos, it's not surprising that those taboos become eroticized.

I want to say too, because we haven't talked about this yet, that one of the most disturbing features of a lot of mainstream porn is how racist it is. The stereotyping and overt sexualization of African American men, for example that they all have penises the size of the Eiffel Tower, and that African American women are voracious and want sex all the time, is linked to the inherent racism found in pornography. A lot of it is this taboo of the out-of-central-casting white man just really wanting to have sex with black men or black women. That stuff is obviously really, really disturbing. I link it with the stuff you're talking about, which is a way of people working out the way they've cathected these things they think of as taboo. It's very disturbing, and it's also very ironic.

It's not that uncommon. It's almost a trope of the famous, fundamentalist preacher at a megachurch who, it turns out, is having sex with men. This happens over and over again. It's kind of the same phenomenon. It doesn't surprise me at all.

MYISHA: What is your view on hookup culture and apps that promote hookup culture?

NANCY: I don't have any problem at all with people meeting one an-other and having casual sex, or even people going online and seeking casual sex with someone else. If both people want to do that and they want to do that on Grindr or whatever, it's all good. However, I think there's a lot of psychological pressure on kids to think that hooking up is going to be a really great way to get the sex that you want. Sometimes it might be; sometimes it is. In some sexual subcultures, it's been hap-pening for generations, in part because of taboos.

When it comes to heterosexual women or bisexual women who have sex with men, it's often the case that they think a hookup is com-plicated. It may not be a simple desire for sex, and it can produce what many young women have told me is something I call a "hookup hang-over," where you think this is going to be a great thing and then it just doesn't go as well as you thought it would. It's kind of awkward, em-barrassing, or sad. I mean, that can happen in any sexual encounter.

I think in the heterosexual world, sex is actually in some respects better for men. Some of that, I think, is physiological. I am referring to cisgender men or people with penises. There are men who don't have penises; that's fine. But a person with a penis, who's had a penis from birth in particular, they have this organ that is there in front of their body, that has erections, that's interesting, and that they're bound to play with when they're little. Little girls may sort of rub their crotches on things or understand that there's some stuff down there. I think it's much more unlikely that little girls would really get to know their sexual organs in the same way that little boys do.

This is a point that Simone de Beauvoir makes, and I think it's true. It doesn't mean anything essentialist. It's just, I think, plausible. It may be the case that an adolescent boy has much more understanding of how to get off than a girl does. And I think it can be, we all know, harder to deal with clitorises and g-spots, vaginas and all that stuff. I think that hookups are likely to be more satisfying in some instances for boys than girls. There's a way in which the hookup culture makes things sexually difficult for women. But the other thing is, I think that for some girls, their sense of self-esteem comes from feeling that they are sexually at-tractive to boys, and their desire for sexual pleasure in some instances takes a backseat to that. I find that worrisome. Frankly, I think adver-tising culture more than porn is a dominant force in acclimating young girls to that mindset very early on. Then, of course, they start seeing porn now at a young age, too. So they get the sense that it's something about them if they're not having an orgasm, or if they're not enjoying the encounter.

26

John Corvino on Homosexuality

MYISHA: What would you say are the three most popular arguments raised against homosexuality? What are your responses to them?

JOHN: I usually divide the arguments into three basic categories: that it's wrong because it's unnatural; that it's wrong because it's harmful; or that it's wrong because it violates my religious beliefs.

On the question of unnaturalness, it really depends on what people mean by "unnatural." One thing they might mean is that our organs all have a natural purpose, what they're designed for. Then one way to respond to that is say, "Well, of course, lots of our organs have multiple purposes. I can use my mouth for talking, for singing, for breathing, for licking stamps, for blowing bubbles, for kissing a woman, or for kissing a man." It seems really arbitrary to say, "Well, all of those are natural except the last one."

So the general strategy with unnaturalness arguments is to try to get people to explain what they mean by "unnatural" and then talk about the different ways in which that does or does not have moral relevance. Because even if you call something "unnatural," that's not necessarily a bad thing. We have to say more to sort of flesh out the moral significance of that.

The harm arguments take all different kinds of forms, but the basic idea is that somehow same-sex relationships, homosexuality, involve a harmful lifestyle. And those arguments tend to rest on a lot of bad social science data. So one way to address those arguments is to address that bad data.

Then, finally, the religious arguments. It really depends on what people's religious traditions are. There are sort of two different ways one can go with that. One is to try to work within that tradition and say, "Well, yes, the bible says this. But when we understand that in the context in which it was written, it seems to imply something very different from how you're using it." The other is to say, "Well, yes, the bible says that and that's what it means. But the bible is wrong about certain things." I say "the bible" with a recognition that different religious traditions have different scriptures. However, the claim made in America today is that the "Judeo-Christian bible" condemns same-sex relationships. I think those scriptures do condemn certain forms of same-sex relationships, but whether we should take that as a blanket condemnation, I think, is much more controversial.

MYISHA: What is some of the social science data that critics appeal to in the harm arguments?

JOHN: A lot of that has to do with effects on children and the idea that children do best in a mother-father family and particularly with their own biological mother and father in a stable marriage relationship. The problem with that argument, even apart from some of the debates about the research and what it actually says, is that it doesn't sort of squarely face the options on the table.

Forbidding people to engage in same-sex relationships or have same-sex marriage doesn't mean that more children are going to end up with their married biological mother and father. It just means that the children of lesbian parents, of gay parents—children who are currently being raised in those households—will get the benefit of the stability and the social support of marriage, the legal support of marriage.

So what's interesting is that with respect to those arguments, you can even grant some of the broad social-science claims about which family forms children have the best outcomes in and still not get the conclusion that people want. Now, I don't think we should grant many of those social-science claims, because they often fail to distinguish between different kinds of households that ought to be distinguished. I mean, there's a difference between children, for example, who have experienced divorce or some other event in their lives that has been disruptive in that way and children who begin their lives either in a same-sex lesbian household, same-sex gay household. And those things tend to get blurred in some of the research.

MYISHA: Let's call the person who uses the religious argument the religious skeptic. This skeptic may say, "Well, the scripture says that homosexuality is wrong. If I am to make accommodations, whether that's a hermeneutical accommodation or another, then it ought to be the case that I should make hermeneutical accommodations as it pertains to other laws and norms in the bible." Where does the buck stop, or is homosexuality the exception?

JOHN: Well, to the extent that it's an exception, it's an exception in that it's one of the places where people don't make the accommodations that they're willing to make in other cases. I mean, probably the best example of that is divorce. So when we had not long ago the case in the news of Kim Davis, the Kentucky clerk who did not want to issue marriage licenses to same-sex couples, she said it's because the bible said that this is wrong and she wanted to enforce God's law, not human law. She was asked, "Well, what about divorce?" She herself had been divorced multiple times, but in a way that's not relevant. But what was relevant is that she had no problem issuing licenses to people who had been previously divorced and her response to that was, "Well, that's between them and God."

Well, wait a second. Okay, that's between them and God. But on this other case you're going to enforce God's law? It's a really inconsistent standard, and I think that what often tends to happen is not that people are really trying to produce this sort of consistent, coherent, biblical standard that they're applying in all cases in their lives. Rather, they have these independent objections, maybe visceral reactions to same-sex relationships, and then they sort of pick out the parts of the bible that help back that up.

I don't want to make that as a general claim about all religious people because I have many religious friends who really do try to hold all of that consistently and be consistent in their interpretations of those things. But when we look at how this plays itself out in the political realm, there is definitely inconsistency with respect to homosexuality versus various other things that the bible talks about.

MYISHA: I remember seeing an infograph about traditional marriage. It read, "Let's go back to traditional marriage" but it was satirical. The infograph went throughout the bible and looked at passages that highlighted a range of traditional marriages that were sanctioned in the bible such as marrying your sister-in-law or polygamy. Those were examples of marriage in the bible, but we are not living those out today, not in an American Christian context. Still the term is employed. It seems that there is something attractive about the concept. What do you think is attractive about "traditional marriage"?

JOHN: Well, I get the idea because I'm kind of a traditional guy myself. I'm one of these people who appreciates sort of tried-and-true norms and doesn't like to rock the boat too much unless there are good reasons to rock the boat. But sometimes there are good reasons to rock the boat. Sometimes we realize that the way we've been doing things, the way we've grown accustomed to do things, actually hurts people, actually makes it harder for people to flourish in their lives and does so needlessly.

There's something appealing about tradition because people don't want to sort of reinvent morality from scratch in each generation, they appreciate sort of tried-and-true norms. But we have to be careful not to let that appreciation for tradition become a kind of moral complacency, which too often it can become.

MYISHA: I think in social movements people have a tendency to fight for their particular agenda without seeing how other people's oppression and their own is linked. There are people in the gay and lesbian community as well as others who do not see how a law like North Carolina's HB2 (which required people to use government-run bathroom facilities that corresponded to the gender assigned to them at birth) could have hurt not only the transgender community but themselves. What problems, if any, do you think anti-transgender legislation brings to a society as a whole?

JOHN: People have come to realize that beating up on gay and lesbian people—or even gay, lesbian, and bisexual people—is not so cool anymore. People are going to push back, they're going to speak up, they're going to recognize the bigotry in that.

Now many people on the right wing are picking on transgender people and doing so in really hurtful and damaging ways. And that's bad because it's bad to treat people that way, but it's also bad because anytime we scapegoat a group (I think that is what's happening with transgender people) we miss the real threats that are facing us. So if we want to protect people from aggressive sexual behavior or if we want to protect people from ways in which sexual assault might occur in bathrooms, it's not transgender people we need to worry about, right?

MYISHA: Right, right.

JOHN: I think it's at best a distraction and at worst a real sort of moral travesty, a kind of perversion of what we ought to be doing, which is to focus on the real threats, particularly with respect to threats of sexual violence.

MYISHA: You mentioned Kim Davis. Is it possible to support religious liberty *and* oppose discrimination?

JOHN: I think it's not only possible to support religious liberty and oppose discrimination, I think supporting religious liberty is a way of opposing discrimination. I think that the legacy of religious liberty is a legacy of inclusion, it's a legacy of equality, it's a way in which we say that as a nation, as a people, we want to embrace diverse groups and not marginalize people just because their practices happen to be different from our own.

When people start using the religious liberty banner as a way of licensing discrimination, it betrays that legacy. It's the opposite of what religious liberty has traditionally been about. And so my book *Debating Religious Liberty and Discrimination* is a point-counterpoint book. The counterpoint is being done by Sherif Girgis and Ryan Anderson, two young natural-law defenders of traditional marriage. But it doesn't just talk about same-sex marriage. It talks about a range of issues that provoke controversy under the topic of religious liberty.

MYISHA: Someone might think, "Although I have a job, what is primary to me is my religious faith. And I may live out my faith in my day-to-day practices, including my job." It then seems that supporting religious liberty in some way may equate to discrimination. So what does supporting religious liberty *and* opposing discrimination look like in practice?

JOHN: I think the Kim Davis case is in many ways an easier case than some of the other cases that come up. The other cases that come up are bakers, florists, and other wedding providers. The Kim Davis case involves somebody who is an elected official whose job it is to administer the law and who is explicitly denying the legitimacy of the law that she is bound to administer. I think that if she feels that she cannot administer that law in accordance with the legal requirements, the appropriate thing for her to do is to step aside. There have been cases throughout history where people have said, "Look, I think the law is unjust, I can't be a part of this," but they don't expect to keep getting paid and not do the job. The thing to do is to resign.

I think the cases of the bakers, the florists, and so on are somewhat different because we're not talking about elected officials. We're talking about private business owners. But I also think that there's something important about the idea that when people enter the public square and open businesses that are treated as public accommodations, they should serve people equally. People should not have unpleasant surprises when, for example, they spend an entire day trying on wedding dresses in a wedding shop and then are told later on, "Oh, no, no, no, we're not going to sell it to you because it's for a same-sex wedding."

That's just to me a matter of basic fairness when we enter into the public square and have to interact with people who may have different moral and religious beliefs but agree to abide by certain rules. I think a lot of people don't realize that most states do not have statewide laws that protect people against discrimination on the basis of sexual orientation or gender identity. So it is perfectly legal in many places to turn people away from bakeries, from flower shops, from wedding dress stores, and so on on the basis of those kinds of beliefs.

MYISHA: This sounds similar to the Jim Crow South and its discriminatory laws and practices targeted at black Americans. Some may be tempted to form an analogy between the civil rights struggle for black Americans and the fight for equality for gays and lesbians today. What are your thoughts about forming an analogy between racial discrimination and LGBTQ discrimination?

JOHN: Analogies can be useful. I also think analogies can be tricky. What analogies do is they take two things that are different in certain respects but are similar in certain respects and try to teach us something by looking at the similarities and the differences. I think there are ways in which the similarities between LGBTQ discrimination today and race discrimination today and in the past—can teach us something about the tendency people have to marginalize those they don't understand, they don't want to understand, and they don't agree with.

The analogy, however, can be overused in certain ways, because I don't think the issues are exactly the same. But we never said that they were exactly the same. Analogies are not about things that are exactly the same. They're about things that are similar and those similarities can be instructive.

MYISHA: America has come a long way in its treatment of LGBTQ folks and it still has a long way to go. We also should not forget international struggles. There are countries in which people can be killed for being LGBTQ. What is your hope for the future?

JOHN: My hope for the future is that we keep the progress growing. And look, you're absolutely right to bring up other countries because the things that happen in other countries in terms of discrimination against LGBTQ people are shocking and horrifying. We often don't pay attention to those things, we don't—we either avert our eyes or we don't bother looking for that information. I think it's important for us, as a matter of basic human rights, to pay attention to those things.

But even here, as you pointed out, transgender Americans are facing increasingly explicit hostility in certain states and in certain venues, and frankly, lesbian, gay, and bisexual Americans are too. For all the progress we've made, I think it's important to remember that our experience in academia, maybe our experience in cities where people have access to more job opportunities, more education, and so on, does not necessarily represent the experience of people all across the country. People are still in the closet, they are still experiencing rejection from their families, teenagers are still being kicked out of the house because they're gay, lesbian, bisexual, transgender, and so on.

My hope is that even as we make that progress, we don't forget the people who are still struggling and we don't forget, going back to the point on analogy, that the struggles that other people are experiencing may be helpfully informed by the things that we've learned through the progress we've made so far.

27

Tom Digby on the Problem of Masculinity

MYISHA: What is masculinity? Is it biologically determined or socially constructed?

TOM: Although biological considerations are not altogether irrelevant to masculinity, prioritizing them often camouflages cultural factors. So in my *Love and War* book, I try to bring those cultural elements out and into the open, to expose them so that there's more freedom around them. To accomplish that, I focus on what I call the "cultural programming of masculinity," as well as other aspects of gender, love, and sexuality. In particular, I describe and explain how all of those things flow from cultural militarism and material requirements of war in societies that rely on war to solve social problems, and that's not all societies, as many people mistakenly assume.

In those culturally militaristic societies, there's a presumption of adversariality (adversarial relations) between one's own society and other societies, as well as between individuals. There's also a faith in force, especially violent force, as a way to solve problems. In societies that rely extensively on war, the presumption of adversariality and the faith in force tend to be important elements of masculinity because men are the ones who are usually singled out for the warrior role. And so masculinity is, among other things, a modality for culturally programming boys and men to fulfill the warrior ideal of manhood.

Another crucial element of masculinity in these war-reliant societies is the ability to manage the capacity to care about the suffering of others and of oneself. That to me is the fundamentally most important prerequisite for somebody who's going to fight war. In actual combat, an effective warrior must be able to manage empathy in that way. He— and I use the masculine pronoun advisedly—must be able to kill and impose enormous suffering on others; and he must be willing to expose himself to the risk of death and enormous physical and emotional suffering.

Now obviously, not all men, even in militaristic societies, are good at being warriors. And many of them would refuse that role even if they were capable of doing it. Nonetheless, militaristic societies culturally program masculine expectations into virtually all boys and men, regardless of whether they're actually going to play that role. In the US today, most boys and men do not actually fight wars, and do not even go into the military, yet we still use things like football to culturally program them to have a presumption of adversariality, of faith in force, and an ability to manage the capacity to care about the suffering of others and themselves. I have to say, Myisha, that it shouldn't be surprising then that we find those adversariality tendencies, of faith in force, and managing empathy even among many professional philosophers who are majority male.

Let me just be really clear about a couple of things. What I've tried to describe and explain are patterns of cultural programming in militaristic societies, not generalizations about all men and not generalizations about all societies. And I should note that there are many other aspects of masculinity than those I have described, many of which have been discussed brilliantly by other folks who work in this area, like Susan Bordo, Bonnie Mann, Tom Keith, Byron Hurt, Jackson Katz, Michael Kimmel, CJ Pascoe, Tristan Bridges, and a bunch of other people.

MYISHA: Would you say that the masculinity that you have described, and I know it varies in different cultures, is what we would consider hegemonic masculinity?

TOM: Yes, it certainly makes sense to use that term because it's inherently focused on domination and control of an enemy in war. But that carries over into the rest of life as well. So it's hegemonic on an individual level. It's also hegemonic in the sense that there's an effort in culturally militaristic societies to culturally program all men and boys into this particular masculine role. It's hegemonic in that sense even though many of them, as I said, are really ill suited for that role and really resist it.

MYISHA: Let's talk a little bit more about what is wrong with this hegemonic masculinity. Someone might say, "Well, I need this masculinity in order to survive in the world, in order to be considered a man." If it is tied to their survival, what is so problematic about this kind of masculinity?

TOM: If you mean morally wrong, that's not something I address, not least because I have a deep philosophical skepticism about moral judgments, and partly because of my growing up in a culture of hate that was grounded in moralism. So I'm very skeptical about moral judgments. But if you mean wrong pragmatically, then I have a long answer to that. I would have to answer that question in terms of the harms of masculinity to both men and women, and especially how those harms to men and women are intertwined.

Let's take the connection between one of the worst harms for women—rape—and those three factors of militaristic masculinity that I described: adversariality, faith in force, and the ability to manage the capacity to care about the suffering of others. Actually, maybe I don't even need to elaborate on how those elements of masculinity connect with the problem of rape. But there is indeed more to the story. Militaristic societies rely heavily on misogyny to both culturally program and police masculinity. For example, to call a man a "pussy" or "bitch" is to throw him over the fence of the culturally programmed gender binary. It's saying that he is not a man at all but rather a woman. It's not like mistaking his eye color. It's a profound insult that only works if women are presumed to be inferior and even detested. Thus, such insults are grounded in misogyny.

So that provides another piece of the explanation of the problem of rape. Misogyny is used to culturally program and reinforce masculinity, so it shouldn't be a surprise that militaristic societies have a problem with men raping. But not all of the victims of those men are women, of course. The thing is misogyny is also operative in many cases, maybe even in most cases, where the victim of rape is a man or a boy. Those are the cases where the rape is understood to make a man into a woman symbolically. In prison he becomes another man's bitch. In the civil war in the Congo, men who have been raped have been called bush wives. There are a lot more examples of how misogyny harms both men and women in militaristic societies, but that may give you enough of a sense of how that works.

MYISHA: There are scholars who are studying masculinity, as you have mentioned. Why isn't femininity examined?

TOM: Well, in societies that rely on war, masculinity and femininity are certainly intertwined. In fact, there's not nearly as much emphasis on those things in societies that are not reliant on war. In fact, in some cases there's simply no such thing as masculinity and femininity in non-war-reliant societies.

The cultural programming of the warrior ideal of masculinity ensures that dominance is an integral factor in masculinity. Correspondingly, submissiveness becomes an integral part of culturally programmed femininity. There are a lot of reasons involved with that. But in any case, it's important to note that these are culturally programmed patterns, not generalizations.

One factor in femininity is obviously maternalism. In militaristic societies, there tends to be an emphasis on maternalism because of the need to keep the population at high levels because of a lot of people being killed in traditional wars. It is important to note now that these are just culturally programmed patterns. I use the word "pattern" the way that Marilyn Frye does, not generalizations. There have always been strong and dominant women just as there have always been submissive men. But part of the cultural programming is to have pejoratives and other sanctions for both of those cases. Women who are political leaders are often called bitches, witches, et cetera. And men who demonstrate devotion to a lover are often described as whipped.

As for people who've addressed femininity, I think the most important and valuable work that's been done on femininity actually comes from someone who was one of my dearest friends, Sandra Bartky. Somebody else who comes to mind would be Susan Bordeaux, who has written brilliantly on both femininity and masculinity.

MYISHA: When I'm walking through a door, and a gentleman before me does not hold the door open, I have said under my breath, "Chivalry is dead." (And don't even get me started with talking about how I feel when men do not pay for dinner dates.) But you claim in your book that chivalry is consistent with misogyny. How so?

TOM: First of all, chivalry implies that men are strong and women are weak; that women need men but men don't need women, and so on. There's an asymmetry going on in chivalry that it is problematic from my point of view. I would say that historically, if not a crucial part of misogyny, it plays a big role in misogyny.

MYISHA: Let's talk about relationships. What has gone horribly wrong with heterosexuality? I wonder if what has gone wrong with heterosexuality can also transfer or infiltrate itself into same-sex relationships.

TOM: I rely heavily on the perspicacity of Nietzsche. Nietzsche wrote toward the end of the nineteenth century at a time when, not only in the US but also in Europe, the notion of equal rights for women and men was in the air. He wrote about the problems that beset heterosexual relationships specifically.

Now obviously, there are plenty of same-sex relationships that go awry, and even some that do so to the extent of violence. But there are problems in straight relationships that are specific to heterosexuality, that flow from the very structure of heterosexuality, namely the "hetero" part; the assumption that there are two genders that are differentiated in specific ways that contribute to the culturally programmed notion of men being dominant and women being submissive. Nietzsche says that that pattern leads inevitably to antagonism. This is easily confirmed by domestic violence statistics. It is for many people, even in everyday life such as arguments and that sort of thing. The notion of women being submissive is rapidly dissipating. We're becoming more accustomed to women in positions of power in politics and business, even religion. Increasingly, girls grow up expecting to occupy those positions of power, even thinking that submissiveness to men is ridiculous. Those attitudes have always been around, especially in certain segments of culture, but they're becoming more prevalent now.

The problem is that masculinity has not evolved in sync with the changes in the lives of women and girls. A lot of men are freaking out, expressing their fears and anxieties with over-the-top misogyny in video-game culture and political discourse, for example. And men have always responded to threats to their domination with violence. I think misogyny is becoming a bit more prevalent. The reason is that this pattern of masculinity has not evolved in sync with femininity, so a lot of men feel bewildered by what's happening in the world of gender.

MYISHA: How can we create more love and less war between genders? What can a solution be? Is there a solution?

TOM: I'm not sure that I have the solution, but a good first step would be to reveal that the gender binary is an illusion. In a society where masculinity is constructed and policed using misogynistic taunts towards men, this is obviously going to create acrimony in their relationships, not just in their love relationships, romantic and erotic, but also in the worlds of work, friendship, politics, religion, and everything else. We can see misogyny in all those areas of life.

I focused on love in the book, but I do often try to emphasize that the implications and ramifications are much broader than just the context of love. Once the myths surrounding masculinity and femininity are debunked, that opens up the possibility of men and women relating to each other with mutual respect, which seems to me pretty obviously crucial to a successful love relationship. It's absolutely crucial then to eliminate the role of misogyny in constructing and policing masculinity. We can't really expect men and women to get along if what it means to be a man is grounded in the hatred of women. Those are some elements. Just in general, a sense of egalitarianism in a relationship seems to me crucial in order for a relationship to succeed.

MYISHA: What do you think of men's rights activists (MRAs), organizations made up of men who feel that they are oppressed as men?

TOM: I guess they would be good examples of the kind of fears and anxieties that men have with regards to the changing roles of women. Women really are gaining more power in the world in every part of culture—politics, economics, technology, business, et cetera. And a lot of men are afraid of that. They have not been exposed to other ways of understanding masculinity and the ways in which masculinity is actually harmful to them. I mean, if a man has been culturally programmed to be able to suppress concern about his own happiness and concern about his own suffering, that has all kinds of horrible implications in men's lives. A lot of studies have shown, for example, that men are less likely to seek medical help when they have health problems. But also, it's emotionally destructive to men to manage empathy in the way that's demanded by masculinity.

I think a lot of these men in MRAs just don't understand the destructive role that masculinity plays in many men's lives, and they haven't been exposed to either a critique of masculinity or to alternative visions of what it might mean to be a man.

MYISHA: As a man, do you label yourself a feminist? Why or why not?

TOM: It depends on the context. Sometimes when I'm teaching, after I have established rapport and respect, and most importantly coolness with my students, I'll proclaim quite boldly that I am a feminist as a way of countering the stigma that is often attached to the word "feminist" among students. I've learned to avoid controversies about whether a man can be a feminist or not. That to me is not a very interesting issue. My own feminism has been a crucial part of my self-identity for well over thirty years. But as far as I'm concerned, in terms of my public life it's my advocacy of feminism that is important, not the label.

If someone wants to say that men can't be feminists, or that I can't be a feminist, or whatever, it doesn't matter to me. I take the lead of bell hooks actually, who emphasized that feminism is really about advocating feminism, advocating different kinds of relations of men and women, and eliminating misogyny; those sorts of things.

MYISHA: How would you convince a man that "feminism" is not a bad word?

TOM: I've had to do that many times, of course. But to keep the answer short, let me share an anecdote. A few years ago, I was giving a public lecture at William Jewell College near Kansas City, which happens to be my alma mater. The fraternity of which I had been a part briefly as a student got word of my visit, and so all the members of the fraternity were required to attend my lecture. There were, I guess, probably about 300 people there and about 50 of them were members of that group. And I wanted to send a message to my "brothers," as they say, not least because so many fraternities have been actively promoting misogyny on college campuses.

During the Q&A, I found my opportunity to send that message when one of the fraternity members asked why feminism wouldn't get in the way of heterosexual love because it takes the side of one person over the other. I started with the definition of feminism; a simple, min-imal definition that accords with most versions of feminism. The def-inition is this: Feminism is a preference that girls and women not be subjected to disadvantage just because they are girls or women. It's very simple and very straightforward. It doesn't involve an ideology or theory; it's just a preference.

I said, "If you look at it that way, anybody who doesn't embrace feminism is effectively embracing the disadvantaging of girls and women, which is saying a lot about that person's attitudes toward girls and women. And in fact, it's just inherently misogynistic to have that sort of perspective. In other words, being anti-feminist or nonfeminist is effectively to embrace misogyny." I said, "I have a message for the men in this audience. If you plan on being a heterosexual man, then you damn well better embrace feminism, because otherwise you're screwed and not in the good way." And I repeated that.

Of course, I was trying to make a point in that particular con-text. I guess it comes across as aggressive. Like I said earlier, I'm still evolving. But it really has broader implications. Any man, regardless of his sexual orientation, is going to be interacting with women and men in his lifetime, in his work, in friendships, and so on. For those relationships to be happy and fulfilling, and even to be successful on an economic level, then you damn well better embrace feminism.

28

Justin Clardy on Love and Relationships

MYISHA: What is love?

JUSTIN: I'm still trying to figure it out. But I think the answer to that question is going to vary depending upon what kind of love we're talking about. Often when I get that question, people mean romantic love. Of course, we must acknowledge that there are forms of love other than romantic love; the love between friends, parents and children, students and teachers, or coworker and citizens.

There are all of these different kinds of love. I don't think that in each mode they admit to be the same thing. I think that romantic love is having a particular regard for a person, and a particular regard for your relationship with that person. It means to value both of them in a way so as to provide you with reasons, and sometimes special reasons, for action.

So basically, you have a relationship with a person, and that person means so much to you as to provide you with reasons for action. It's valuing your relationship with a person in a certain kind of way, and it's valuing that person in a certain kind of way.

MYISHA: It's the value that I have for that person and that relationship that gives me a reason to act?

JUSTIN: Right.

MYISHA: I have a reason to buy them flowers.

JUSTIN: Right.

MYISHA: Ok, I get it. I have a reason to call them every day. I have a reason to tell them "I love you." These actions are based on the value that I have towards them. Does this same definition apply to love between a mother and child?

JUSTIN: I think so. But it's important to note that when we're talking about relationships themselves, we could be talking about two kinds. We could be talking about attitude-dependent relationships and attitude-independent relationships.

An attitude-dependent relationship is a relationship, where whether or not there is a relationship between the people that are said to be within that relationship depends upon the attitudes that those people have toward one another. I can't be said to be Sally's girlfriend or boyfriend unless there exists some attitude towards Sally that holds that "Hey, I'm Sally's boyfriend!"

But in attitude-independent relationships, the relationship itself does not depend on the attitudes of the people within that relationship. So, you might have Bob and Sally who are brother and sister. Bob might get mad at Sally and say, "Oh man, you're not my sister no more." But they have a biological tie, and the biological tie is what binds their relationship in a certain kind of way. That binding does not depend on any attitude that the two participants have. So, Bob will always be Sally's sister even when he's pissed off or mad at Sally.

MYISHA: Which of those relationships do you think are more complicated? Some social media profiles ask, "Are you in a relationship?" We know the social media site is really asking, "Are you in a romantic relationship?" I don't know if this is still an option, but it used to be the case that one of the options were, "It's complicated." That's also only related to romantic relationships. But I've found that some of the most complicated relationships are really those relationships that you call attitude-independent relationships. Do you feel the same way? Why or why not?

JUSTIN: I don't want to say that family relationships and, say, friendship or romantic relationships—that one admits to being more difficult than the other. Because what it seems like to me is that each comes with their own set of problems, as well as their own set of triumphs and successes.

I tend to look at them as just different sorts of relationships. I like to look at relationships individually as opposed to saying, "Okay, well, look, here's this class of relationships that we'll admit to universally having these characteristics, such that the only good types of family relationships are the ones that admit to x, y, and z." I don't know if a good family relationship admits to having such a formula, nor do I think that a good romantic relationship admits to having such a formula.

MYISHA: There is a R&B ballad by singer Musiq Soulchild called "Teach Me How to Love." It's a beautiful ballad, but after listening to it so many times I began to think to myself, "Really? If you can't love by now, I don't know what I can teach you." Do you think love can be taught?

JUSTIN: Insofar as love involves this particular valuing, I don't know if you can teach a person how to value. But I do think that maybe if not love itself is being taught, there are other things that we tend to associate with love that can be taught; certain patterns of behavior that might be caring, tender, or compassionate. So maybe even if we can't be taught how to love, we can be taught how to be nice, I guess.

It's hard to say whether or not love can be taught. I do think that if you come from a certain family, or if you have had certain sorts of experiences, or whatever, they might put you in a position to be a better or worse lover later. Again, that's hard to say, because I tend to think that, at least when it comes to romantic love, the success of that love will not depend upon me matching some set of conditions that are independent of me. It will depend upon the level of satisfaction that my partner tends to receive from me. That's something that is just kind of hard to say can be taught, because I don't know who my partner will be or so on and so forth.

MYISHA: Do you think there's a difference between loving and being in love?

JUSTIN: Oh yes, I think so. When we say, "being in love," we use the term to signal a distinct mode of love, and that mode is usually romantic love. But more generally, a person can love; they can have this particular regard for a person and their relationship with another person, without being said to romantically love them. I think that friends do this most commonly, but you also have, again, other forms of love like family love or parental love.

So there is a difference between simply loving and being in love; whereas we use the term "being in love" to designate or to signal romantic relationships or romantic involvement.

MYISHA: I must admit that in my life, I've loved my romantic partners, but I wasn't necessarily in love with all of them. How can you explain that?

JUSTIN: I think that the mode of being in love itself can vary. Remember, it's a particular valuation. How you value a person, and your relationship with them, might not always be the same. Our partners, in the course of relationships, behave in ways that give us reasons to not, in a sense, value them less as people; but they might give us reasons to value our particular type of relationship with them a little bit less. I don't think it's uncommon that, if we've been in love romantically, at some later point it's also true that we say, "Oh, well, no, I just love this person." I think that love is not something that is permanent; it can go back and forth depending upon the reasons that you have.

Insofar as love involves providing a person with reasons for action, we have to realize that some of those reasons would imply that an action should be that we break up with a particular person. If we can have that type of reason in a romantic relationship, I don't think that it would be too far of a stretch to also think that we could have a reason in a romantic relationship that causes us to value the relationship with that person a little bit less.

MYISHA: What is your view on monogamy?

JUSTIN: Well, it's always interesting when people want to hear my perspective on monogamy. A lot of times people might have read what I've written in a particular blog post, "Marriage and Commitment," and think that I'm anti-monogamy; or they might have seen a recorded talk of mine on polyamory and think, "Oh, he's anti-monogamy."

But I think that's a misunderstanding and I'll try my best to explain. When it comes to monogamy, it's a type of romantic relationship. But by no means is it the only type of romantic relationship. I also don't think that it's the only type of romantic relationship that is valuable. Now, we've got to be careful if we think that monogamous romantic relationships are the only type of romantic relationships that are valuable, because a similar thing has been said throughout history about heterosexual relationships, which has excluded the homosexual community as well as other alternative relationship styles. If monogamy is the only type of romantic relationship that is valuable, well, what is it about a monogamous relationship that makes it the only type of valuable relationship? If other types of relationships can be said to admit these characteristics, we have to realize that they're not different; they should be treated similarly, or the same.

A lot of times people point to the value of monogamy as being held by commitment. It's valuable because people are committed to each other. When you're with only one person, that shows that you can be committed. Polyamory means there are people who have more than one open romantic relationship at a time, where it can actually be said that they are loving more than their one partner, or two partners, or three partners. What is found in these relationships sometimes is that there are commitments present within them. A triad, a polyamorous couple of three people, might commit to one another to not add a fourth person; or a quad, a polyamorous couple of four people, might commit to one another as to not include a fifth person. These are different types of commitments, or alternative commitments, but commitments nonetheless. We could have multiple commitments to our friends; we could have multiple commitments to our children if we have more than one child. So it's hard to argue that when it comes to a romantic relationship, the only type of commitment that we can see exhibited is to one person.

So I'm not anti-monogamy. I think that actually, my perspective allows me to be tolerant of monogamous relationships and say, "Yeah, that's cool if that's what you're into"; but it also says, "Hey, polyamorous folks, homosexuals and asexuals, and all these other alternative relationship styles—y'all are cool too." Whereas what I found most prevalent in our society is this harsh attitude toward persons who might find themselves having polyamorous desires, or people clinging so highly to the value of monogamy that they ostracize and exclude other individuals, without considering them or their feelings.

Again, relationships don't have conditions in them independent of the people that are in them. If my partner and I, or Bob and Sally are fine with including Susan, there can't be anything that I can say as an external observer about their arrangement that means that it's less valuable. I might not prefer that arrangement myself, but I have a hard time saying, "Hey, yeah, you folks' arrangement is flawed, and you cannot be said to be in love in the same way as I am."

MYISHA: What do you think about married swingers? Does that complicate the polyamorous view of commitment you just articulated?

JUSTIN: I don't have a problem with it. Again, I think that the terms of a relationship ought to be left to the participants of that relationship. I have a very hard time with external persons telling people within a relationship how they should behave within their relationship. I can't tell, for instance, my brother and his romantic partner, "Hey, you guys should be doing it like this." Like dude, that's your relationship. That's not my jurisdiction. So, if you guys don't have a problem with having sex with persons outside of one another, I can't really say that that's wrong, or that type of activity is contrary to the way that you all value one another within your relationship.

But we do so; often without considering what we're saying and how it's affecting the people that our comments are aimed at. Swingers have feelings, too, and to be the recipient of harsh treatment on the basis of their romantic preference is no different, I think, or it's different in some regards, but not entirely different than us treating homosexual or lesbian people differently on the basis of their romantic preferences. We have to be careful when we make those claims.

MYISHA: So let's get into the political side of things. What is the role of love in politics for you?

JUSTIN: To answer this question, we've got to realize that societies are made up of people who have emotions. We already have governmental institutions that can and do affect the emotions of the citizens within a particular society. This is done through the national anthems we sing, the holidays we celebrate, and the public spaces we create and inhabit. What we have to realize is that in just the same way as listening to Big Sean or Kanye West makes you feel some kind of way when you're listening to them, singing the National Anthem also evokes a certain type of emotion in a citizen that is geared toward the country as its object. It makes you feel a certain kind of way about your country.

If we're saying that love is an emotion as well, then it might be possible for us to use these very same government institutions to inspire in people, or to cultivate in people, emotions that are more favorable to love like compassion, tenderness, care, and sympathy. I think that insofar as we all tend to value love, it can have a proper place in society. And one way we could bring it about would be to use our institutions to cultivate these sorts of things that are favorable to love.

Section 6

EMOTIONS AND ART
IN PUBLIC LIFE

29

Paul C. Taylor on Black Aesthetics

MYISHA: You talk about the problem of racial invisibility in *Black Is Beautiful: A Philosophy of Black Aesthetics*. What is this philosophical problem of racial invisibility?

PAUL: Well, on a certain level it's what it sounds like. On another level it's the kind of thing that towering artists like Ralph Ellison and Toni Morrison and towering thinkers and critics like Michele Wallace have written about. It's a multilayered problem that has to do with the degrees to which and ways in which people of color tend not to register properly in certain kinds of social contexts. So the kinds of consideration and regard and concern you'd show to your fellows in society somehow just gets by a certain group of us. And in varying ways, that's what the problem of invisibility is.

If you think about those famous opening lines or passages from Ellison's *Invisible Man*, there's that strange encounter on the street with the guy who bumps into him. And the guy is surprised like "Oh, I didn't even see you there." Invisibility is just that black folk in particular don't register as persons, as people with perspectives, or as people with subject positions that are worth considering in ethical transactions.

MYISHA: Tell me a little bit more about how Ralph Ellison and Toni Morrison in particular have informed your thinking about black invisibility.

PAUL: It actually started with Morrison. I, like a lot of people, encountered both of these texts in high school and didn't know what to make of them because we weren't given the resources to understand them properly, I think, at least in my high school. The first one I came back to, as someone with more resources to bring to bear, was Morrison, and I read *The Bluest Eye*. That text is animated by this remarkable, phenomenological reflection that involves this young woman finding herself in a position in which she's completely unable to register her own personhood in a certain way. She desperately wants blue eyes, which she doesn't have, which, being a certain kind of person, she's not going to have unless she has technological interventions of certain kinds. And she cannot imagine herself as beautiful for that reason, and other people have the same issue with that. That's where it started for me. That's not Ellison's invisibility problem yet. That's a deeper problem. That's the kind of thing Frantz Fanon writes about. That's a kind of internalized inability to register your own subjectivity, personhood, worth, and value.

Then Morrison goes on and talks about invisibility in other contexts. The version of it I get from her is about the inability to register black perspectives or personas. She talks about it later on in *Playing in the Dark* in connection with this remarkable passage from Hemingway, which is meant to stand in for all sorts of ways in which black folk don't show up in literature except as devices of a certain kind—plot devices or narrative devices, machinery.

The easiest way to think of this is the generations of North Atlantic literature that describes characters in racially unmarked terms until they get to the Negroes and then it's, "The Negro did this" or "The black person did this," whereas everyone else is just Fred, Tom, and Sally. That's the clearest point of entry into that kind of invisibility. It's, paradoxically, a kind of hypervisibility. You're invisible as a person. You cannot be racially unmarked because you're hypervisible as a racial object, a racialized object.

Then I came back to Ellison, who gives you an interesting way of thinking through the more basic or more straightforward versions of this peculiar failure to register another person's presence.

MYISHA: There is this popular argument that says something like "Well, the beauty gap is narrowing because blacks wearing their hair natural is now considered beautiful, more beautiful than it was ten or

twenty years ago. People are also now admiring black female bodies."
But you disagree with this conclusion. What is the beauty gap? Why do
you think the beauty gap is *not* narrowing?

PAUL: My dear friend and colleague Eddie Glaude has written a wonderful book called *Democracy in Black*. At the heart of that book, he puts
an idea out called the "value gap." The idea behind that is that there's a
kind of comprehensive divide between the way places like the US value
white people and the way they value people who are not white. It's a
very simple idea but very powerful idea because we can see it playing
out in all sorts of domains.

We see it playing out less often in the kinds of ways it used to in
the grainy civil rights footage from the mid-twentieth century US civil
rights movement, in terms of explicit acts of oppression and aggression
based on race. We see it playing out more often in terms of things like
colleges inviting us to talk about terms such as implicit attitudes and
that sort of thing. But it's there and we see it. One way we can see it is
by tracking all the other gaps. We can track the achievement gap and
the gap between the mortgage rates that similarly situated people of
different races get.

The beauty gap is one other version of this deeper sort of values
gap. The idea, of course, is that there are all sorts of ways in which
people who are socialized by appealed hegemonic aesthetic norms,
norms of bodily aesthetics in places like the US, have decided and act
as if people of color are less attractive than white people.

Now, is this as much the case as it used to be? Well, no, of course,
not. But we—in deference to the thought that our way of engaging this
version of the value gap has changed—spin this sort of false narrative. We say, "It used to be the case that black bodies were universally
demonized and despised, and now that's changed because "we" desire
them, they are objects of desire." That is James Baldwin's "we," the sort
of abstract hegemonic American subject. "There are all these ways in
which we now credit the beauty of black bodies."

To which I and many other scholars—I'm not the first one to talk
about this—say, "Well, just look at the history and you'll find that black
bodies were always desired?" The desire was just bound up with all
sorts of weird other things. So Thomas Jefferson and Sally Hemings—if
that's about anything, it's about desire. It's about lots of other things,
of course.

It's about power, it's about all kinds of things. But I mean, you can
see this in Jefferson's notes in the state of Virginia. He talks about the
tragedy of these boisterous passions overcoming white people and

they're put in a situation where they've got a wolf by the ears and they can't let go. This is an expression of the very peculiar kind of ambivalence that's at the heart of white supremacy that can bind together desire and aversion all at once.

We see this. So it can't just be linear progress from "black bodies were despised to black bodies are desired." It has to be more complicated than that. My suggestion is that the complexity is something we can track from the beginning of the US to now, and it plays out in different ways. But the one thing it does not do is give us a kind of linear-progress narrative.

If you look at the things that are meant to be markers of progress now—the example I use in the book is black female artist Beyoncé on the cover of *GQ* Magazine. People look at that and then claim that that wouldn't have happened fifteen years ago. *But* that can happen even as in other contexts, black bodies are still demonized and despised and subject to aversive responses in ways that are mediated by aesthetic judgments. The sort of linear-progress narrative is too simple, even though it is surely the case that things have changed.

MYISHA: What do you say about the popular phrase that, "Beauty is in the eye of the beholder," which is the idea that we can't help who we find beautiful and who we're attracted to? Do you agree with this phrase, or do you think that behind all of our attractions and perceptions of beauty is this social under-grounding that we're unaware of?

PAUL: Yes, to all of the above. Yes, beauty is in the eye of the beholder, but the eye is a socially constructed phenomenon. The eye is not an innocent eye. This is Toni Morrison's point. The eye, the bluest eye, is something that is an artifact of social processes unfolding in a certain way. One of our burdens as responsible agents, as hopefully responsible agents navigating our social terrain sensibly, intelligently, and critically, is to take responsibility for the persons that we become at the intersection of the various social forces that aspire to create us in the old mold.

This is when we have to distinguish first-order and second-order kinds of responses. There's the beauty that my eye beholds and then there's the critical reflection that I undertake to interrogate the eye that's doing this beholding. So it's not just a one-stage process. Yes, the eye beholds things in a certain way, but then I can subject that process to criticism and self-criticism and self-reflection and say, "I shouldn't respond in this way to that thing."

We've all had this experience in other contexts. At least many of us, most of us, I hope, have had this experience. There are things we like; then we find out more about them and we think, "Wow, gee, I probably shouldn't like that as much as I do." Then, lo and behold, it turns out we don't like it as much as we did because we know more about it. And the thing that we behold is now a different thing and we can respond to it differently, even at the level of immediate—what John Dewey would have called "immediate responses."

So yes, it is the case that on a certain level your responses just are your responses. But as a critical being that can cultivate virtue, better habits, and dispositions, we have the opportunity—I would say in many cases we have the burden, the obligation—to subject ourselves to the kind of criticism that allows us to interrogate that immediate act of perception and retrain our perception so that we have different responses.

MYISHA: If I find people from different races attractive, find them beautiful, and I also even date them, have I transcended some racial barrier?

PAUL: Maybe. You've transcended some barrier. You've transcended the sort of minimal aversive barrier that would have ruled out a certain segment of the human population for you. So yeah, you've transcended something, and good for you. (Laughter.) That probably wouldn't be the end of the story. Because, then, we have to ask questions about fetishization. We have to ask questions about what's going on in you when you comport yourself in this way.

These are the questions that, again, I want to suggest that people ought to ask themselves. Sometimes when we have these conversations, people either are or sound as if they are passing judgment on their fellows. That's probably not usually a productive or an appropriate way to proceed. The way I prefer to think of it is that we're providing resources to our fellows to interrogate themselves, because I don't know what's in your head. You probably don't know what's in your head until you think about it. This is why God invented therapy.

What we do in these conversations about these kinds of things is give each other the resources to interrogate ourselves in our moments, our critical reflective moments and say, "Well, why is it that I like this? Why is it that I only date white guys?" Whatever race you are, "Why is it that this is where my affections and my attractions lead me? Is this something worth interrogating? Is this something that connects to other things about me?" These are the questions we have to ask ourselves.

And so yes, if I get to the point where I say, "Oh, I see someone who's from a different race and my momma wouldn't want me to date her, but, well, I can imagine it," then maybe I've overcome something that I might have uncritically let govern my behavior. But that shouldn't be the end of the story. We should always be subject to self-criticism and self-reflection.

MYISHA: What is black music?

PAUL: That's it? That's the end of the question?

MYISHA: That's it.

PAUL: It's a short question but it's a hard question. So the easy answer is the answer that I refuse at the beginning of my book. The easy answer is: Black music is whatever Negroes have produced. So if a white person plays the blues, that's a problem because blues is black music and that belongs to black people, so then you've imported notions of cultural possession and property; what Stuart Hall would have called "cultural insiderism." But as an abstract sort of philosophical matter in the way that philosophical aestheticians usually think about this, that's not where you want to begin. You don't want to start with ideas about cultural possession.

So what is black music? For me, black music is a label that we can use in provisional and evolving ways to point to the musical practices that have specifiable, discernible roots in music of the African continent—or in parts of the African continent, and there are ethnomusicological stories to tell about this. There are certain kinds of practices that we can trace from West Africa to the Caribbean to the southern US and so forth.

That's where it starts for me. It's a straightforwardly, empirically, verifiable, or disconfirmable account of certain kinds of musical practices. But then it becomes a political question. What is it that we pull from these historical traditions to continue the process of racial formation in, for example, liberatory context?

So it's a complicated question, but it's a question—maybe this is the way to put it: The question is in a certain way both harder and easier than it appears. It is harder than it appears because we'd like to be able to point once and for all to specific idioms and say, "That's black music," and we can't do that.

But it's easier than it appears because the burden is lighter. When we ask the question, "What is black music?" we sometimes act as if we want to answer that outside of a story about racial formation processes. For me, black music—that label—points us to a set of phenomena that are bound up with racial formation processes. So they are part of this contest over racial meanings. They are part of this contest over how to distribute the benefits and burdens of social cooperation in a racialized society. Black music is an evolving thing that has specifiable roots, but it can grow in unpredictable directions.

MYISHA: Are white artists not being "authentic" when they do black music or when they do it in a so-called black way? Is it always a practice of cultural appropriation when they do black music?

PAUL: It's not always an invidious form of cultural appropriation. There's a rich story to tell about what cultural appropriation is, and I don't think we have told this story adequately yet. There's some very good work out there on it now, and there's more coming. But we typically use it as a term of criticism. To appropriate is "bad in this way," and so I want to talk about that as invidious cultural appropriation.

It's not always invidious. This is what Alain Locke had in mind when he said, "Cultures have no color." In a perfect world, a world in which ethno-racial boundaries weren't bound up with politics (some of us think that that's unavoidable, that's what race is), culture would work in racialized contexts the way it works in other contexts. People borrow things from each other. People steal things from each other. Mozart stole from Handel! That's just how culture works.

So it's difficult to start immediately talking about appropriation whenever somebody borrows something from another context or learns something from somebody who doesn't look like them. That's hard because that's just how culture works.

But when you build back in the politics, the power asymmetries and the access and opportunity that come with racialized boundaries and terrain, then we start to get some traction for ideas about invidious cultural appropriation.

One way of raising worry about contemporary white artists is the way people used to raise worry about Elvis, the way people raised worry about Vanilla Ice. People used to raise worry about Art Pepper, in modern jazz. The worry is that these people are doing things people who look differently have done for a long time but didn't get credit for. And now you put a white face on it, and then look what happened. That's the worry.

It's Michele Wallace's worry about restraint of trade. It's about unequal access to certain kinds of opportunities. Those opportunities are segregated by race. That's where the worry comes in. We present it sometimes as a worry about the nature of the enterprise, of the body. So a person with the wrong kind of body cannot perform or participate in this performance tradition. It feels like a metaphysical claim.

But my view is that it's better understood as the beginning of a political claim. It's an expression of skepticism about the degree to which the relevant opportunities are equitably distributed. And so the worry is, "A white artist like Iggy Azalea just ain't that good a rapper and nobody would care if she looked differently." I'm not an expert in this performance tradition, so I don't know—I've listened to her and I don't think she's interesting musically. But to me that's the interesting version of the worry. If you looked like Shaniqua on the corner and you were making those noises, nobody would care. But because you look the way you do, you get more attention, which means you get more money, which means you get more play, which means you end up in a better place. And that seems inappropriate.

MYISHA: How about the issue of authenticity?

PAUL: Authenticity is really interesting, and like everything else we were talking about, complicated. Because there are different levels of it, different degrees of it. We talk about it in different ways and different contexts. Sometimes when we talk about authenticity, we're worried about something like fakes or forgeries. So you present something as one thing and it's really something else. But in other contexts, it's more straightforwardly an existential kind of consideration, that in some sense participating in a certain performance tradition is not faithful to what you really are. And it's hard to tell that story unless you're committed to a certain kind of racial ontology. The story goes like this: the white artist is the kind of creature in virtue of which he cannot authentically participate in this performance tradition. Again, that's a hard story to tell. The easier story is the political one.

Where does authenticity fit into that? Well, this is where we might invoke a kind of existentialist ethic and say, "Well, it's incumbent upon that white artist to figure out how he can in good faith inhabit this space." Has he really grappled with the power relations that inform the space of cultural production that he inhabits so that he can do that honestly and sincerely and so forth?

That's one way to get the authenticity question. I think it's the only way. Then we're thrown back onto the burden of self-interrogation and self-reflection. I can't tell you you're being inauthentic. But you can figure out for yourself whether you've entered into a productive relationship with the forces that make you who you are.

Behind all of this is the complexity that informs the very spaces we inhabit at these moments. There's a wonderful book by a great historian named Charles Hughes called *Country Soul*. In this wonderful book, he goes through the three principal sites at which R&B music was produced in the middle of the twentieth century. We can tell similar stories about the old blues performers like Son House. The black performers that we think of as paragons of black music could play all kinds of things. Some of them loved country music and they wanted to play country music, but then they got funneled into this industry that was committed to a certain kind of racial politics in virtue of which the black guy can't play country music. He's got to play this new thing; we're going to call it R&B. And the white guy who hung out with the black guy can't play R&B; he's got to be a country musician.

So there are these moments in which we artificially, in a certain sense, prop up the boundaries that allow us to raise the worry about authenticity. We have to engage the question of where these boundaries are at on an even deeper level. The authenticity question again becomes a matter of interrogating your relationship to, among other things, certain kinds of power relations.

If I'm the white guy, Muscle Shoals, and I can sing Aretha Franklin's songs the way that Aretha sings it but they won't let me record it, should I think this is just basic unfairness? Or should I accept the fact that, if it is a fact, that by virtue of my skin color I have a different prospect, I have a different relationship to certain kinds of opportunities?

We have to tell these stories in a fine-grain way by appealling to what's going on in those contexts. But they can't be simple stories about the metaphysics of certain bodies and the way those bodies inhabit certain cultural spaces divorced from politics.

30

Amir Jaima on the Power of Literature

MYISHA: What kind of questions does philosophy of literature attempt to address?

AMIR: Philosophy of literature isn't exactly a traditional, classic subfield of philosophy. It's really under aesthetics. Aesthetics is asking questions about what kinds of knowledge can be acquired through a sense of perception, or just through experience in general. Classic questions that emerge out of aesthetics are: what is beauty, and what is art? But it includes other questions like: what is style, and what is the value of appearance? So when you get to writing in particular, you have this sort of division between how the text appears and what it says. Aesthetics traditionally looks at how it appears as really the realm of art and literature, and then what it says as the realm of philosophy and thought and reason.

The thing that I'm interested with in looking at philosophy of literature is trying to break down that distinction of thinking that "Well, how we say something affects what it says." You hear this all the time when adults talk to children, or when your parents gave you advice and whatnot. You say you're sorry and it sounds like you didn't mean it. It's like "Oh, sorry." But if you say it like you mean it, it actually can communicate some content because how you say it matters. That's an analogy for thinking about what I think of as writing in general. When I look at philosophy of literature, I think, "Well, there's something about the way that literature communicates its content, but actually, it also is communicating something in addition to what it's saying."

Then if you look at philosophy in general, the opposite or the converse of that argument is that "Well, the way that philosophy traditionally communicates ideas also communicates something." The argument that Nussbaum makes in her work, *Love's Knowledge*, starts off by saying that the choice to write a drama, novel, or an essay communicates something already that affects what it is that we're going to say using this form. And maybe there are some things that we can't say using one form or another, without there being sort of an implicit contradiction.

MYISHA: So it would appear that literature and philosophy are worlds apart. How do you see them?

AMIR: I see them as rather continuous. I think that it's a false distinction to look at one as just art, and the other as the work of reason and theory. The way that I like to think of them is that they are basically two ways to ask questions and to engage ideas. In ancient Greece with Plato, this distinction was collapsed, where all of the dialogues are unmistakably literary works. As we move through a history of philosophy, a lot of figures do write using literary forms. But in the twentieth century, we've sort of made this sharp distinction between them. I think it's a matter of convention that that's happened, and it does a disservice to philosophy. The distinction we make is greater than the distinction actually is, to use a rather cryptic way of putting it.

I think that traditional ways of writing philosophy can learn things from literary forms that would redeem them in many ways that would make them better. It would bring philosophy back to, I think, what it should be doing, which is helping us live our lives and solve real problems.

MYISHA: Is literature philosophy?

AMIR: I think so. It's not all good philosophy in the same way that I don't think all philosophy is good philosophy. So for the same reasons I think literature is definitely philosophy.

I think a lot of times when literature is not good philosophy, it's because maybe the writers don't think of what they're doing as philosophical projects; that sort of in spite of themselves, they are engaging in a philosophical project. That's part of the general convention that literature is not philosophy. I know there are some writers who are like "Oh, I'm just telling a good story and I'm not trying to understand the world." But I don't think there's any way to tell a story, a believable story about the world, that doesn't also say something of the world in a way that I think is similar to what philosophy does.

MYISHA: What is it about black literature that makes it so philosophically rich?

AMIR: Excellent question! The short answer is that I think black literature is the venue where a lot of black philosophy has taken place. It's sort of been relegated to that space. Historically, black figures have been excluded from philosophy for a number of reasons. One of the reasons is just the history of racism. It was assumed that black thinkers weren't really thinking; they're just experiencing.

On the other hand, the question of identity, what does it mean to be black, is a question that a lot of black literature has engaged. The question of what does it mean to be anyone, to be a particular kind of person, is a question that starts from a very particular place. It starts from our experiences. There's a long history in philosophy, of making "experience" a dirty word. If it's just your experience, it falls to relativism. But in fact, there are a lot of questions that really begin with our experience. The black experience, particularly the black experience of racism, and experiences of confronting violence, oppression, and domination, are all examples. These are things that begin with experience, and it requires a story to even explain the contradictions and injustices, the things that don't make sense, or why these are even questions.

Something happens and the first question we ask is, "Well, why did that happen?"; we try to make sense of it. Then that's the starting place of a whole philosophical line of inquiry. Why did this happen? There's a particular set of questions that I think are unique to the black experience for historical reasons, and that's where black literature makes this huge contribution. There have been a lot of philosophical figures who have taken that question up in traditional philosophical forms. So it's not to say that literature is the only place that you can raise these questions, or the only manner. But the places where those questions emerge, and sometimes I think the best place to engage them, is in the literary form. Historically, black literature has been doing that work.

MYISHA: Tell me about what you admire about Toni Morrison's work, and why you believe she is a philosopher?

AMIR: She's one of these literary figures who I think is self-consciously philosophical. In one of her nonfiction works, she explains that if any of her work is not about the community, then she has failed. She is trying to understand her own experience, the experience of her community.

She is trying to make sense of it, to assuage it; to provide vocabulary, understanding, context, and community through these texts. I think she's deliberately trying. Her first novel, *The Bluest Eye*, describes the tragic experience of a little black girl who wants blue eyes. Morrison is imagining the self-hatred that goes into thinking that in order for her to be beautiful, her own eyes need to be changed in ways that are impossible. The burden of being beautiful against a white standard of beauty is tragic. That's the story of *The Bluest Eye*.

I think Toni Morrison's novels engage aspects of the black experience in their contradiction. She is sometimes critical, sometimes praising, but she is not just shining a light on them and saying, "Here is what it means to be black." No, no, no. Toni Morrison, in telling this particular story, is making arguments. She's making proposals for how we should think about ourselves, and how we should engage racism and develop communities. The protagonists become exemplars or heroes. The antagonists, of course, are then ways not to be. So in some ways these are ethical problems. But Toni Morrison is doing this deliberately, self-consciously, and she does this in every work on purpose.

MYISHA: Philosophers make arguments explicitly and in a certain form. You say that Morrison is making arguments. Say more about how argument making happens in literature. Help us, as readers of literature, to see these arguments more clearly.

AMIR: There are a number of ways that I think that happens in literature. In order to tell a story, it requires doing something; it requires the reader suspending disbelief. They're telling a work that's explicitly fiction, but the reader has to say, "Well, maybe this could happen."

We could think there's sort of an implicit argument that the author must make for the reader to suspend disbelief successfully. In science fiction, for example, or superhero narratives, there are characters like Superman. However, people can't fly and Krypton is not a real place. But if Krypton did exist, and that person came to Earth, maybe this is what that person's life experience would be like. So we could extract deductions that start from our basic laws of physics and say, "Well, this is what the world would have to be like for someone to be able to fly in our world on Earth." That happens also when we look at characters who are very much like ourselves, though not as dramatically different as in science fiction or fantasy. But we think, "Here's an interaction that people are having." And then we'd say, "Well, is this a believable interaction? Is this person realistic? Is that actually how someone in this situation might behave?" We test stories against our own experience all the time. Again, even if they're fictional, we test them against what we think of as reality. In a good story, the novelist makes that case persuasively. That's one way that I think the arguments appear.

Then also, if the characters make certain kinds of choices that we wouldn't make, or if there's an argument that maybe this is a better choice, perhaps we could understand the reasoning given the story or given the context of this particular character. We could then say, "Well, maybe that's an argument also."

Another way arguments occur, or are presented in stories, is whether or not someone is even a hero at all. We think, if it's a moral argument or a political argument, is this person actually the protagonist of this story in a meaningful way that I identify with? I think that's sort of an argument. Then of course, the crudest ways that arguments appear in stories is when people have debates in novels. In Plato's Dialogues, for example, you have Socrates literally debating with his interlocutors.

MYISHA: There are philosophers who have written novels. Sartre wrote novels, and W. E. B. Du Bois wrote *The Black Flame Trilogy*. What can you do in a novel, philosophically, that you can't do in essay form?

AMIR: Most of the things that novels do, essay forms can also do but they haven't done. One thing that novels do really well, that I think essayists should draw more upon, is novelists are extremely aware of who is speaking and who they're speaking to. The narrator is addressing someone, a "narratee" of sorts. Essayists traditionally have not done that, although the good ones do. The good ones are keenly aware of their voice. They're aware that they're addressing a particular audience. Those are the more effective essays. Novelists always do that. They must do that. It's just what the form demands of them.

There are things that novels do that essays can try to do, but won't be able to do as well. Novels think about things like luck and chance. They think about contradiction and the particularity of our experiences. They resist abstraction and logical formalization, and yet they still pose philosophically relevant questions. If you want to have a philosophical inquiry about hunger, humor, love, loyalty, or our emotions in general––which are things that are so experiential—essays can talk about those in general. But if you don't ground it in a setting, a time, or even put those emotions in a body which is a character, then frequently, essays will seem empty.

And then sometimes when we're thinking about problems that seem to just be paradoxical or contradictory, stories can hold those next to each other without collapsing and being a fault of reason. Essays can frequently use nonlogical tools, in addition to logic and reason, and have a more holistic experience of thinking things through. Again, the question that you're trying to engage will determine which form might be more appropriate. But I think when we think about things that are particular in that way, novels have an advantage.

31

Adrienne Martin on Hope

MYISHA: You have been doing work on hope for a while. Your book *How We Hope* was released in 2013, and you have a forthcoming book on the same subject matter. It seems like a simple question, but there are several accounts of hope. What are the ways in which people have tried to talk about hope, why do you reject those approaches, and what is your view?

ADRIENNE: There are a lot of reasons that a person might ask that question, "What is hope?" What prompted it for me was wanting a deeper and clearer understanding of how hope influences people's reasoning and motivation. In my book, a big part of what I was aiming to do was understand hope as a mental state rather than, say, as a religious stance or phenomenon.

The philosophical and psychological work on hope has had a boom in recent years, so there are a lot of options on the table. But it's probably still fair to divide up the views into two rough categories. There's what I call the "orthodox definition," which you'll find in a lot of modern philosophers like Descartes, Spinoza, Hobbes, and others. According to this view, hope is basically a combination of a desire (you want what you hope for), and some kind of belief that what you desire is attainable. You think what you hope for is possible, or maybe you assign a probability estimate to it between zero and one. That's one set of views, and there are variations within that rough description.

Then there's those, including me, who think that you need something more to get to hope. For me, the fact that you need more is most salient when I think about cases where two people both know that what they deeply desire is highly unlikely. I think it was Luc Bovens who pulled *The Shawshank Redemption* into philosophical literature. In that book, you've got two prisoners, one cynical and one hopeful. They both yearn to be free and they both believe that the possibility of attaining the freedom is vanishingly small. But if one is cynical and one is hopeful, there has to be something more than the yearning and the possibility to get to hope.

My view, which I articulate in the book, is that the something more is an additional attitude that the hopeful person takes toward the possibility of, say, freedom. He sees that vanishingly small possibility as enough to go on, as enough to permit him to talk and dream about freedom; and even in the book, to build a pretty wild plan around it. The cynical prisoner doesn't do any of that. He just tries not to think about the possibility of freedom. That's where my view sort of fits into the various options.

MYISHA: President Obama had the "hope" slogan. In your view, did Obama get it right? Or should we look back at that slogan differently, given your view?

ADRIENNE: Actually, what got me interested in hope was in part the hope rhetoric in the campaigns of Obama and Hillary Clinton. I was doing a postdoc at the National Institute of Health (NIH) at the time and there was a lot of talk about hope. I said, "Well, what is this thing that everybody thinks is so important but everybody's kind of worried about it? Am I giving you false hope?" There also was Obama's hope campaign. He's certainly not the first politician to put the concept of hope right at the center of his campaign, but it was very prominent. Then there was Hillary Clinton saying, "Hope is not a plan." I started thinking: It's really interesting that some communities find appeals to hope very motivating in a concrete and pragmatic way; whereas for other people, as soon as you start talking about hope, they think you're talking about fantasies and dreams. That made me want to understand what hope is such that there could be such a broad disagreement about it.

MYISHA: There's a Christian scripture that says, "Faith without works is dead." I know you differentiate between faith and hope, and we'll talk about that later, but I wonder about the "works" aspect of hope. It seems that if I hope, there could be a window of justification for me to be passive. What is the relationship between hope and motivation? That is to say, does hope influence motivation? If so, how does it, and when does hope not influence motivation?

ADRIENNE: I started thinking about hope mostly because I wanted to understand how it influences practical deliberation and motivation, because that was the worry at the NIH. The worry was that hope would lead patients to make bad decisions or to enroll in studies where they didn't understand the risks, that kind of thing. I think there's this very common view, that hope is like this special kind of battery. Cheshire Calhoun sometimes calls it the "energizer-bunny view of hope"; it just keeps going and going and going. To give someone hope is to give them a boost; and to take away hope is to do some kind of energy suck.

But like you say, it's not too hard to think of cases where hope seems to make a person passive. One of the things I rant about a bit in the book is that I think, especially in the US, there's a number of considerably powerful forces socializing people to be passive hopers, or maybe misguided hopers. They're leading us to hope in a way that primarily involves fantasy, without any real attention to or uptake of what it would take to actually realize those dreams. I think get-rich-quick schemers are often in the grips of this kind of hope. They have this sort of vision, this dreamy vision, but there is no connection between that and the actual means that it would take to achieve it.

The book is called *How We Hope*, and that's for me the key to answering this kind of question. We can hope in ways that are productive. We can also hope in ways that are not productive but that are distracting or contribute to errors like confirmation bias. We can substitute hopeful fantasies for agency. I think we can also hope in ways that are not productive but are just nevertheless harmless occasional escapism. I don't think there's anything problematic with that. But I do think a lot of people develop a disposition to hope in these ways that is very distracting from the actual facts on the ground.

MYISHA: What are some productive and positive ways that we can hope? My immediate thought is: "Well, if I'm hoping that I get a tenure-track job, I'm going to work on journal articles. I'll do everything that's required to make myself attractive on the job market." Is that all that's needed to hope productively, just taking the necessary steps to achieve what I am hoping for? Or is there something else going on?

ADRIENNE: I think the issue here is really dispositional and a matter of character. It's less of a matter of when it comes to any individual thing I'm hoping for, that I should think about the ways that I should hope for it; that I should be realistic about the possibilities of it being achieved, and realistic about what it would take to bring it about. But this doesn't seem like a deep insight.

I think the deeper point is that we have to work on our characters. We have to try to develop habits of attention. A whole lot of what I talk about in the book is the relationship between fantasy and hope. For a lot of people, to hope for something is to spend a lot of time imagining what it would be like to have it. I think we're really encouraged to think that way. If you look at all of the self-help literature that really surged in the '80s and early '90s, a lot of it really concretely recommends, "Sit and imagine the thing you want. Have a vision board." That alone, in itself, does not seem problematic. The problem is if that's what your hope consists of, it's too easy to think that, well, now you've kind of done the work of hope. I think that we should think of hope as a much more virtuous hope, a useful hope, much more closely intertwined with planning activities.

MYISHA: Can we hope too much?

ADRIENNE: What is too much? A person can be unrealistically optimistic about the things they want, and a lot of people think that that's hoping too much. That's what you find in the bioethics literature, for example. There are people who think that dangerous hopes are the ones that involve just believing your cure is more likely than it is, or that your medical benefit is more likely than it is.

For me, unrealistic optimism and hope are pretty different things. A person can hope too much in the sense that they hope in a way that substitutes for agency. But I don't think that's intrinsic to hope itself. That's hoping badly. I also think a person can be guided by very powerful hopes in a way that works very well for them. It seems to me like there isn't a single dimension along which you can say, "Too much, too little."

That's kind of the point of the analysis that I give. While there are definitely desires and beliefs involved in hope, there is also the possibility of seeing your hope as enough to go forward. That gives you a different dimension of evaluation. What I want to say is that a lot of people tend to think that to hope too much would be to either assign too high a probability to the hoped-for outcome or to want it too much. I actually think the more likely way that hope goes wrong is when people pin too much on their hope, and you can do that even with a good probability estimate and a perfectly appropriate desire.

MYISHA: What is the difference between hope, faith, and wishing?

ADRIENNE: Okay, let me start with just hope and faith. In Christian theology, hope and faith are two of the three theological virtues, and they're sort of the volitional and intellectual faces of trust in the existence and grace of God. I'm an atheist, but I was raised in a broadly Judeo-Christian culture. I think of faith as a kind of ironclad hope. I think there's also an attitude that doesn't necessarily have to have God or anything supernatural as its object but that still deserves to be called "faith."

Jonathan Lear talks about what he calls "transcendental hope" in connection with Chief Plenty Coups, who was the leader of the Crow Nation during the period where they survived colonial onslaught. They survived it by changing their way of life. Chief Plenty Coups, Lear argues, had a vision of a Crow future where although what it would mean to survive and still be the Crow Nation outstripped the conceptual resources, it was nevertheless a vision and it was a guiding one. That's what I could call faith. I'd call it hoping for something that you're not yet equipped to conceive.

MYISHA: And wishing?

ADRIENNE: I don't have a ready analysis of wishing. Aristotle says that wishing is much like hope but not bound by the probabilities. You can wish for something that you take to be impossible, whereas to hope for something, you have to take it to be at least within the realm of possibility. That sounds about right to me. Wishing is a very similar kind of attitude that involves wanting something but doesn't preclude wanting something that you take to be essentially impossible. I think it probably makes sense to say that wishing also has some additional attitude involved. It's not just wanting, but it's wanting and then taking that desire as enough to justify thinking about it or crying over it.

MYISHA: I'm thinking again about the relationship between possibility and hoping. It seems that anything is possible. There may be certain laws of physics that cannot be violated, but it is possible that a poor person could indeed become a billionaire. Are there boundaries to these possibilities or is it limitless?

ADRIENNE: I actually don't even think that hoping is necessarily bound by the probabilities of the laws of nature and the laws of physics because, if you're someone who believes in supernatural forces, then you can hope for the intervention by those supernatural forces. I actually think it's subjective what the relevant probability, or what the relevant conception of possibility, is that constrains hope. For someone who's a naturalist, their hopes are going to be bound by what they take to be physically possible. Maybe one could say that what we're bound by is what we take to be metaphysically possible, and naturalists and supernaturalists disagree about what's metaphysically possible.

MYISHA: Sometimes we place hope in people, and you write that this is a distinctive and fundamental way of relating to people interpersonally. What do you mean by this?

ADRIENNE: That's the center of my current work, and I sketched it in a programmatic way toward the end of *How We Hope*. I don't even use the word "hope" that much anymore, but I'm still talking about the same idea. The idea is that we invest in each other. We can invest a lot of different things in each other. We can invest time, emotions, labor, money, care and concern. I still think it makes sense to lump all of these together under the description of "placing hope in a person."

When we do invest in a person, we create or strengthen interpersonal bonds. Those include normative bonds like debts and obligations. I argue that this is a distinctive way of relating. I mean that it's distinctive in the sense that these aren't exactly the same kinds of bonds and obligations that moral philosophers tend to focus on. They're not rights and perfect duties, for example. The bond created by a promise has a claim of right at one end of it. The person making the promise gets to enforce the promise in various ways. Whereas placing hope in a person produces a bond that isn't primarily about having an enforceable claim on a particular action. It's more like having a call upon that person to give due attention to the value of the hope as they go about their lives.

That's what I'm investigating right now. I'm thinking about the kinds of interpersonal bonds that aren't attended to within traditional deontic frameworks, but that still have that kind of call-and-response structure to them. You're supporting a friend in their project. That seems to give you some kind of legitimate influence over them so that if they, for no good reason, completely drop the project in the gutter, you have standing to express disappointment in them.

It's a special standing. Your uninvested bystander doesn't get to say, "Oh, you really let me down," but you do. If you invested in your friend and then they squandered your investment without any good reason, then you have the standing to say, "You really let me down." That seems to me like you're expressing an attitude that belongs among Strawson's reactive attitudes. It's not resentment; it's something more like disappointment. But it is nevertheless deeply interpersonal, and I think it plays a huge role in our lives.

MYISHA: It seems that part of having an interpersonal relationship with another person *is* hoping in them to some extent.

ADRIENNE: I think it's rare to find an interpersonal relationship that doesn't involve some kind of investment of hope. Right now, I'm thinking about the investment of hope interpersonally as a way of sharing agency. I actually invest my agency in my children, for example. What that does is charge them with taking up that agency, and then using it in certain ways. Most human relations involve that, but I don't know that I think it's definitive.

MYISHA: Do you think it's important to hope? Why or why not?

ADRIENNE: I keep being surprised to discover that people think I'm this very pro-hope person, despite the fact that in the book I spend a lot of time talking about how hope can make us passive, it can substitute for agency, can distract us from important information, and can make suicide appear rational.

So, is it important to hope? Imagine hoping for a particular outcome like a solution to climate change. I would mostly recommend against that hope, or I would recommend against it unless you are an unusually strongly pragmatic, pessimistic person. I think the key to Barack Obama, and why his hope was actually very functional, is that he's a very pragmatic, pessimistic person. I know it's because he talks about hope and because he works really hard to bring about change in the world. But I think that in the way that he does it, it's clear. If you look at the way he approached various projects when he was in office, he was always prepared for the worst. If you think you're that kind of person, and I think if you mostly interact with and influence other people who are like that, then go for it; hope for whatever you want.

But I think your hope is likely to be either largely indistinguishable from your plans or take up very little emotional space in your life. More commonly, if you're a bit of a dreamer, if you've grown up on a steady diet of Disney, rom-coms, and Forrest Gump; or if you're going to be heard by a lot of people who have, then I recommend against invoking hope in connection with efforts to mitigate particular disasters that we currently face. I think that it's just passive making and distracting. That's kind of the bad news.

There is good news. I think interpersonal hope is where it's at. Cornel West talks about being a hope. I say that's where it is. Figure out who's invested hope in you and live up to those hopes. Invite more people to place hope in you, and place hope in other people and create and strengthen those bonds and obligations. Do it because those are the things that make life meaningful and those are the things that give you reason to do shit even when despair is obviously rational. That's the kind of hope that I think is important and that we need to try to maintain.

Conclusion

A Note on Conversations

Conversations are hard to have!

Imagine the feeling you get in your gut when someone says to you: "We need to talk." The words sound like an indictment. Immediately, you feel transported into a dark, cramped room with one dimmed light and a hundred possibilities in your head for why this person needs to converse with you. Your thoughts race, and your heart thumps, jumps, and refuses to calm down until the person explains what's on their mind. The longer you have to wait, the more intense the pain. "Why am I in trouble?" you wonder. Needing to have a conversation signals a serious situation. You could have gotten the silent treatment. They could have gotten over it. But no! Your failings are so great that only a conversation will do.

Initiating a conversation is not easy either. When you're the one to confront someone, and make them sit down with you to have a Serious Talk, you risk being perceived as irrational, sensitive, or insecure. "I feel" statements are supposed to make your conversation partner lower their defenses—at least that's what my twelfth-grade conflict resolution teacher told me—but they can expose you, and make you feel dangerously vulnerable in the process. Who knows how it will all turn out anyway? You may spark the conversation in hope of being understood or resolving an issue, only to be dismissed or ignored in the end.

Then there's the conversation that springs forth—somewhat unexpectedly—from our everyday interactions with each other. No one in the group is in trouble, at least not initially. A gathering that was meant to celebrate Kareem's engagement or Fazza's birthday can easily turn into a panel discussion about Palestine, Black Lives Matter, hetero-normativity, or health care. Do we participate or exit? Do we hold back or speak our minds? If we do share what we think, how much can we say? How far can we go? And at what cost will it be to our friendships, social calendars, and overall flourishing?

Having conversations is a way for our social, linguistic species to express and explain, correct and collaborate, make sense of things and make things happen. Anything that can do all of these things will never be easy.

In this book, I engaged in thirty-one conversations with folks from a variety of backgrounds and social positions—who also have PhDs in philosophy. We talked about prejudice, oppression, and social justice. We also talked about monogamy and polygamy, love and hope, money and distrust. As a result, I now know more about any of these issues than I ever did before. I also understand my interviewees more—as people and thinkers—and have more insight on the wider world as well.

But what only a couple of people know is that I was *always* nervous before each conversation. The uncertainty, I must admit, frightened me. I had no idea how the conversations would actually go. I also wondered: Would they take me seriously? Would our conversations be productive? Would the philosophers I talked to be as interesting in person as their written work was? When I did not understand some-thing, I had to push myself to ask for clarity at the risk of sounding stupid. When I disagreed with something, I had to find the balance between being a passive listener on the one hand and an obnoxious ac-ademic on the other.

At times, they challenged me to revise or restate questions that I thought were initially brilliant and clear. Most of the time, they made me question my own "wokeness," forcing me to get over myself and do it quickly. These conversations led to other ones, this time with listeners online and in person. Not all of these conversations were teeming with praise. There was disagreement and criticism. No one said conversations would be easy!

By prompting and leading the conversations that air on UnMute, I've made myself vulnerable, and in this book I'm doing that yet again, but promoting conversations is worth it to me. It's something we all need to do more of. Why? We live in a world in which conversations are happening less, superficially, or not at all. We all know that couple who sits at the restaurant across from one another with forks in one hand, cellphones in the other, making no effort whatsoever to make eye contact. Or the person who randomly appears on your social media feed with the purpose of being Super Rational Man—whose sole mission is to save the day by demolishing every comment that does not have the proper logical structure or spelling. Or the person at a water cooler near you who wants to have conversations only on her own terms. Or the person who doesn't really care about a particular issue at all but only uses the conversation to prove that he has a liberal arts degree from the University of Judith Butler and Ta-Nehisi Coates. He has all the postmodern terms and ambiguous liberation phrases to prove it, too. These everyday phenomena discourage conversation, right when we need it the most.

In our current political climate, many have emphasized the importance of talking to the other side. The belief is that we are "politically divided like never before." I must admit that this always sounds like an exaggeration to me, similar to when I hear people call a recent game "the greatest upset in sports history." Usually in these cases, the speaker has no working knowledge of sports history and no standard of comparison. They just mean they're worked up. So when people say that we are politically divided *like never before*, it makes me wonder if they're missing the historical context and just making a dramatic statement. What do they think was happening when the country was about to divide in two over the issue of slavery, or when the Vietnam War brought the country to a vicious cultural war whose traces still influence politics today? People were plenty divided then as well. But hey, how can you properly measure division anyway? I digress.

The solution to the current political divide, many believe, is conversation. But the conversations that people promote, in answer to the divided political climate, tend to look like either listening to understand or arguing to learn or win. (If it seems paradoxical to "argue to learn," wait and see what I mean.)

The first kind of conversation, listening to understand, is an approach to conversation that many vouch for as a way to comprehend why others think, act, or vote the way they do. The objective seems to be to get at the heart of their concerns in an effort to address them and reconsider our assumptions and labels. "Not all red voters are racist and here's why," they say. Having empathetic understanding for others is important for deliberation, collaboration, and connection. My concern is not with the conversation per se, but the discretion used when calling for it. Unfortunately, *this call* for understanding is often one-sided. It is often not directed the other way around. It tends to be a call only when certain groups are misunderstood. This sends the message that only certain people are worth our understanding, while others are not. But conversations are, by definition, not meant to be one-sided. That is to say, in our conversations there is not supposed to be one speaker who soliloquizes and an audience who draws conclusions. Conversations are about engagement, exchange, and empathy on both sides.

Then there's the view that conversations are arguments. This has three faces. Joshua Knobe and colleagues (2015) make a distinction between arguing to learn and arguing to win. When we argue to learn, we present an argument, listen to the other, and move forward to an agreement. When we argue to win, we present an argument so that we can score points and defeat the other. They suggest we do the former.

Social psychologist Robb Willer thinks that a way to have better political conversations is to understand the moral values of the other side and then appeal to those values in our arguments. If purity is a conservative value, for example, then Willer recommends that we use that term and not "climate change" in our attempts at persuading them to take care of the planet.

These researchers' suggestions are insightful. But they tend to treat all conversations as arguments. I do not think that they all are. Nor do I think that the purpose of all of our conversations is agreement. Often times, our most fruitful discussions are those where we discover we disagree. These conversations are not unproductive. I will refrain from making a judgment on what should be the end goal of conversations here. These suggestions, however, do bring us closer to my own recommendation. And what better way to introduce it than to provide an example of a somewhat "horrible" example of the argument model.

I present to you Socrates: the Athenian founder of Western philosophy. By asking what is piety, justice, and love, Socrates placed humans and human affairs under philosophical investigation for the first time in the West. In comparison to his Eastern and African philosophical neighbors, he was late to the party. But when he arrived, he was off and running, chatting with everyone. Throughout the work of his student Plato, we learn of Socrates's wise words and observations, such as, probably the most famous, "The unexamined life is not worth living." He also made himself known for engaging everyone around him in dialogue. He was the gadfly of Athens, whose ideas—judged to be corruptive to the youth and disrespectful to the gods—lead to his death by hemlock poisoning. He started too many conversations, you might say, but in doing so, he changed Western philosophy forever. He left us with ideas that pervade thousands of years later and showed great character when, for example, he refused to escape prison to save his own life.

But I ask you, would you have wanted to have a conversation with Socrates? Would you have wanted to examine life with *him*?

Let's assume the role of a fly on a Grecian wall as Socrates converses with others. From a fly's-eye view, we can see him beginning to spark a philosophical conversation after leading in with talk about more ordinary things. He then isolates a key term and presumes ignorance. But he only does it so that after many efforts by his expert interlocutors, their own ignorance is revealed (and often publicly). Socrates constantly pushes back and at each turn offers no insights, only counterexamples, one after the other. So it's not surprising that the end result is always the same: his interlocutors find a reason to end the conversation and then leave. We are made to feel sad for Socrates, perhaps even pity him because no one has the tough skin needed to seek out truth with him. However, if Socrates wasn't so arrogant at his worst, and dismissive at his best, his interlocutors probably would have continued to speak with him. While one might argue that Socrates is a poster boy for what happens when our conversations aim at winning, I think he is a perfect example of something else that is wrong with our conversations: Us.

What if I told you that conversations are not our most pressing problem? (Ok, I am telling you that.) The problem is who we are in our conversations. Despite our differences with each other, we are often— like Socrates—not the kind of person with whom others can or would want to have difficult conversations. If you suddenly feel that you have been transported into a dark, cramped room with one dimmed light and a hundred defenses for why I cannot be talking about you, breathe. Let me explain.

We cannot isolate conversations and their content from the people who engage in them. It's hard to digest advice from a hypocrite, share with someone who makes you feel insignificant, or correct someone who thinks he knows it all. This is because character matters in our conversations. I believe if we aim to be a certain kind of conversation partner by exercising particular virtues, our conversations will be better regardless of the topic or the disagreement.

Epistemologists and ethicists like José Medina, Linda Zagzebski, and Aristotle have offered up insights on virtues we can have as knowers and moral creatures. I do not profess to add anything novel to their contributions, so I will only appropriate them for our purposes here. Together they remind us of the beauty of traits like humility, sincerity, and tactfulness. These character traits are "conversation starters" in that they allow us to be the kind of person others can begin and continue to converse with. I note in brief just a few here to convey my point. I leave it up to you to add others to the list.

Humility is when a person recognizes their epistemic limitations. A person who has "conversational" humility can admit that they do not know it all. They have what Medina calls a "humble and self-questioning attitude." Those who are humble are not self-righteous. They recognize that at any moment, anyone (including themselves) could be wrong. *Curiosity* is an interest and willingness to know. People who are curious have a motivation to gain knowledge, and it doesn't matter from what body that knowledge reveals itself. They are not naive. They are simply indiscriminate in whom they talk to, believing that anyone is bound to teach them something. Being *diligent* helps a person keep their curiosity in times in which dialogue with others is either shut down or difficult to have.

A person who is *open-minded* acknowledges and respects alternative perspectives. Being open-minded entails being willing to consider new ideas. Open-minded conversationalists are not quick to reject what others have to say. They are likely to see the beauty in disagreement. This eye allows them to be more accepting and less controlling. *Moral courage* is the fortitude to move beyond one's comfort zone. A person who is courageous faces the fear of the unknown. She is also willing to face criticism or misunderstanding. She knows that this is often the risk one takes when talking with others. When a person is *sincere* in a conversation, she is herself. She is not playing a character in order to get approval. Sincere conversationalists do not come to conversations with ulterior motives or masked as something more accepting. They are unpretentious.

Conversation partners who are *generous* are not quick to judge or speak. They are willing to give their partner the benefit of the doubt. They are not so enamored by their own voice that they never let others share. A generous person is often quite *patient*. When talking with them, others often feel that they can be heard and finish a sentence without being interrupted with the infamous preface, "not to cut you off, but . . . " Patient conversationalists do not think their thoughts are more important than the thoughts presently being spoken by others. Therefore, they often wait their turn. Their patience also helps them keep their composure when others are not as virtuous.

Tactful people are experts in tonality and linguistics. They know what to say, how to say it, and what context to say it in. They do not force others to always have thick skin when talking with them. (It is often uncomfortable and doesn't fit them anyway.) Tactful conversationalists do not allow their vices to drive the bus and so it is rare that they justify their tactlessness with "I'm just keeping it real" or "This is who I am."

We can add other virtues to this list such as honesty, discretion, security, and self-awareness. As I have mentioned, the list is not exhaustive. There is an assortment of virtues waiting for us to put in practice. I have tried to practice these virtues in the conversations in this book. But I have also been challenged to be and do better beyond academic discourses. Here are some questions I am constantly asking myself: How can I extend the same curiosity and humility to ordinary folks on Main Street that I have shown to professors on College Road? How can I have the same moral courage in conversations with my friends, peers, or supervisors as when I have conversations with philosophers; when there's everything at stake just as much as when there's very little at stake? How can I be more sincere and honest when I stand to lose so much? How can I be less defensive and more self-aware when the people I care about muster up the courage to say to me that "We need to talk"? Socrates was right. The unexamined life is not worth living.

Let me offer a word of caution. In our technological age, we use texts, audio messaging, live video chats, and social media threads as ways to engage in conversations. There's no need for us to wait until we are in the same city or even know each other's real name to converse. But the very innovations that facilitate our exchanges can also distort the aforementioned virtues and thus disrupt our conversations. People can mistake the tone of our texts, misinterpreting what was intended as a kind response as a mean rant. (A skit entitled "Text Message Confusion" from the sketch comedy show *Key and Peele* illustrates this perfectly!) Our dismissive zingers and not our open-minded replies are often rewarded with likes and follows, and our brains recognize this. It's hard to practice courage when death threats loom in your Twitter mentions and the Internet never forgets. While social media brings so many advantages, if I never have to be in your presence or know you to "talk" with you, then some might ask, "What do I owe you or myself when we engage in discussion?"

Even if we are able to jump over these technological hurdles and see the virtues of others, I cannot guarantee that conversations will instantly become easy. It is hard enough to talk about moral and political issues. Topics like prejudice, oppression, and social justice are the elephants in the room—they are what many people think about but few dare to discuss. Some topics are hard to talk about because we have prolonged the conversation for so long; they can implicate us; or obligate us to do something we probably do not want to do. I don't think talking about controversial topics will undermine our democracy. Yes, conversations are hard, but they could be had if only we weren't so hardened.

By saying that we have to practice virtues, and improve our character, in order to improve our conversations, I don't mean to say that only perfect people have what it takes to be worthy conversation partners. What I am claiming is that we cannot separate conversations from the people that engage in them. Be the person that you want to have a conversation with. This has nothing to do with being smart, progressive, or right. It has everything to do with being a person with a character that makes conversing a human experience, for the people on both sides.

Say What?
A Glossary of Terms

Academics have a way of speaking that can be confusing and perhaps, some might say, annoying. One of the biggest annoyances is
the use of terms that only they seem to know the meaning of. But this
use of specialized vocabulary is not restricted to academics. It is also
used within activist circles and "woke" or "conscious" communities.
In the interviews in this book, we have tried to explain concepts and
terms as best we could. However, this doesn't mean we did not fall
into the trap of using specialized language with the assumption that
everyone would understand what was meant.

The purpose of this glossary is to pull out that recurring vocabulary
and "make it plain." This glossary is not meant to be exhaustive. There
are books and articles that provide a more detailed explanation and
also challenge assumptions behind some of these terms. However, this
brief account aims to provide a clear understanding of their meanings
as used in this text and perhaps encourage readers to explore them further in other contexts.

Think of this as not only a glossary but a comprehensive guide.
I dedicate this guide to those new to philosophy; those who lack a full
grasp of common academic vocabulary and philosophical vocabulary
in particular; those who have been faking their understanding of said

vocabulary for years; and those who have been bold enough to respond to their usage with "Say What?"—only to receive a more confusing definition in return. This is for you!

A

To have an **account** is to have a position on a matter. To give an **account** of prison abolition, for example, is to provide a philosophical position on the matter of prisons. This position not only explains one's take on a subject, but it may also include reasons for that particular position. In this text, Elizabeth Barnes provides an **account of disability**; Luvell Anderson provides an **account of slurs**; and David Livingstone Smith provides an **account of dehumanization**. "Account," "position," and "view" are often used interchangeably.

An entity that is able to act intentionally in the world has **agency**. One possesses **agential capacity** when one has the ability to act in the world and make free choices. A person who is able to do so is an **agent**. While slaves may be a paradigmatic example of people who lacked **agency**, this example is too simple. Given that they were still able to resist and marry (i.e., act and make choices), they can be described as having had **limited agency**.

I know **a priori** and **a posteriori** may sound weird at first. That's because the terms are Latin for "from the earlier" and "from the latter," respectively. Although Latin is no longer spoken conversationally, academics still love to incorporate Latin terms and phrases into academic language. Don't ask me why. Let's just roll with it. **A priori** is knowledge that does not depend on sensory experience or evidence. This knowledge comes from reason alone and not experience. Consider the statement: "Every retired teacher has taught a class." Through logical reasoning, I can deduce that if a teacher is retired, then they have taught a class. The clue is in the word "retired." I need not observe every teacher in the world to come to this conclusion. Thus, this is an **a priori statement**. And I know the truth of this statement through **a priori knowledge**. Theorizing that arises purely from **a priori** knowledge is usually referred to as "**armchair** philosophizing."

The statement "Charlie is a teacher" is different. This statement is a fact about a particular individual. I can only know the truth of this statement through experience. For example, I would need to have evidence that Charlie teaches at least one class in order to come to this conclusion. This requires experience in the world. Thus, this statement is an **a posteriori statement**. I know the truth of this statement through **a posteriori knowledge**.

C

Capitalism is the major economic system in the world today. One of the most basic features of capitalism is private ownership of factories and other businesses. These two things are often referred to as "the means of production." In its most ideal form, capitalism is a system based on the primacy of the free market. This means that the free market determines income and profit and the way goods are produced. The rights and liberties associated with a functioning free market include rights that protect against theft, rights to own what we acquire on the market, rights against fraud and deception, and the free exchange of property rights. A **capitalist system** is often contrasted with socialism—a theory that advocates, for example, that the means of production be owned and controlled by the community and not the individual.

Carceral refers to any form of or unique practice within prisons, jails, or confinement. Theorists define the **carceral state** differently, but it can refer to actors and institutions within the criminal justice system (e.g., police, judges, or probation officers). It could also refer to the ways in which public space and social programs are designed to promote surveillance and supervision. Lori Gruen mentions **carceral logics** in this text to refer to ways of seeing and understanding the world through a punishment and incarceration lens. Thus, a **carceral logic** is a punishment mindset.

Cis is a term used to refer to those who identify with their biological sex assigned at birth. A **cismale** and **cisfemale** are those whose gender identity matches their biological sex. Those whose biological sex doesn't align with their gender identity are considered transgender. A return back to Latin may be helpful in unpacking how cis/trans functions. Cis refers to that which is on the same side of a given boundary or feature, while trans refers to that which is on the "other" side. Thus, the province of Gaul was divided into "Cisalpine Gaul," which was on the same side of the Alps as Rome, and "Transalpine Gaul," which was on the "other" side of the Alps.

Colonization is a political relationship between two or more communities in which one community attempts to exert power and control over the social organization of the other. Historical practices geared toward initiating, maintaining, or legitimizing relations of colonization include **direct forms of colonization**, where the "mother" country attempts to directly control the political institutions of the **colonized**, or eliminate them entirely. The United States was a colony of the British Empire in this sense before the American Revolution, and much of Central and South America were colonies of the Spanish, Portuguese, and Dutch empires in this sense. There are also **indirect methods of colonization**, where the "mother country" attempts to influence and steer the political institutions of the colonized, while leaving them wholly or partially intact. The Indian subcontinent was colonized by the British Empire in this way. This is, arguably, the sense in which the third world or "Global South" are colonies of the first world/Global North in today's world. Historically, **colonial powers** have used a combination of these approaches, preferring direct tactics with some kinds of people and institutions and indirect methods with others.

Kyle Whyte and Andrea Pitts use **settler colonialism** often in this text. The term refers to practices of **colonization** in which the colonizers—rather than rule from the mother country—settle and live in the territory under their control. **Settler colonial states** include the United States, Canada, New Zealand, Australia, and South Africa. The term **colonizer** is also used in everyday parlance to refer to persons who enter into spaces traditionally occupied by others (e.g., a Hispanic neighborhood) and then seek to control or change it, while often dismissing the people who have occupied the space and even admitting a sense of discovery when they learn practices or inventions of the traditional group.

D

Deontic or **deontological** refers to duty or obligation. **Deontic moves** are ways of holding people accountable by reminding them of their duty. Traditional **deontic frameworks** are duty-based structures underlining relationships such as those between spouses, and employers and employees. These duties are usually explicitly expressed in marriage vows, employee manuals, and other contracts.

E

Epistemology is the study of knowledge. It is a subdiscipline in philosophy that answers questions such as "How do we know?" It also explores topics such as testimony, belief, evidence, and truth. There are different **epistemologies** or ways of knowing. **Feminist epistemology** comes out of an acknowledgment that a lot of knowledge claims and practices of inquiry that have been treated as universal are actually from a male perspective and thereby gendered. **Epistemic** relates to knowledge or knowing and often precedes terms like **epistemic limitation**— a restraint a person has to knowing. In that vein, **epistemic injustice** refers to injustices that are committed within the domain of knowledge such as when we do not give credibility to a speaker because of their social identity or when a group lacks resources to understand their situation. When a black professor is perceived as "not knowing what she is talking about" because of her race and gender, she is experiencing an **epistemic injustice**.

Something is said to be **empirical** if it can be derived from observation or experiment. **Empirical evidence** is material that is obtained by studying the world. This can occur, for example, by conducting a survey or series of lab studies with human or nonhuman animal subjects. The evidence is used to support or disprove a hypothesis or position. To say that something is an **empirical matter** is to say that it cannot be proven through logical argumentation or theory but requires the gathering of data through observation. While I could provide a logical argument for why it is unjust to stop black and brown men solely based on their race, it is an **empirical matter** whether such police encounters have resulted in actual arrests. This is because it would require statistical data. One cannot obtain this information by theorizing alone.

A property is **essential** if it is an inherent, intrinsic quality that makes a thing what it is. **Essentialism** is the belief that things have features that make them what they are. **Essentialism** in race theory is the view that racial essences or qualities exist. Black people have an "essence" that is fundamentally different from white people and vice versa. Therefore, race isn't a **social construct** on this view and racial categories are not invented. Some racists are obviously **essentialists**, but so too are many Negritude thinkers and Afrocentric thinkers.

H

Hegemony means dominance, or predominant influence. **Hegemonic ideas** are a dominant set of ideas that come to be commonplace or common sense often through coercion and consent. In this text, Tom Digby talks about **hegemonic masculinity**—the dominant way of "being a man" in a particular culture. A country can have **hegemony** over other competing states. For example, **US hegemony** refers to the United States's dominance as an economic, political, and technological power.

While there are different varieties of **humanism**, the basic idea behind its usage in this text is that it is a system of thought whose focus is on human values and concerns. A **humanist** believes that humans matter. A **transhumanist** thinks that humans have not reached their full potential. They are still developing. While **traditional humanists** believe that the human condition can be improved through the humanities such as education and culture, a **transhumanist** believes that the human condition can be improved or enhanced by creative technologies that will enhance human intelligence and physiology. Examples include technologies that enable us to use more regions of our brains and technologies that help us live forever. **Transhumanism** and **posthumanism** are often used interchangeably.

I

Ideal theory imagines what a well-ordered, just society would look like while either ignoring actual unjust conditions or adding in favorable conditions such as colorblindness and tolerance. These favorable conditions are also referred to as **ideal conditions. Nonideal theory** imagines what a well-ordered, just society would look like while considering actual, unjust conditions. These unjust conditions (e.g., racism and classism) are often referred to as **nonideal conditions.**

Ideology is a set of values, beliefs, or theories often held by a group or society. **Ideology** affects how we see the world. These values and beliefs are often political, social, or economic in nature. Examples of **political ideologies** are Marxism and liberalism. Examples of **cultural and social ideologies** are racism and feminism. The way we act, the way our social institutions function, and which institutions we have in the first place might all depend on what **ideologies** are at work in a society, since we often act based on what we believe and find important.

The Combahee River Collective originally conceived of **identity politics** in their 1977 statement. They wrote that "the most radical politics come directly out of our own identity." Because their identity as black women is on the nexus of class, race, and sex, they believed that in addressing their concerns, one necessarily addresses the powers that oppress us all. **Identity politics** now generally refers to political positions based on the interests and perspectives of the social group that one identifies with. Examples of social movements and groups that practice identity politics are the LGBTQ community and the civil rights movement. While some might think that only marginalized communities practice **identity politics**, some thinkers have argued that straight white men also engage in **identity politics**, citing the 2016 US Presidential elections as an example.

Imperialism is closely related to **colonialism**. Empires attempt to expand the range of influence of their political community and institutions, often by colonizing other communities, but also by attempting to exert control over territory like land and sea. **Imperialism** can refer to this practice itself, or to the ideology that encourages and sustains it.

Intersectionality is a theory of how overlapping identities of race, ability, class, ethnicity, religion, and sexual orientation impact the way that minorities experience oppression, disadvantage, and discrimination. Kimberley Crenshaw coined the term in 1989 to help explain discrimination that was occurring among a group of black women plaintiffs. They were not discriminated against because of their race because black men were not discriminated against. They were not discriminated against because of their sex because white women were not discriminated against. Crenshaw found a way to explain how their identities as "black" *and* "woman"—both race and gender—were **intersecting** to create discrimination in varying configurations and intensity to their counterparts. It wasn't simply a case of racism or sexism; rather, they were experiencing both racism and sexism. Their multiple identities together shaped their experiences of oppression.

Thinking intersectionally is to think of how oppression affects identities differently. It is to resist reducing all sexist oppression to the experience of white women and all racist oppression to the experiences of black men. It is also to resist ignoring the unique experiences of disabled women or immigrant transmen, and so forth. **Thinking intersectionally** considers how these multiple identities work together in the lives of others.

An **interlocutor** is a person who engages with others in dialogue or critical debate. It is a person to whom you present your arguments to and who may object to or agree with them. When reading Plato's Dialogues, we are introduced to several of Socrates's **interlocutors**. Euthyphro and Thrasymachus are examples. These two **interlocutors** engaged with Socrates on questions of piety and justice. Socrates often disagreed with their conclusions and challenged them at every turn.

L

Liberalism is a political philosophy that developed in eighteenth-century Europe, during what's often referred to as the Age of Enlightenment. The crucial political and ethical values in this philosophy are freedom and equality. **Liberal** thinkers advocate for many different political principles and kinds of political institutions from this starting point, but usually tend to favor political arrangements that treat the individual (rather than, say, the family or the community) as the site of political value, the subject of political responsibilities, and the bearer of rights.

Logics are ways of thinking, understanding, and reasoning. The terms **carceral logics** and **settler-colonial logics** are used in this text to point to particular understandings. For example, **settler-colonial logic** is a way of thinking as a settler colonizer. This understanding can range from thinking that whites are superior to thinking that indigenous peoples are not self-sufficient and that individuals should own natural resources.

M

Metaphysics is the study of what is real, what doesn't exist, and what seems to exist somehow or other. For example, cars exist and ghosts don't. But what about sports teams? Obviously they exist, because sports fans root for them. But maybe there's nothing to being a team beyond the people who make it up, and everything we say about teams is just shorthand for things you could say about some people. **Metaphysics** comes up with tools to help us better understand cases where we feel pulled in two directions about whether something exists.

To describe something as **metaphysical** is to point out that object's relationship to the themes of existence, reality, and being. For example, a common philosophical mannerism is to name a **metaphysical question**. A speaker might say, "I'm drawing a distinction between the **metaphysical question**—what a sports team is—and the ethical question—how should sports teams behave during competition. Notice the difference between the two: the **metaphysical question** examines the team's existence, and the ethical question examines the team's behavior.

N

What needs to be the case in order for something to be true? Here enters the topic of **necessary and sufficient conditions**. **Sufficient** means that something *is enough* to make a statement true. **Necessary** means that something *is needed* to make a statement true. However, it is not necessarily all that is needed. Basketball is a perfect example to illustrate these two conditions.

Consider the statement: My team won the NBA championship. What *needs* to be the case for this statement to be true? **Necessary conditions** for the statement to be true would be for my team to get through the playoffs, practice and strategize, play hard, and so on. But playing hard is not a **sufficient condition** or *enough* to win the championship. My team could be so good and the competitor so bad that my team is able to win without putting too much effort into it. What would *be enough* to make it the case that my team won the NBA Finals Championships? They won four championship games before their competitor did. Winning four championship games before their competitor is a **sufficient condition** for winning the NBA championships. This is enough for the statement to be true. Conditions can be **necessary but not sufficient; sufficient but not necessary; and necessary and sufficient**.

Normative relates to a norm or standard. **Normative claims** are assertions about what people should do and how things should be, and judgments about what actions are good or bad. "Lying is never good" and "Children should respect their parents" are examples of **normative claims**. To ask "Where is the **normativity** in your argument?" is a way of asking the speaker "What are you instructing us to do or not do?" or "What moral judgments are one making?"

O

Ontology is a branch of metaphysics that is concerned with what kinds of things or structures exist. **Realists** affirm the existence of some category of objects. **Antirealists** deny the existence of some category of objects. **Racial ontology** is concerned with the questions "What kind of thing is a race?" and "Is it real?" One can be a **realist** about race by thinking that there is a thing "out there" to which the category of race picks out. One can be an **antirealist** about race by thinking the category refers only to something "in our heads."

P

Pan-Africanism reflects a range of political views. The most basic idea is that people of African descent share in a common history and destiny. They also share a common interest—freedom from racism, slavery, and colonialism—and should be politically united to fight against these oppressions. **Pan-Africanists** aim to strengthen the bonds and solidarity between all people of African descent. In this text, Chike Jeffers notes that Du Bois was a **Pan-Africanist**.

   Patriarchy is a social system in which there is an unequal power relation between men and women. In other words, in a **patriarchy** men have more power than women and they often hold power over women. In a **patriarchal society** men are respected more than women and men have more privileges than women. Masculinity is also valued over femininity. As a result, masculine cismen are often rewarded over women and other men. We see **patriarchy** in everyday life through the over representation of men in political and economic institutions; the gender pay gap; domestic violence; and rape culture. A behavior, attitude, or value that reflect the preceding description can be viewed as **patriarchal**.

S

A construct is something that is built or created. A **social construct** is a category or phenomenon that is not natural but built by society. Many argue that gender is socially constructed and thus a **social construction**. This is because, unlike sex, gender is not biological or natural. Instead, gender is constructed by society. Saying that femininity is socially constructed is to say that what counts as "feminine" originated within and does not exist independent of human societies and that we are "trained" to perform gender in particular ways.

Acknowledgments

The idea for this book emerged from support I received from hosting and producing the Unmute Podcast. Interviewing the contributors in this book was an intellectual joy. Without their contribution there would be no book.

To my former students who inspired the podcast and subsequently this book: Robert Pleasant, Dammion Williams, Anthony Womble, Lillian George, Ismael Cedeno, Lachristin "Jazzmin" Mack, Raymond Vaughn, Anthony Shell, Benjamin Mensah, and Allan Alexander. You did this!

To Lucy Randall, who took me seriously when I "hit her in her DMs" on Twitter by suggesting I had a book proposal I wanted to show her. Your enthusiasm gave me so much confidence. Thank you! Much appreciation to Hannah Doyle, whose patience and suggestions made this book better.

This book was completed while in residence as a Advancing Equity Through Research Fellow at the Hutchins Center for African and African American Research, Santayana Fellow in the Philosophy Department, and an Associate in the African and African American Studies Department at Harvard University, respectively. Thank you, Abby Wolf and Krishnakali Lewis at the Hutchins Center, for providing me with financial support for transcriptions. Much thanks to my Hutchins Center Cohort of Fellows for giving me extra affirmation as you read through sample chapters.

Thank you, Dr. Cornel West, for not only writing the foreword to this book but for being a public philosopher par excellence and an intellectual who practices what he preaches (i.e., freedom, justice, and love for all people). Twenty years ago at a book signing, teenage me came up to you and said, "I'm going to be the next Cornel West when I grow up." Thank you for telling me to be the next me. I haven't regretted that decision!

I am grateful for the careful eyes, wonderful suggestions, and youthful energy and excitement of my research assistants, Hilda Jordan and Ismail Buffins. You both are two of the most brilliant young people I know and the true definition of Black Excellence. Your enthusiasm gave me much needed energy in the final hour.

Thank you, Chris DeArmond, for transcribing these interviews into print. Your ability to make sense of what you heard, despite not being a philosopher, is awe-inspiring. Thank you Devin Mawdsley for illustrating us. You captured what I originally imagined, so brilliantly.

The glossary section was a community labor of love. I am grateful for the folks who engaged in conversation with me and provided suggestions and feedback on drafts to ensure I didn't make too many mistakes. Thank you, Rose Lenehan, Axelle Karera, Lidal Dror, Douglas Ficek, Mordecai Lyon, Olufemi O. Taiwo, Michael Monahan, and John Torrey.

If a creative or intellectual is ever successful, it is because of the people that are by their side in their private and vulnerable moments. I am truly grateful for my family (Chekida, Cearia, Marquis, WaWa, Juice, and John) for loving me no matter what. I am also grateful to my best friends, Jason Reynolds and Mafaz Al-Suwaidan. Jason, you are a role model of excellence and a constant reminder of what we said we would do in the world with our words almost twenty years ago. Mafaz, you have no idea how our giggles, secret language (HQC!), and nourishing friendship got me through the days that I was not only writing this book but a dissertation and so much more. Many thanks also to my community at Harvard University and the University of Illinois, Chicago, for their belief in what I do and their constant encouragement and support.

Index